CONTENTS

PREFACE

Producing a book often means going along a lonely and tiring trail. Many have eased the burden. Dr Bill Goldthorp, consultant obstetrician and gynaecologist, must take credit for flaming my interest in medicine and teaching me much: we had a very rewarding research partnership in the 1970s.

I should also like to single out Dr Jim Lord. Over the years he has always given freely of his time, providing help and valuable scrutiny. Many thanks are also due to the staff efficiency of the Polytechnic Library; especially from inter-library loans and the Didsbury site. A final thanks is reserved for Corinne Wilshaw. She took on the daunting and rushed task of audio-typing the book; and performed wonders.

MEDICINE AND HEALTH

Sarah Burley

Joel Richman

LONGMAN
London and New York

LONGMAN GROUP UK LIMITED
Longman House, Burnt Mill, Harlow
Essex CM20 2JE, England
and Associated companies throughout the world

*Published in the United States of America
by Longman Inc., New York*

© Longman Group UK Limited 1987

First published 1987

BRITISH LIBRARY CATALOGUING IN PUBLICATION DATA

Richman, Joel
  Medicine and health.
  1. Social medicine
  I. Title
  306'.46   RA418

ISBN 0-582-29686-2

LIBRARY OF CONGRESS CATALOGING IN PUBLICATION DATA

Richman, Joel.
  Medicine and health.

  Includes index.
  1. Social medicine.   I. Title.   [DNLM: 1. Health.
2. Medicine.   3. Sociology, Medical.   WA 31 R532m]
RA418.R53   1987   362.1   86-10692
ISBN 0-582-29686-2

Produced by Longman Singapore Publishers (Pte) Ltd.
Printed in Singapore

INTRODUCTION

The book is offered as an overview of some of the current debates on health. Its thematic packaging may be irksome to some specialists in medical sociology. That rendition has been deliberate. The presentation tries to find a comfortable path between the academic 'robustness' of the epidemiological direction, stuffed to the brim with tables and correlations, and the philosophical abstractions of the social theories of health. The task is not to be a sapient guide leading the 'uninitiated' through the labyrinthine ideas of great minds, and then determining what Marx, Foucault and Parsons, etc. really (meant to have) 'said'.

The core of the material is Anglo-American, but prongs have been attached to other health formats; namely from traditional and modernising societies. The latter are more than cultural examples. Western scientific medicine, though cosmopolitan now in influence, is having to recognise its own limitations and will be increasingly impacted by other health beliefs. Although the thematic approach leads to an artificial compartmentalisation, many health topics do bounce their way through the whole book, appearing in new guises within different contexts. The notions of 'patient', 'doctor' and 'treatment regimes' cannot be transfixed, and frozen, within one frame.

Chapter 1 acts as the 'trailer' and attempts to show how health beliefs and theorising are central to all societies. Disease often challenges the moral order, by raising key questions on 'naturalism' – the elusive taken-for-granted baseline. Some diseases have shaped the semiotic repertoire. The pay-offs for different vested interests in cross-cultural medicine are also illustrated. For example, the cold war between USSR and USA is played out with health indicators.

Chapter 2 looks at the interplay between technology and medicine, setting the debate within the wider issues of social change and control in industrial society. Moral philosophy has been revitalised by the new challenges. The potentialities of *in vitro* fertilisation and similar developments have sharpened ethical demands. Medical technology offers, too, new definitions of patient; stipulating, accordingly, other obligations.

Chapter 3 takes the central concept of 'sick role', launched by Parsons, and navigates it through the shoals of critical scrutiny. Parsons' prescriptive model of how patients should respond to their illness has been much modified by later empirical research. How people come to know that they are ill, the referral stages and subsequent illness behaviour have been the mainspring of many studies.

Chapter 4 provides a window on the secret garden of the doctor–patient relationship. The lay and professional dimensions of time frequently clash and strategies are devised for handling these dilemmas. How the front-line doctor, the GP, has been buffeted by rapid change – more incurable illness and increased client unemployment, etc. – is one focus. Gender differences in diagnosis are another.

Chapter 5 is concerned with professionalisation. This dominant occupational trend and its implications for medical practices are explored, while at the same time some of its varied derivations are chased. The rules of the professional game are well established and act as a model for would-be aspirants. Illich's indictment of the medical profession and posited solution have now lost some of their original shine, but nevertheless still remain forceful and worth rehearsing.

Chapter 6 explores the hospital, which is more than the strategic site in the fight against disease. It is also the workplace for a complex mix of occupational and status groups. Two major aspects are explored. First, how the hospital, as an organisation, has been made to fit into structural and political ideas developed in other areas. The Griffiths recommendations for reform are but one set of proposals in a long line of attempts to get the hospital structure 'right'. Second, hospitals have induced patient alienation by their processing mechanisms: strategies of intervention, mainly for pre-operative patients, have been devised. Their efficacy is analysed.

Chapter 7 is devoted to an interpretation of medical errors. For a long time the scientific mask of medicine has projected a progressive face, inhibiting external scrutiny of its practices. Medicine has developed 'creative' tactics and ideology for handling its own errors – often transforming them into professional learning aids. Errors are more frequently blamed on the deviant patient, who disobeys doctor's orders. The view from the patient's side will be offered. Psychiatry is also under renewed pressure to rethink its diagnostic categories; the implications of cross-cultural values are considered.

Chapter 8 is concerned with the new buzz-word, 'community'. Both the political right and left are promoting it as the way forward in health and other activities. Some of its tortuous history in social thought will be outlined, as well as current practical applications. In the nineteenth century the belief was strong that community had been 'lost'. The major Italian experiment of 1978, when many psychiatric hospitals fully decanted their patients, will be traced. Primary health care in the less developed world is another variant of the mystique of community; some of its pitfalls will be highlighted.

Chapter 9 looks at that pastiche usually referred to as 'alternative medicine'. The list is endless: acupuncture, primal analysis, homoeopathy and reflexology are only the top line of a large menu. The public's interest is intensifying. Reasons for this are posited: dangerous drug reactions, bureaucratisation and impersonality of 'orthodox' medicine – to point to the obvious ones. The relationship between cosmopolitan and alternative medicines has never been an easy one. Some rapprochement is promised with the talk of the 'holistic' approach.

Chapter 10 takes us into the area of unemployment and health. Some have likened unemployment and its consequences to the 'new plague'. The post-industrial society of superabundance for all, a figment of academic imagination in the 1960s, will not materialise. Large-scale unemployment is likely to persist and experts, like Brenner, argue that medical and social 'pathologies' will increase. The determining variable is considered increased 'stress'. This claim will be reviewed. Doctors have used 'return to work' as a criterion for confirming recovery. If this indicator is no longer available for many, medical norms become more problematic.

A final note, the book is not intended as a flagship to signal a new brand of medicine. Hopefully, it is a prompt, to help some in their attempt to theorise about health in general, and their own existence.

Joel Richman

Chapter one

HEALTH BELIEFS AND CULTURE

All societies have notions of health and its variants. It is universally acknowledged that to be healthy is desirable. Health concerns can entwine all aspects of social structure. Everyday greetings often probe a person's well-being. 'How are you?', can elicit a range of responses, graded according to the relationship between the enquirer and respondent. In a fleeting contact, as on the street, a quick and generalised response of 'fine', or 'not too bad', suffices. Between those who share mutual trust, etiquette demands elaboration and more self revealment. Details of anatomical functioning are then permissible. A sharp pain in the left shoulder can be supported by either 'simple' or 'detailed' theories as to its cause.

Societies differ, however, in how they produce and accept 'reasonable' explanations for health conditions. In our society a plausible explanation from a middle-aged man could be that he 'suddenly' engaged in a strenuous activity and damaged a 'weak' muscle. In a *traditional* society, like the Azande, described by Evans-Pritchard (1937), those with 'an unusual' shoulder pain may seek out the 'real' cause of the condition. The cause, in unusual circumstances, is often thought to lie outside the body, in the tensions generated in interpersonal relations with others. Those who envied, or quarrelled with him, may have resorted to witchcraft. The Azande, like us, know that the shoulder pain *can* be caused by physical exertion but, in 'unusual' circumstances, are prepared to extend the relevance of explanation by incorporating others as the 'primary' cause. We would normally rely on the medical profession to provide the 'real' explanation for our misfortune.

Health beliefs also surface on departures: with the entreaties to 'keep well' and 'take care'. Moving from familiar places can present unknown risks. Before commencing difficult journeys the *Romans* initiated collective invocations; with the use of sacrifice and libation they called upon household and clan gods to protect the departee's health from external, unknown forces. Prior to the destruction of the first temple, the *Ancient Hebrews* carried a piece of tribal land when travelling beyond it. At that time, Jehovah was not yet considered a universal god. His protective powers were restricted to one's tribal territory. In today's societies, preparations for sustaining health *en route* are similarly ritualistic: vaccinations, health documents and a personalised medical chest are the normal accoutrements. But the focus of our health beliefs is different: the internal structure of the individual is the major, explanatory base. Nevertheless to maintain, or restore health, necessitates *in all cultures* that prescribed patterns of behaviour be followed. This ritualistic component of healing does however vary, with Western scientific medicine according it only a secondary and unintentional effect.

To promote the message that health care and culture are indivisibly entwined, the following related themes will be raised. Firstly, attempts will be made at finding common ground for defining 'health' from the vast array of its uses. Secondly, we shall examine some ways health and disease have been linked to social change when, for example, plagues have decimated populations. Thirdly, we shall explore the explanatory value of some belief models: these are the cultural principles which articulate the mechanisms responsible for the 'cause' of disease. Fourthly, we consider how illness and disease can shape the symbolic values of society. Fifthly, we tease out the significant characteristics of *traditional* and *western scientific* medicine. Dunn (1976) prefers to call the latter, *cosmopolitan medicine,* for its domination is accelerating world wide. This leads to a discussion of some of the issues which inevitably arise in a cross-cultural analysis of medicine. The developing countries are often used as a comparative 'laboratory' for testing European derived theories of health.

WHAT IS HEALTH?

To be healthy implies to be in 'harmony' – how and with what, raises huge *epistemological* questions of an essentially philosophical hue. Embedded deep in this puzzle are problems of: what is 'natural', i.e. society's base-line for according social judgements about human conduct. *Cosmological* frameworks must also be deployed for explaining how the total physical and social components of a society are 'ultimately' meant to mesh – notions of health and sickness permeate all dimensions. Not least, society's reasoning about health is ultimately based on a deciphering of the 'primordial contract' – i.e. a perception of the 'original' and intended version of humanity. The body then becomes the significant framework through which moral order is represented. To be sick means a deviation from accepted standards of well-being. Changes in bodily functions/social conduct, represented by signs and symptoms, constitute the cultural repertoire for recognising, diagnosing, or defining (according to cultural emphases) the condition. So intense is the theorising about health, that the attributes of health become attached to other contexts – as when we talk of someone having a 'healthy attitude'. Distasteful behaviour, similarly, can be labelled as 'sick'; many criminal acts of violence are thus headlined. References to 'mindless violence', often applicable to 'vandalism', clearly reflect the mind/body dichotomy underpinning much of western medical beliefs. The mechanistic conceptualisation of the body owes much to the influence of Newton and Descartes.

The universal conjunction between health and harmony needs further emphasis. The Ancient Greeks, as represented by Plato's writings, very much equated health with the soul, which was synonymous with perfection. To them, the world was in a steady-state equilibrium. Souls gave it the essential and residual form. To understand health, one had to go beyond appearances and first impressions, since these relied on perceptions, which often varied. Health was *not* a perceptual entity to the Ancient Greeks. Moravcsik (1976) shows that although Plato never had a theory about health, *per se*, he (and other Greek philosophers) used health and the body as the resource for wider ethical reasoning.

To maintain health was worthwhile, but not at all costs. To extend life beyond the dictates of 'nature' would be abnormal. Maximisation of pleasure and elimination of pain were not necessarily indications of health; although Plato argued that on balance a healthy life would tend to be more pleasurable. Physicians would be in dereliction of their duties if hedonism – the idea that pleasure is the most important thing in life – was made their chief tenet. Although health and nature were regularly ordered, it was recognised that there could not be one complete set of evaluative signs appropriate for all. Indications of what constitutes health for children, the aged or warrior amputees will clearly differ though the fundamental principle of health would not.

From this crude cameo it should be obvious that the concerns of the Greeks remain with us. They can be translated into the ethical dilemmas of using life-support machines when 'brain death' has occurred. The 'pleasure principle' has parallels with the ambiguous status of cosmetic surgery for heightening sexual arousal. With rapid demographic change doctors have the task of agreeing appropriate, normative standards for evaluating the health status of different groups. Questions of 'normal' ageing and the probability of the health deterioration of President Reagan during a second term of office, have been a matter of electoral significance.

The health–harmony thesis can also be elaborated, contrastingly, in the Sande society of present-day Sierra Leone. MacCormack (1982) has extensively reported their practices. The Sande is a woman's sodality (men have their own, Poro), whose senior members take responsibility for women's health and pregnancy. Briefly, the Sande cosmology locates water as the home of ancestors and sky as the place of the creator god. Both powerfully influence earth where humans live with plants and animals, who share the supernatural properties of the sky and water forces. For a successful pregnancy a woman must abide by strict taboos, often dietary, lest misfortune befalls her. She avoids eating birds, for they articulate the balancing domains of the sky creator and water ancestors. Abnormal births are considered the product of a malevolent spirit. They must be left to die in order to neutralise its evil intrusion on birth and to stabilise everyday life.

Major medical systems have formulated clearly their health-balancing principles. The Chinese focus on the opposition of Yang and Yin. The male and female components provide contrasting life energies in the body's meridian flow.

Unani medicine, widely practised in the Islamic part of India, and now in England, relies on balancing the four humours: black and yellow bile, blood and phlegm. Each humour can be either hot or cold, or wet and dry. (The Chinese recognised six humours.) The excess of one element can be neutralised by the taking of an appropriate substance, proportionately, with the opposite properties. Hot and cold do not refer to the properties of temperature, but to its delegation within a 'natural' classification. For example, pregnancy is considered 'hot', while lactation is not. Meat and fish are also considered hot, to be avoided during pregnancy. Unani medicine is founded on the Greek tradition of Galen and Hippocrates, whose ideas diffused to India via Arab traders in the eighth century. The humoric basis of cosmopolitan medicine was mainly extinguished by the nineteenth century.

In Central and South America another version of the hot–cold distinction is also prevalent, mainly among peasants. It is likely that this health scheme preceded the Spanish conquistadores. McCullough (1973) claims it has biological, evolutionary implications. The peasants in the hot Yucatan plains take care not to over-exert themselves in the hot sun; a hot condition is regarded as highly dangerous. The chances of heat-induced diseases are also reduced by cooling down with salt water drinks.

Worsley (1982) has cautioned against the readiness of some to jump abruptly to the conclusion that the opposition/complementarity of these health axioms provide an easy accessibility to the decoding of their societies' cultural apparatus. French 'deep' structuralists, like Lévi-Strauss, would regard them as a lever for exploring the 'unconscious' culture of a society. Worsley calls for systematic observations of the health principles in use, by groups with different interests, before general rules are gleaned.

Concentrating on the health–harmony equation has detracted from the other linked issue: what is disease and illness? The tendency has been to regard disease as a deviation and an abnormality. This is misleading. Assuming a consensus on what constituted 'harmony' or 'normality', it is problematic if individuals could maintain that condition for long. To be completely disease free is, so far, an illusion. The oft-quoted World Health Organisation definition is messianic in its intent '. . . a complete state of physical, mental and social well-being, not merely the absence of disease or infirmity'. The 'social well-being' dimension does not question the appropriateness of different value systems to foster individual health. To experience a 'frequency' of illness in one's lifetime could be considered normal, for it would be a realistic outcome. The question now becomes: what level of frequency (for a disease or disease pattern) is within tolerable limits? All societies have taxonomies of disease. Cosmopolitan medicine has been rapidly enlarging its disease lexicon, but has not produced satisfactory explanations on the causes of all. To label a disease does not necessarily mean that its parameters are fully known. The mountains of sick notes and death certificates have their explanations geared more towards administrative convenience.

What is accepted as disease is often a matter of cultural notation. Bilharziasis, transmitted by water-borne fluke, has not always been recognised: most fellahin in the Nile region had it. In nineteenth-century England high blood pressure was a symptom, now it is recognised as a serious disease. The over indulgence of alcohol was once regarded as a social evil of the lower working classes; alcoholism is now a disease common to all.

The terms 'illness', 'disease' and 'sickness' are usually slurred together, to add to the confusion. Kleinman's (1978) distinction is useful, but limited. Disease is reserved for the abnormalities in the structure and functioning of the organs; the pivot of the biomedical model. These need not be culturally or individually explicit. Illness refers to an individual's experience of disease and other related conditions. Sickness can be used interchangeably for aspects of illness and disease. When applied cross-culturally these categories can fracture. Some traditional societies locate disease outside the body. Industrial society refers more to 'stress-related' disease, also implying some external causation. The pattern of disease and treatment distinguished by each culture reveals the practical reasoning on which its wider social order is based. Despite cultural variation in disease recognition, a number of common features are shared: diseases have origins, characteristic indicators, and undergo stages of development. Pre-1940 cosmopolitan medicine frequently referred to the 'crisis' point of an illness, when a sudden change for the better or worse, occurred.

The Greeks placed great store on dramatic changes in the disease trajectory occurring on special days, based on multiples of seven. In the past, when doctors were unable to effect a cure, they accrued prestige by their capacity to predict disease outcomes. Kahana (1985) shows how traditional healers are still able to maintain their legitimacy by this device. In Ethiopia, with Christian Amhara and Jewish Falasha, the belief in possession by Zar spirits is very strong. Zar healers do not lose credibility if they are ineffective, as long as they can explain their limitations in handling the superior and unpredictable spirit.

Paradoxically, as scientific research on disease has increased, the more abstract and problematic has the concept become. King (1982) notes that the word 'disease' embraces two separate propositions. One derivation is from 'morbus', a word used by sixteenth-century physicians when Latin was the common, medical language. Morbus is derived from the Latin 'mors', death – disease in this sense heralded its strong possibility. The English word 'disease' has its source in the Old French 'aise', meaning comfort. Dis-ease therefore meant to interfere with comfort (or be ill at ease) – not death-threatening episodes. Death-threatening diseases are readily acknowledged. The Tay–Sacks disease (amaurotic idiocy) with high incidence among Ashkenazim Jews, was first described by the British ophthalmologist, Tay, in 1881, and results in death between the second and fifth years of infancy. Mental retardation, convulsions and paralysis are part of the tragic trajectory.

On the opposite pole of the disease spectrum there is often no firm agreement about what should be incorporated as a disease. Sun-bathing to achieve a healthy-looking tan is socially desirable. It has been advocated for those with vitamin D deficiency (e.g. some house-centred Bangladeshi women in England). Too much exposure can be damaging: not only with the immediacy of sunburn. There can be long-term degenerative effects to oil cell structures; some susceptible people (fair-skinned) will develop skin cancer. The boundary between bodily change and disease cannot be precisely fixed, often falling prey to sorites.

Of increasing relevance is the question of the ideal standard of beauty, being more readily purveyed. Those dissatisfied with aspects of their body, to the point of social incapacitation, could be said to fall within the disease orbit. The medical status of cosmetic surgery is ambiguous, responding as it does, to changing 'consumer fads'. The affluent also use it to delay ageing – at least its outward signs. In many cultures it is women's shapes which are socially sculptured. Some East African herding tribes elongate the necks of young girls with rings, Victorian ladies were tightly corseted into hour-glass figures. The disease consequences are clear. Should the rings be removed asphyxiation would occur, as a result of the atrophied neck muscles; corseting produced liver damage.

An allied point; if disease (especially non-infectious) is a developing phenomenon, whence does it originate? Eighteenth-century physicians located it either in the specific organ 'under attack' (idiopathic), or originating there but then colonising other organs (sympathic). To locate a disease does not necessarily result in its explication. Diabetes, affecting the pancreas, 'appears' in children when around six years and in others at twelve years. Huntington's Chorea, associated with hereditary degeneration of parts of the brain, is often apparent when over forty. Where (and what) were the diseases before their clinical emergence? To proclaim they are the product of a virus, defective gene or chemical imbalance, does not remove the question asked. Although doctors may recognise a pre-disease stage – as with women who have untypical cervical cells, called dysplasia, who are then treated for 'early' cancer – there is still no certainty that without treatment disease would develop. Some cancers and multiple scleroses have 'spontaneous' remissions, permanent or otherwise, as part of their trajectory. This only re-emphasises the question: where is the disease?

This fundamental issue can challenge the social order of societies. The problematics of some diseases pose a threat – moral, legal, social and political. How each culture responds reflects its theorising with the body of knowledge used to sustain its own version of social reality.

The history of western medicine reveals oscillation between two competing perspectives. One is the *ontological* view which considers disease as a specific entity, unrelated to the individual's personal and social characteristics. The Ancient Greek and Roman schools of medicine were responsible for the earliest formulation. The mechanistic vista of the universe stamped on our imagination by Newton in the seventeenth century and again, later, by discoveries in bacteriology by Pasteur and Koch in the nineteenth century and by post-1930 discoveries in antibiotics, all contributed to the powerful position that for each specific disease there was a distinct cure.

One corollary of this doctrine was that the body is merely the receptacle for disease. This sacred text urges medical research to go hunting the 'holy grail' of disease, as if it were a thing. Both Presidents Nixon and Reagan pledged electorally to discover 'the' cause (and cure) of cancer. Opposing this heroic view of medicine is the notion that disease is an 'abstraction', indivisible from the individual's total existence. This focuses attention towards the complex relationship between an individual's personality, social network and environment, and these two contrasting modes are not unique to western medicine; other cultures play out these themes, as we show later.

SOCIAL CHANGE, DISEASE AND ILLNESS

There are many theories to explain why societies change. Durkheim, in the last century, argued that a major and sudden population increase will cause a new 'moral density', necessitating a more complex division of labour. Marx's often repeated argument is better known: that the economic contradictions and resulting conflict between the owners of the means of production and labour will lead to irreconcilable conflict and change. Others have emphasised the 'determination' of new technology, the juggernaut effect; and the appearance of entrepreneurial personalities. Most theories rarely appeal to health and disease as important factors, but Marxists obliquely incorporate health deterioration in the the process of miserisation and intensified economic competition.

Historians, subscribing to the 'great man' view of history, are often directed to inspect the health profiles of their subjects when considering decision making. However, it is difficult to prove directly that a ruler's sickness did alter the course of history. For example, Martin Luther (1483–1546), who helped to transform the religious face of Christendom, lists many influences on his development: the severity of his childhood upbringing; the harsh discipline in his local Latin school; the inspiration of Occamist philosophy. Yet it was the 'fear' of death from lightning that led him to become a monk in the Erfurt Monastery. In later life he suffered badly from 'irregular' bowel movements. How do all these things add up? Nearer our times, was Nazi Germany defeated because of Hitler's 'nervous' disease, or because of his 'fixation' with the strategy of geo-politics; culminating in the disastrous invasion of Russia and the war on two fronts? Could the partitioning of Europe after the Second World War be laid on the shoulders of the very infirm President Roosevelt at the Yalta Conference? We can never know.

The relationship between disease and changes within social structure is much clearer. Anthropological historians, like Ackerknecht (1953), have traced the longevity of some of our modern diseases. Versions of arthritis were common in the earliest hominids, and in some animals, even dinosaurs. Degenerative knee disease was an occupational hazard of hunting bands, male Eskimos having the highest rate. The constant jarring movements on hard ice were responsible.

It was the introduction of sudden, 'unmanageable' disease which had the greatest impact. In medieval Europe, plagues brought devastation and loosened the social fabric. Rufus of Ephesus presented the first accurate description of the fatal disease, originating primarily in North Africa and Syria, but it was not until the sixth century that Europe first experienced it. Bede chronicled its appearance in England between 664 and 683: some forms were bubonic, while others were pneumonic. The culmination was the Black Death in the fourteenth century; it was estimated that one-quarter of the European population died, perhaps more in England.

The plague's reputed origin was Central Asia and its spread followed the trade routes. In England the high mortality among villeins weakened feudalism. Moral uncertainty fostered alternative religious forms (heresies) for salvation, like the Lollards. As a footnote, the plague has been recorded this century in the USA, but with minor consequences. In San Francisco 1907–08, there were 159 cases and 7 deaths.

The introduction of new diseases decimated the indigenous populations of the Americas, accelerating its colonisation by Europeans. Measles, smallpox and influenza were deadly to those lacking immunity. In North America those diseases often followed the fur trails, and settlers deliberately spread smallpox by passing infected blankets to Indians. Malaria also followed the Europeans into the New World, arriving via their black slaves who had evolved an immunity to it in Africa. Paradoxically this immunity was at the expense of proneness to sickle cell anaemia. Indians could not survive the malaria in lowland sugar plantations. The introduction of European-based diseases into the Pacific, as in Polynesia, greatly disrupted the traditional cultures. The high and random death rates fractured networks of gift exchange. As the appropriate gifts were lacking, the legitimacy of social transactions like marriage was undermined.

Medicine has increasingly been used as an adjunct of state policy. Most descriptions of the 'good society' have emphasised the virtues of health. After the Boer War, for example, there was much debate on the poor 'physique' of working-class recruits. Britain's declining economy prior to 1914, relative to its competitors like Germany, renewed the concern for the health of its industrial workers, who were thought to lack the 'appropriate' work discipline. Corrective occupational health measures were introduced. The wider issue of a eugenic policy was also aired. It was hoped that encouraging the 'less fit' and poorest to reduce their family size would cause the 'moral' and health status of the country to rise. Current debates on cutting into the 'cycle of deprivation' echo this policy.

Nazi Germany carried to extremes a eugenics policy with its medicalised killing camps. For the new Reich to last a thousand years, racial 'purification' was essential. The obscene doctrine was supported by influential academics – doctors, geneticists and physical anthropologists – who subscribed to the formation of an Aryan master race. Medical imagery permeated the extermination policy. Jews, Slavs and gipsies were portrayed as inferior species; presenting a health threat. If left untreated, they could infect the gestation of the new Germany. Propaganda films frequently interspersed scenes of ghetto Jews with those of rats; the message that both were the harbingers of plague was clear.

Lifton's (1982) psychological study of the medical behaviour in Auschwitz argues that the Nazi hierarchy could aptly be called a 'biocracy'. Their authority was based upon supreme biological principles. The institutional rhetoric of the extermination camps was laced with medical insignia. Selection for the gas chambers resembled a collective, medical screening; the inmates were told to undress in the 'medical blocks'. Although the camp doctors did not always participate in the killing, they supervised the acts of junior staff.

The inmates formed a large, passive reservoir of 'specimens', who were used for experimentation designed to promote the health of the new Germany. Some were injected with infectious diseases, like typhus, for testing new vaccines: others were bombarded with X-rays; testes and ovaries were then removed for evaluating the effects of sterilisation. Lifton describes, too, the coping strategies used by doctors, normally dedicated to saving life, for participating in these death orgies. Professional integrity was maintained by translating their immoral acts into 'scientific' and 'technical' questions. Extermination and mutilation were 'normalised', as just 'ordinary' work. Doctors developed also the ideology that it was they who were undergoing a medical ordeal, because of the enormity of their 'task'. Japanese doctors, imbused with similar racist doctrines, also experimented on defenceless prisoners with germ and freezing techniques; they too crossed the line from healer to killer.

Germ warfare is one of the least discussed of the fatal options available in a superpower conflagration. There are charges and counter-charges about its use today. Cuba has accused the CIA of responsibility for the outbreak of Dengue Fever in 1981. The disease was previously unknown in Cuba and was spread by the mosquito *Aedes Aegypti* from three different sources. Over 300,000 cases were reported, with 158 deaths.

HEALTH BELIEF MODELS (HBM)

It is necessary to classify the multifarious descriptions of health beliefs and practices. These, it has been stressed, are culture laden. Classification permits 'shorthand discussion' of principles across cultural boundaries. The hot/cold equilibrium is one such model. Others are described below.

Supernatural and natural

This distinction is perhaps the oldest. It owes much to nineteenth-century evolutionary theories. Belief in supernatural causation was considered by armchair anthropologists, like Frazer, to characterise those at an earlier and 'primitive' stage of reasoning – animism. This belief was considered infantile; environmental features (like rocks, trees and animals) contained spirits, affecting everyday existence. When missionaries heard Australian aborigines claim affinity with kangaroos – 'the kangaroo is my brother' – they misunderstood the account. They considered that the aborigines were suffering from delusions; in fact, kangaroos played a significant, totemic role in the aborigines' world order.

Reliance on natural causation was equated with more 'scientific' reasoning; substantiated by some empirical evidence. At best, supernatural medical models were considered as 'misguided' and generally harmless, sometimes curing by 'chance' hysterical conditions, whereas natural HBMs offered from European ethnocentrism, more potential effectiveness. The supernatural HBMs were considered to contain the following agents of illness: wrathful gods and ancestors who inflict suffering on those transgressing moral codes; witches and sorcerers operating for self-gain; loss of the soul and other vital parts (e.g. mana of the Polynesians) by dreams or other stronger powers; convulsive, alien spirit-possession of the body. The natural HBM was considered a closer progenitor of scientific medicine, e.g. as typified by humoric balance.

Much depends on the prior definition of 'natural'. At one time western medicine contained large elements, which by today's criteria of natural, would be considered supernatural. In the sixteenth-century astrological causation of illness was considered natural, by the conventions of the time. Illness resulted from the influence of unfavourable coincidences of celestial bodies. Modern research has demonstrated, incidentally, that rates of bleeding during operations can be correlated with lunar phases! Ayurvedic medicine, the dominant form in India, is very much underpinned by medical astrology. Horoscopes reveal the individual's susceptibility to illness and prognosis. The planet Mercury exerts undue influence on the nervous system, leading to mental derangement.

Personalistic and natural

This HBM was suggested by Foster (1976, 1983) for cross-cultural analysis within traditional medical systems. It was developed with an awareness of the semantic and philosophical difficulties conveyed by the category of 'supernatural', already referred to. 'Personalistic' explains disease etiology by the 'purposeful' intervention of agents deliberately pursuing their victims; causing them to fall ill. The malevolences can be human (witches), non-human (ancestors and other spirits) or 'supernatural' (deities). A naturalistic model is founded on the broad principles of impersonality, common to everyone's existence. Sickness becomes the product of some imbalance in the human condition, whether it be humoric or loss of excessive heat/cold forces. Foster notes the geographical distribution of these two schemes. Pre-European Africa, the Americas and Oceania have a predominance of the personalistic type, whereas Indian and Chinese medicine have a greater frequency of the naturalistic model. Other medical regimes can also be considered naturalistic; homoeopathic medicine, acupuncture and the germ theory of cosmopolitan medicine.

The healer's role differs in the two schemes. Personalistic healers do not probe symptoms in great detail. Diagnosis is channelled into tracking down the motives of those who have vented displeasure on the sick. Once revealed, the appropriate remedy can then be applied. One solution is to exorcise the offending agent; sometimes by absorbing it within the healer's own body. His own superior powers can later neutralise it. Christ did the same, when he absorbed the sins/sickness of mankind. Another course is for the victim, by a change in moral conduct, to offer recompense to the offended agent. Naturalistic explanations of disease involve the application of more specific treatments on the body. For example, 'cold' herb therapies and frequent bleeding can be used to counteract excessive body heat. Prohibitory behaviour, often dietary, is often used.

Foster is aware of the limitations of his taxonomy. Most societies are mosaics of both natural and personalistic causation. Ayurvedic medicine, although predominantly naturalistic, can accommodate personalistic explanations, such as the evil eye and witchcraft. Among the Zulus, described by Ngubane (1976), the belief in sorcery (ukuthakatha) causing disease is combined with the notion of balance (ukufa kwabantu). Zulus accept that their existence is meshed with nature; plants, animals and people. As humans and animals move to other places they leave behind 'aspects' of themselves and simultaneously 'absorb' parts of the place (e.g. atmosphere or tracks of animals). Disease can be spread when a serious illness, taken from one person, is left suspended for another to catch.

In Britain today, 'victims' of road accidents can understand the mechanics of their injuries, but will frequently demand to know 'why it has happened to them'. Further, the principle of balance central to naturalistic explanation, also operates within the personalistic model. Good health is restored when the patient is reintegrated with the offended spirit, with their social discord removed.

Retribution HBM

Others have teased out for comparative analysis the personal theorising engaged in by the sick. Serious illness not only incapacitates but it also confronts the pysche with demands for new explanations about the shattering of the moral world, which was formerly taken for granted. This is common in all cultures, as exemplified by our road accident victim. The sick search their past for clues which might illuminate their present misfortune. Ito (1982) has referred to misfortunes assigned to retribution as 'retributive comeback'.

The range of explanations offered are classifiable, reflecting, as they do, different tension patterns found in each society. These can include; parent–child relations, wider kin and contractual work obligations, etc. Ito's study ('comeback' was the actual term used by his respondents) among urban, Hawaiian women, elaborates the inter-connections between social obligations and medical theorising. The older Honolulu neighbourhoods were sampled. They contained the largest percentage of native Hawaiians; most were poor and marginalised. Detailed biographies were given of six women, who had sixty-two children between them.

Ito located two sources of retributive comeback. There are inter-group disputes (Hukihuki), as between families. Third parties, especially 'defenceless' children, are the likely sickness victims. The other type is due to an individual's thoughts or actions. Rudeness is a serious breach of convention. The retributive comeback can be conveyed by spiritual (Hawaiian, Christian gods, or unknown mediums) and human forces. Hawaiians undertake detailed bio-graphical searches for their diagnosis. The parallel with western psychotherapy is overt. Psychic complaints are believed rooted in 'earlier' experiences. The latter have to be reconstructed, made meaningful and then they become acceptable.

Internalising and externalising

Young's (1976) formulation is a further attempt at eradicating the ethnocentric bias of cosmopolitan medicine's claim to be the best measure of disease recognition and treatment. Empirical proof of medical practices is not the monopoly of cosmopolitan medicine. All seek it, according to the central tenets of the respective medical beliefs. The Amhara (living around the old Ethiopian capital, Gondar), followers of an early form of Christianity, monophysitism (the belief that there is only one nature, a synthesis of the divine and human) have been used by Young to advance his argument.

Their medical explanations include attacks by demons (Ganel), animal spirits and sorcery. Protective amulets are frequently worn. By scientific criteria this practice is atavistic and useless. However, if the amulets fail to protect, the Amhara, like us, seek empirical reasons. The religious text in the amulet could have been contaminated by rain and sweat; or the sacred preparation of the text was inappropriate. We also claim that failure of vaccines was due to a 'faulty' batch. Symbolic proof of medical efficacy has greater warranty among the Amhara. This proof is increasingly promoted by cosmopolitan medicine's treatment of the many chronic. The aura of 'contentment' and 'quality of life' are offered as proof of success with chronic and terminal patients.

Young presents *internalising* and *externalising* as polar opposites; with all HBMs gradated between them. Internalising systems emphasise physiological functions; externalising ones emphasise events outside the body. The latter are presented as anthropomorphised narratives. Thus in externalising systems anatomical differentiation is simplistic; e.g. the body may only be divided into an 'upper' and 'lower' part. The Chiapas Indians of Mexico regard their bodies as a 'black box', merely as a vessel for external change agents. Externalising beliefs frequently offer a single cause for a range of body symptoms. In contrast, internalising beliefs posit many explanations, for the same symptom/disease – as with cosmopolitan medicine.

Young, referencing the Amhara, shows the cultural match between the status of the sick, disease etiology and choice of healer. It is public knowledge that spirits 'prefer' women and the very poor – both of low status. Less powerful and cheaper healers are called in. The cleric healers (deriving their powers from God) inevitably deal with high status clients, like wealthy traders. These are the victims of the most potent, external threats. The hierarchical principles of a society are therefore reinforced by its HBMs. Amharic medical beliefs, in common with others, have their ambiguities, often generated by social change. It is these problematics that healers/doctors are called upon to reconcile within their collection of medical knowledge.

Cross culturally, internalising models are closely associated with those societies with a more complex division of labour; producing an economic surplus supportive of a literate elite. The healers can create a monopoly of their medical knowledge. To conclude, the important point to remember about any health belief system is how it orders and blends both internalising and externalising etiologies. The Amhara, for example, know many anatomical parts, but they only credit the heart and stomach with special health significance. The stomach contains worms for digestion; sickness occurs when they are disturbed and attack the stomach.

IMAGERIES OF DISEASE AND ILLNESS

This section enlarges an earlier comment – how selected illnesses become culturally charged and convey sets of ideas about moral identities within society.

For the individual, illness often means facing the 'unknown'. For society some illnesses, too, can take on additional significance. This can be due to the sudden appearance of an unknown illness (herpes/AIDS); or because of the persistence of a serious sickness, defying medical endeavours (cancer); or when a 'common illness' suddenly flares into a virulent form for 'no apparent reason' (Spanish flu after the First World War); or because a major disease becomes closely associated with an 'outgroup'. These variables operate, of course, within the overarching moral order of the day. Condemnation and fear of some sufferers can be accompanied with demands for their segregation, lest they pollute others and precipitate 'moral decay'. Colonies for epileptics were still present this century.

In medieval Europe, leprosy was once the great social divide between the pure and the impure. Lepers had to give warning of their presence. They were compulsorily zoned outside the walls and were considered victims of divine wrath. Foucault's (1973) impressive thesis explains how madness replaced leprosy as the next great divide. (For a while, venereal disease held sway as an exclusion marker, but did not last: the powerful and upper strata also became unwilling victims of the 'French and Spanish pox'.)

Formerly, folly (madness) was praised and was the inspiration of powerful imagery in literary and artistic works. Did not King Lear offer to exchange his crown for the cap and bell to find wisdom, asks Foucault? With the coming of the age of reason, madness was denigrated. It became equated with all forms of error, being the great underminer of scientific precision and progress. The mad were banished. Burghers paid merchants to convey them elsewhere. Public whippings were also part of the exclusion rituals. Asylums sprang up to house the mad. These operated outside the normal, legal framework. The mad, as irrational, had no civic rights. Sontag (1979) has continued the Foucault theme of how illness can become a metaphor. Whenever the causality is problematic, it has this potential. She particularises TB and cancer. Before TB was treatable, it was a mysterious illness. In the nineteenth- and twentieth-century literature it was portrayed as a spiritual illness, which could expand consciousness. This imagery was evoked, partially, because the lung was in the upper spiritual part of the body. The tubercular look, as exemplified by Chopin, was a model of refinement. Invalidism, with the genteel cough, could be an interesting occupation, especially for leisured ladies. The mysterious trajectory of TB – punctuated with sudden cravings for food and sex – added to its 'mystery'.

The contemporary imagery of cancer as a 'dreaded disease' is sustained because its many forms still defy the armouries of rational, scientific research. Sontag argues strongly that its semiotic potency also proclaims that its diffusion is due to nature's revenge on an overtechnically ordered society.

Sontag erects the interesting hypothesis that the respective, metaphoric dominance of TB and cancer coincided with different stages of capitalism. The nineteenth-century version emphasised strict accumulation of wealth; human energy must be conserved otherwise the body would weaken. The economy of 'spermatic conservation' was the ideal. *Tubercular* patients were also ordered to conserve their ardour and energy. Today capitalism is out of control, like a runaway train. There are no solutions to the 'inevitable' economic and nuclear self destruction and the promise of economic abundance for all will not materialise. The corresponding *cancer* imagery is one of uncontrollability and pessimism. However, a note of reservation has to be added. It is doubtful whether the romanticisation of the high culture on TB, projected from literature, was meaningful to the suffering masses. Some of Sontag's explanations rely heavily on the mechanism of psychological reductionism.

The latest disease to evoke powerful imagery and terror is AIDS – Acquired Immune Deficiency Syndrome. The media headline it as a plague – frequently the 'gay plague'. Cancer, often Kaposi's sarcoma and leukaemias, accompany AIDS and the body's defences fail. Fear is generated because its origin is not fully understood. Theories abound: that it is derived from the African green monkey virus; that it originated from 'outer space'; and that it is the consequence of a 'failed experiment' in genetic engineering. There is no medical cure, just a promise of one if the resources are made available for research – the 'cancer story'. There are many conflicting reports. There have been over 14,000 (1985) reported cases in the USA. One estimate has the number of British cases doubling every six months. The Royal College of Nursing's extrapolation is that by the 1990s there would be one million victims.

Uncertainty is projected by the knowledge that about one in ten with the AIDS antibody will later develop the disease. The incubation period can be four years. Avoidance taboos have been set in motion. Bodies have been avoided in mortuaries. Medical directives have been given to avoid, where possible, autopsies on victims. Fire and ambulance personnel have demanded breathing tubes to avoid the possibility of mouth-to-mouth resuscitation with carriers. Prison officers have 'quarantined' their establishments, restricting transfers. It was reported that a bus driver had refused a homosexual's fare! Parents of haemophiliacs do not want to be told whether their child has the AIDS antibody, to avoid possible refusal by schools. Although it is known that the disease is transmitted through semen and blood, others suggest saliva, breast milk and tears, as well. The fear of unknown transmission is strong. For haemophiliacs, who use Factor VIII to induce clotting, one estimate is that half these children have already got the AIDS antibody. The imported Factor VIII from the United States has been contaminated.

AIDS is thought to have originated in the central African states, primarily Zaire, where it is endemic and infects heterosexuals. Five per cent of Zaire's population is believed infected. It 'spread' to the USA via Haiti. AIDS' close link, in the USA and Europe, with marginal groups, homosexuals and addicts, has amplified the 'moral threat'. Religious fundamentalists go further; they assure that the disease is caused by divine wrath, punishing transgressions against God's natural laws. There are also overtones that AIDS is also the penalty for society's encouragement of promiscuity, sexual exploitation and hedonism. Queensland, Australia, has made it an offence for gays to donate blood. San Antonio, under the Texas Communicable Disease and Prevention control Act 1982, has taken the most extreme measures. AIDS sufferers face a 2–10 years' imprisonment for having sexual intercourse with healthy people, or donating blood and tissue. It is indicative that AIDS is not called the Zaire plague, in the same way as we have the deadly Lassa fever.

Marxists could argue that emphasising the homosexual/bisexual/prostitute connection deliberately deflects from some essential debates on the capitalist exploitation of health. Contaminated blood, in the transfusion network, is not the only threat to health. Lives are at risk from reduced services, NHS 'savings' being used to finance the military machine, or to offer tax benefits to the more prosperous. Hagen (1985) has revealed how blood products, e.g. plasma, manufactured and distributed by Western international companies, have been derived from less developed countries, including AIDS-infected supplies from Haiti, Zaire and elsewhere. One Canadian based company is alleged to have had a turnover of around 20 million dollars in 1979. Blood from these sources is much cheaper; poor families there supplement incomes by selling blood on a regular basis. Thus the spread of AIDS, as part of the Western exploitation of the Third World, has rarely been given prominence.

TRADITIONAL AND COSMOPOLITAN MEDICINE

It is now useful to collate some of the themes represented in HBMs and realign them by making broad comparisons between these two dominant medical forms. Traditional medicine, simply, refers to that indigenously practised in developing societies; often peasant based, tribal and ethnically laced. There are crucial exceptions. Japan is highly developed, technologically, but traditional medicine is still widespread in the form of acupuncture, moxibustion, herbal therapies and massage therapy (amma), etc. In Japan, industrialised on a feudal base, traditional values are still strong.

It is not possible to detail all the debates. For example, comment has frequently centred on the appropriateness of the designation of 'medicine man' and 'shaman' – the traditional 'healer'. Hultkrantz (1985) has returned to the topic; although they are frequently used interchangeably, he argues for their distinctiveness, the shaman not being a variant of medicine man. The term medicine man, too, can be confusing – being gender bound; and some mainly use ritual performance, like singing, not medicines. Hultkrantz argues that shamanistic activity is primarily concerned with mediating, ecstatically, by trances, between this and other worlds on behalf of clients, although medicines, as an adjunct, may also be used. Shamans tend to predominate in hunting and herding societies.

Traditional medicine

There is much diversity in health activities and beliefs covered by this heading. Some have complex etiologies. Others, like the Dobu, have only one explanation of disease – witchcraft/sorcery. They have no special practitioners; some, like the Amhara, worry constantly about disease, while the Cheyenne adopt a 'fatalistic' attitude. Their major anxiety is maintaining an adequate food supply and they believe, too, that disease is caused by the invisible arrows shot by the spirits of animals, like deer; not by magic and taboo breaking. Taboo breakers are weakened and punished in combat, not by sickness. Despite these variegations, it is still possible to sketch common principles.

Since Ackerknecht (1971) chided medical historians for being obsessed by the evolutionary idea that 'primitive' medicine is the predecessor of the modern, and consequently was not worthy of serious study, medical anthropologists have made it an important domain. With immigration from former colonial territories, cosmopolitan medicine is being jostled, intellectually and practically, by it. Closer inspection of traditional medicine has revealed 'scientific' ingenuity. Its pharmaceutical potential is still to be unfolded. The Eskimo used baby incubators made from the skin of seabirds, lined with feathers, and hung over lamps with small flames.

Traditional societies tend to be small scale, public centred, highly ritualised and with their members interrelated with multiplex ties – i.e. kinship ties carrying all sentiments: political, economic, social and religious, etc. Fulfilling reciprocal obligations is the dominant norm. Personal disputes can soon threaten the social order. It is easy to explain why illness causes are often matrixed in interpersonal tensions, and why they are overlaid with moral injunctions. Other common complaints like colds, eye infections and toothache, have different explanations.

Most public rituals have healing purposes, as with the sun dance of American Indians. Navaho males can spend a quarter of their 'productive' time participating in healing ceremonies. To be cured means social reconciliation with kin, ancestors and nature. Treatment is family and community orientated therapy. Dramatically, with the Navaho the family will call in a 'singer' to cure their member. He will chant for nine days; supportive relatives and others will drop in and contribute. We can find examples of 'wound chanting' in Homer.

Healers are local. Their legitimacy can spring from their having been cured from a serious illness. Spirit mediums (shamans) usually practise after receiving the gift of a special spirit. Healers in general have expertise in deciphering the kaleidoscopic, interpersonal tensions enmeshing their clients. Their 'bedside' manner is a major prerequisite. The Cherokee healers would not recruit into their association those with unfavourable dispositions. Healers are client orientated. Clients can evaluate their performances, having seen them many times in public. The Greeks also banished from their cities inefficient doctors.

The pull of clients mitigates against healers innovating, by experimenting to advance knowledge into the realm of 'abstract laws'. Their success rates, against the criteria of cosmopolitan medicine, are unknown. Surgery was not prominent; mutilation of bodies was often evidence of flesh-eating sorcerers. Autopsies were performed, but in order to find evidence of whether witchcraft had caused death. The Azande sought that 'proof' in the bile. Bleeding was an acceptable treatment. Many societies knew how to heal wounds. The Dakotas used sinews as sutures. The Masai used thorns, but their skilful surgery was exceptional, considered by Ackerknecht on a par with Renaissance standards. Splints were used by cultures as different as the Eskimo and Hottentot. Technical, healing procedures were supplemented with protective magic. The Manos of Liberia knew the intricacies of snakebite and used tourniquets; but they also plastered rings of white clay to 'aid' the healing process.

To conclude, traditional health beliefs can only be understood within their social context. Concepts of health permeate their major symbolic structures, through which social order is made intelligible. Healing makes dramatic appeals to these, often manipulating these residual symbols for restorative and harmonious ends. Frake (1961), with his study of how the Subanum classify skin disease, pioneered traditional, medical classifications and pointed us towards their logic. Although he exaggerated the discreteness of each sickness category, he rightly emphasised how the severity of a given symptom, or sickness, is very much dependent on the set of relationships through which it might come to be mediated. The body location of a skin condition can very much affect, for example, marriage transactions.

Cosmopolitan medicine

This has many faces. Its official and powerful face claims that it is derived from natural science; that it is progressive and self-corrective in its search for verifiable universal laws, having overcome past superstitions. Disease becomes a discrete entity, reified and decontextualised.

But cosmopolitan medicine, like any other, cannot be separated from its cultural context. It replicates the structuring of industrial society. That is, one based on increased specialisation of knowledge and tasks, consisting of different classes within a strong centralised state, and shifting towards private life-styles. Cosmopolitan medicine is arranged around a set of specialities, each invested in a body aspect. But the medical process becomes one of 'cultural dismembering' of the body, by its narrow foci of interest. Doctors' knowledge is considered exclusive: clients have little understanding or control over medical procedures, which contrast sharply with the client/healer relationship.

As Foucault (1973) and others have pointed out, cosmopolitan medicine is a discourse, imposing new social constructs upon the world, with its own special vocabulary and new symbols. The term, 'patient', becomes a person with new obligations – to obey doctor's orders. The medical gaze often distorts the individual's (patient) self-concept, adding to his alienation, and enlarging the symptoms. Cosmopolitan medicine is multiplying rapidly in sickness categories. The latest offering is TMJ syndrome, involving the temporo-mandibular joint. Symptoms include facial pain, severe headaches and shoulder pains; all due to teeth grinding. The doctor/patient relationship is an exclusive one; with non-patients rarely incorporated. There are exceptions: in paediatrics parents, usually mothers, become translators of their children's symptoms. In psychiatry, where the patient's condition relates to others, family therapy may be used. But hospitals, as healing places, are insulated from society by medical gatekeeping. To be in hospital, by definition, means to be sick.

Although cosmopolitan medicine stresses its own evolutionary distinctiveness, especially from traditional medicine, it does contain many magical elements. Magic is used for handling uncertainty, not just sickness, but also for ecological purposes. Its prescribed rites creates confidence for the users. In Melanesia, the ritualistic performance relies on the recitation of lengthy spells. African magic makes more use of significant objects and cosmopolitan medicine has its slavish adherence to technical procedures and bureaucratic rules. The taking of blood pressure, the daily rounds of pill-giving and bathing, etc., all take on ritualistic dimensions and generate an aura of 'predictability'. Hospitals see themselves under siege from unknown germs and fear contagion. Many precautionary measures taken, however, are important for their symbolic import.

Magic is a closed belief system resting on an initial untestable premise – namely, that magical forces exist. The evidence for their effects is all around. If we care to examine the 'facts'. 'Inconsistencies' challenging the working of magic can be absorbed by 'secondary' elaborations of belief. If, for example, after the correct, protective magical rites a patient dies, their efficacy is not disputed. Explanations for failure are sought elsewhere: one of the participants in the healing ceremony may have been ritually impure; or a more powerful spirit may have negatively intervened.

Posner (1977) has shown how aspects of cosmopolitan medicine are not immune from such 'witchcraft thinking'. She takes her example from the treatment of diabetes. This is predicated on the initial premise that it can be controlled by 'normalising' the blood sugar level. There is no hard scientific evidence for this assumption. Patients who are 'well controlled' can have severe complications, and the reverse. Many secondary elaborations of belief are deployed to explain away the blatant inconsistencies and keep intact belief in the blood sugar level. Patients can be blamed for negligent self-medication; the pharmaceutical company's insulin may not suit a particular patient and so on.

Summarising, it is increasingly difficult for cosmopolitan medicine to maintain its stance of being founded on scientific rationale, apart from cultural influences. Some of its drugs, like quinine, are derived from traditional medicine. Cosmopolitan medicine is now scavenging herbal treasure troves to extend its pharmaceutical base. Traditional medicine uses between 25,000 and 75,000 species of plants. The Masai alone use over 600. Political and economic exigencies are increasingly setting the medical agenda for health delivery and research. *In vitro* fertilisation and the distribution of dialysis machines are but two recent instances. Medicine and the state have always worked in tandem.

Weindling (1981) gives an apposite example of the influence of German Nationalism after 1871. The state promoted the rise of paediatrics to aid its policy of strengthening the family, for maintaining an adequate supply of industrial labour. Imperial concepts were mirrored in cytology (cellular research). Cells were described as having 'borders', 'cultures', 'colonies' and experience 'domination' and 'invasion'. British medicine has also played its cultural repertoire: since the Second World War it has consistently reinforced the cult of motherhood.

SOME ISSUES IN CROSS-CULTURAL MEDICINE

Cosmopolitan medicine has developed a range of cross-cultural interests. First, there is the pragmatic one of diffusing its own model, especially to the less developed countries: considering it one of the 'blessings of civilisation'. Some recipients do not share this opinion. Rather, they may regard it as colonialism in disguise: promoting an over-dependency on Western technology; sponsoring hierarchical division in the shape of a new professional elite; devaluing community and preventive medicine; and trivialising the skills of local healers.

Cosmopolitan medicine is moving towards the uniform classification of sickness to add 'precision'. Psychiatric diagnosis has been more vulnerable to the charge of erraticism and confusion. Computer-based diagnostic systems, like CATEGO, have produced a 'standard' version of mental illnesses. The *Diagnostic and Statistical Manual* of the American Psychiatric Association (DSM III) has multiplied and 'refined' its categories. Among Western psychiatrists disputes rage over their appropriateness to fit symptoms found within industrial society. For example, for schizophrenia the precondition that symptoms must be present for over six months, will 'slant' the diagnosis to the more 'extreme' cases.

There is the danger that Western-derived constructs of mental illness will be slotted indiscriminately on symptoms with a different cultural context. Malay beliefs, that spirits of dead animals and men (badi) can poison their victims, will easily match Schneider's first rank symptoms of schizophrenia – hallucination and loss of control over the body's boundary. Ndetei and Singh (1983) have attempted to obviate this cultural bias in a study screening eighty psychiatric African patients in a Nairobi hospital. They found that first-rank symptoms in Kenyan schizophrenics are as frequent as in English patients. Other studies had indicated cultural variations: Sri Lankans having low rates, etc. However, the researchers had deliberately chosen their patients on criteria matching English schizophrenics, which tells us very little about the general incidence of schizophrenia in Kenya.

Cosmopolitan medicine is increasingly using cross cultural analysis for extending the range of its own theory base. Those seeking the 'cause' of cancer are incorporating more 'environmental' influences. Exploring cultural variations, may pinpoint these more precisely: Japanese having the highest rate of cancer of the stomach; Chinese the highest rate of cancer of nasopharynx; Filipino men the highest rate of cancer of the liver; Haitian women the highest rate of cervical cancer; while Moslems, Jews, Parsees and nuns have the lowest rates – all provide us with different pointers in unravelling the enigma of cancer.

The overall cancer rates for the USA and Japan are similar: being second to cerebrovascular disease as the major 'killer'. However, the cultural responses are different. American doctors adopt an open approach with their patients. Japanese doctors conspire with the male members of the family of the cancer patient, to keep secret the diagnosis. The Longs (1982) argue that cancer is considered a polluting disease, defiling the individual's inner spirituality. Buddhism and Shintoism place great merit on being ritually clean; rinsing hands and mouths before entering sacred shrines. Japanese link cancer with disfigurement and lingering death; contraventions of the Samurai tradition of 'dying well' with self control. The old pray at 'sudden death' temples for a dignified, quick release from the burdens of old age.

Some isolated communities constitute a 'human laboratory' by having extreme incidences of genetically puzzling diseases. Drake (1984) has reported that in a remote part of the San Luis province, Venezuela, the incidence of Huntington's Chorea is six hundred times greater than in the USA, the Soto family having the world's record for this disease. Examination of these members reveals, for the first time, the chromosome linkage.

Investigations into senile dementia are following clues posed by the disease Kuru, found among tribespeople of New Guinea. This affects the reflexes of women and children, causing uncontrollable trembling. They participate in the ritual cannibalism of deceased relatives, eating the brains. The men hunt and eat fresh animal meat. The brains of young Kuru victims display plaques similar to those found in Alzeimher's disease, indicating a virus connection.

Health/disease as measures of a country's beneficent, are long-standing. In the Ancient World, Galen maintained that the first duty of rulers and other powerful dignitaries (land owners), was the well-being of their subjects. But Plato considered the need for many hospitals and doctors as indicative of bad government!

The USA and USSR, as part of their cold war rivalry, are competing over the merits of their respective health trends. The core of the debate is this. Marxists claim that capitalist exploitation has produced a distinctive disease pattern. Witness the class gradients of morbidity and mortality. The inferior life chances of the poorest are deliberately contrived; being the class casualties of the economic system geared to the needs of the wealthy. Further, the life expectancy differential between males and females in agricultural societies has been reversed, women now live longer. The rapid introduction of new technological processes (e.g. those of chemical toxicity), without adequate testing, to sustain profitability, has caused a new 'plague' of diseases. Increased alienation has also increased stress related diseases.

The Marxist thesis has been countered by Cooper and Schatzkin (1982). They claim that it is industrialisation, not capitalism *per se*, which is responsible. The so-called 'capitalist pattern' of health is present in the USSR. There is a ruling class of techno-bureaucrats, who control the state machinery. This elite has more favourable access to health facilities, with reserved clinics. The 'coronary factor' is present in the USSR: those of lower educational achievement are more at risk. The state has failed to take drastic, preventive measures. Cigarette and alcohol production are state monopolies. Their 'profit' contributes towards the military machine. Butter is still a luxury. To reduce the fat content of the Soviet diet would be a reminder of past food shortages – a dangerous political move. Also, for part of the 1970s infant mortality rose where it declined in the West.

Szymanski (1981) has defended the Soviet position, accusing its adversaries of using disinformation to discredit its health achievements. Concerning the rise in infant mortality – which in the USSR was probably from 23:1,000 in 1970–71 to 31:1,000 in 1975–76, this was localised in Central Asia. (The USSR does not lodge all vital health indicators with the WHO. East Germany, with a lower infant mortality rate than West Germany, does.) Muslim migration to the cities now involves hospitalised births, which are recorded more accurately. In the established industrial centres, infant mortality resembles that in the West. Also, in the 1970s the infant mortality rate for the Ukraine and Estonia, at 17:1000 was two and a half times that of Muslim Uzbekistan. Szymanski also contends that the only other age group to show an abnormal mortality was that of 40–59 years. This band experiences the 'survivor' trauma. Many of their kin were killed in the Second World War in which Russia lost over 20 millions. The 'irrational' guilt felt by these survivors makes them very susceptible to illness. (The same syndrome has been recognised with Jewish survivors from concentration camps.) One final retort by Szymanski, directed at the USA, declares that if black mortality is scrutinised it is much higher than both the USSR and USA national figures!

The final issue is the question of whether there are any mental disorders unique to a specific culture. Psychiatrists and anthropologists are divided on this possibility. the term culture-bound-syndrome has been applied to a pot pourri of conditions. To list a few.

'Amok', found in South East Asia, has actually been incorporated into the English language to mean a frenzied lust for blood. A normally withdrawn quiet person will attack without warning others, and things, with knives, uttering piercing screams. If restrained, the attacker has no recall of events. Early explanations considered 'Amok' as the product of a 'primitive' mind and an 'epileptic dream state'. Recent speculations classify it as a non-organic psychosis, contoured within a special cultural form. Drug addiction, malaria and syphilis have supporting causation.

Murphy (1972) offers another direction, and traces how 'Amok' has undergone a number of cultural redefinitions. In the sixteenth century, the behaviour was associated with kamikaze-style warriors in battle. Then it became associated with those who preferred to die fighting rather than be captured as colonial slaves. Today few cases are reported. 'Amok'-like symptoms are described elsewhere. The 'wild man of Borneo' who figured in European circuses, is a representation of the menacing behaviour (wild gesticulations) displayed in New Guinea. 'Depression' does not precede the 'attacks', nor is a victim killed. Interpretations range from the European ethnocentric ones of hysteria to the tribal explanation of spirit possession for communicating messages.

Windigo (Wendigo, Whitiko), cannabalistic cravings, has been exhaustively researched among the Algonkin Indians of north-east Canada. The sufferer believes he has been transformed into a windigo, an ice-monster. Windigos are often returning hunters, who have been unsuccessful. They reject food and express the wish to eat their kin; perceiving them as fatty animals. The Algonkins recognised the early symptoms and formerly killed the 'pre-windigos'. One treatment was bear fat, as an emetic to expel the heart of ice. This led to the European explanation that windigo is caused by dietary deficiency. Many Algonkins have dietary deficiency (especially vitamin B), but do not develop windigo.

Psychoanalytic theory has been operationalised as an aid. Those who lose prestige, by being unsuccessful hunters, sublimate their anxiety by assuming the form of the windigo. This feared monster now has to be given recognition. Although there are no reliable statistics, it is believed that windigo was more common in the nineteenth century, when European colonisation was most disruptive of Algonkin culture. Although psychiatrically windigo is recognised as 'reactive psychosis', this label fails to encompass the wide variants.

CONCLUSION

The chapter has advanced on a large number of fronts. The thrust maintains that health theorising is central to all societies, raising fundamental questions about the foundation of their moral orders. Society's dilemmas are often dramatised within the 'medical' encounter, and they prompt and promote sets of definitions of the self. Imageries of sickness are a dominant part of the symbolic frame of society, and are frequently called upon to sustain its continuity.

REFERENCES

Ackerknecht E A 1953 Paleopathology. In Kroeber A L (ed) *Anthropology Today*. University of Chicago Press

Ackerknecht E A 1971 *Medicine and Ethology*. Johns Hopkins Press, Baltimore

Cooper R, Schatzkin A 1982 The pattern of mass disease in the USSR: a product of socialist or capitalist development?, *International Journal of Health Services* 12: 459–76

Drake D 1984 Huntington's chorea, *Philadelphia Enquirer*, Aug. 26: 20–35

Dunn F L 1976 Traditional Asian medicine and cosmopolitan medicine as adaptive systems. In Leslie C (ed) *Asian Medical Systems*. University of California Press, Los Angeles

Evans-Pritchard E E 1937 *Witchcraft, Oracles and Magic Among the Azande*. Clarendon, Oxford

Foster G M 1976 Disease etiologies in non-western medical systems. *American Anthropologist* 78: 773–6

Foster G M 1983 An introduction to ethnomedicine. In Bannerman R H, Burton J, Ch'en Wen-Chieh (eds) *Traditional Medicine and Health Coverage*. WHO, Geneva

Foucault M 1973 *The Birth of the Clinic: An Archaeology of Medical Perception*. Pantheon, New York

Frake C (1961) The diagnosis of disease among the Subanum of Mindanao. *American Anthropologist* **63**: 113-32

Hagen P J 1985 *Blood: Gift or Merchandise?* John Wiley, New York

Hultkrantz A 1985 The shaman and the medicine-man, *Social Science and Medicine* **20**: 511-15

Ito K L 1982 Illness as retribution: a cultural form of self analysis among urban Hawaiian women. *Culture, Medicine and Psychiatry* **6**: 385-403

Kahana Y 1985 The zar spirits, a category of magic in the system of mental health care in Ethiopia. *The International Journal of Social Psychiatry* **31**: 125-44

King L S 1982 *Medical Thinking*. Princeton University Press

Kleinman A 1978 Clinical relevance of anthropological and cross-cultural research: concepts and strategies. *American Journal of Psychiatry* **135**: 427-32

Lifton R J 1982 Medicalised killing in Auschwitz. *Psychiatry* **45**: 283-96

Long S O, Long B D 1982 Curable cancers and fatal ulcers, attitudes towards cancer in Japan. *Social Science and Medicine* **16**: 2101-8

MacCormack C P 1982 Health fertility and birth in Moyamba district, Sierra Leone, in MacCormack C P (ed) *The Ethnography of Fertility and Birth*. Academic Press, London

McCullough J M 1973 Human ecology, heat adaptation and belief systems: the hot cold syndrome of Yucatan. *Journal of Anthropological Research* **29**: 32-42

Moravcsik J 1976 Ancient and modern conceptions of health and medicine. *Journal of Medicine and Philosophy* **1**: 337-48

Murphy H B M 1972 History of the evolution of syndromes: the striking case of Latah and Amok. In Hammer *et al.* (eds) *Psychopathology: Contributions for Biological Behavioural and Social Sciences*. Wiley, New York

Ndetei D M, Singh A 1983 Schneider's first rank symptoms of schizophrenia in Kenyan patients. *Acta Psychiatrica Scandinavia* **67**: 148-53

Ngubane H 1976 Some aspects of treatment among the Zulu, in Louden J B (ed) *Social Anthropology and Medicine*. Academic Press, London

Posner T 1977 Magical elements in orthodox medicine: diabetes as a medical thought system. In Dingwall R *et al.* (ed) *Health Care and Health Knowledge.* Croom Helm, London

Sontag S 1979 *Illness as Metaphor.* Allen Lane, London

Szymanski A 1981 On the uses of disinformation to legitimise the revival of the cold war: health in the USSR, *Science and Society* **45:** 453–74

Weindling P 1981 Theories of the cell state in imperial Germany. In Webster C (ed) *Biology, Medicine and Society 1840–1944.* Cambridge University Press

Worsley P 1982 Non-western medical systems, *Annual Review of Anthropology* **11:** 315–48

Young A 1976 Internalising and externalising medical belief systems: an Ethiopian example. *Social Science and Medicine* **10:** 147–56

Chapter two
TECHNOLOGY AND MEDICINE

The popular image cosmopolitan medicine likes to project is one of dedication to civilisation. Driven by science and technology an inexorable momentum will be sustained. Given time and 'adequate' financial resources cosmopolitan medicine will conquer disease and make the world a better place. Nature's secrets will be revealed and improved upon. The media is ready to acknowledge the latest medical discovery; whether it be a new enzyme or surgical technique. TV programmes such as *Your life in their hands*, which let the masses temporarily participate in the medical communion and high drama of an operation, draw large audiences. It is rare for the media patient to die on the operating table; errors are not a major consideration.

In the United States the medical dream of eternal life has been accepted by some rich. Those who have died of incurable illnesses have willed their bodies to be preserved by deep-freezing in liquid nitrogen. When the appropriate medical remedy has been perfected, they expect to be revived. Cryonic companies store these bodies for a fee (some have gone bankrupt!).

The interplay of technology and medicine will now be examined from a number of angles. First, the impact of technology on the changing identity of the patient and on the organisation of medicine will be explored. Second, some ethical issues will be pointed up: modern techniques (like life-support systems) have revitalised the long, historical debate as to what exactly constitutes life and death. Also, computer use is accelerating and the question will be posed as to whether it will reinforce the established medical frame, or shift it in new directions.

CONTRASTING PERSPECTIVES OF TECHNOLOGY

Before discussing medical implications it is worth locating technology within two competing camps. The 'technological determinist' school paints an optimistic picture of the future benefits, as described above. Their argument runs as follows. The same technology will have universal application; with its own built in rule structure on its social use. In Kerr's (1973) version, there is a logic of industrialism directing all societies towards the same final, common society. Although societies have industrialised at different times, they will all inevitably converge around the same culture. This technological thrust will transcend existing political dogmas and social differences, in the same manner as social class. There will be an end to antagonistic ideologies and strife. It is assumed that the blessings of technology will produce a post-industrial society without scarcities. A variant of this idyllic futurology forecasts that the post-industrial society will be knowledge-based. The 'rational' thought of science producing the 'correct' solutions for the human condition. The guardians of this supreme knowledge (the professions) will be guided by high ethical standards. These optimistic scenarios are mainly the product of the 1960s, when western economies were buoyant and the spectre of residual unemployment had not yet materialised.

In contrast, there is a pessimistic view of technological progress, one which long antedates the current Marxist and Ecologists' critiques. Saint Augustine was the forerunner of the 'use–abuse model'; protesting against the production of armaments falsely promulgated in the name of peace. Technological advance is thus the major threat to the continuation of civilisation; accelerating environmental and human exploitation, with their uncontrollable and fatal consequences. Rather than enhance freedom, technology has done the reverse, reinforcing the existing power structures (whether they be in medicine or industry) radiating from the centralised state. Under capitalism, argue its critics, science and technology have been enlisted as agents for overcoming the increasing difficulties of maintaining production and political control. One such view sees the majority suffering further degradation of labour (Braverman 1975) as the work process becomes more fragmented, requiring less individual discretion; all in the name of increased efficiency. People become indistinguishable from the commodities they produce and, paradoxically, become addicted to the very goods rooted in their alienation. These goods are required for sustaining a lifestyle through which they hope to rescue some token of individuality from the 'mechanical repression' which has instrumentalised them (Marcuse 1969). In this scenario technology/science is by no means neutral and at the service of all.

TECHNOLOGY AND MEDICINE

So far, no definition of technology has been offered. It is usually taken for granted that we all know what it is. It is all around us: machinery, television, rockets and X-ray machines. The Council for Science and Society (1983) in its influential review, *Expensive Medical Techniques*, saw no need to offer a definition. But what we see all around us as technical objects are the symbolic presentation of types of knowledge and reasoning: if you like, the 'outward' packaging of specialised sets of ideas. Technology also cannot be separated from the social and organisational procedures devised for its use. McDermott (1972) notes this point, but still considers technology as all the products of medical science that are beneficial in preventing or altering the course of a disease – like drugs, or diagnostic procedures. He coined the term 'samaritanism' for the doctor's performance, itself an artefact, with the technology, which reassures the patient. But he acknowledges that it is not always possible to relate directly the doctor's intervention with the final outcome when dealing with many complex illnesses.

It is doubtful whether more medical technology has produced beneficial effects. Much depends on the methods used to evaluate medical performances. Wolf and Berle (1982) make another valuable point. Technology can be classified further, not just into simple and complex divisions. There is the technology the practitioner directly uses, as his own tool, often enlarging his medical role: the stethoscope being an 'early' example. There is also 'high' technology, applied by others to the practitioner's patient, hiving off part of his role; thus 'separating' the patient from him. Now follows a summary of the major effects of medical technology.

TRANSFORMATION OF THE PATIENT

It is difficult to choose a precise 'pre-technical', baseline for comparison because there were many variations. The poor treated themselves. John Donne's *Devotions upon Emergent Occasions*, describing his experience of typhus (1623), may not be typical; he was attended by the king's private physician, among others. Hawkins (1984) compares Donne's pathography with that of the author, Cornelius Ryan's personal *battle* with cancer, 1979. Television advertisements for pharmaceutical remedies inevitably portray them as 'shooting' straight at the appropriate part of the body to bring quick relief. There is no major intervention within Donne's body; except for imbibing cordials to protect the heart from dangerous humours and the taking of purgatives. Pigeons are placed at his feet to attract the vapours from the body. The disease's course was in God's hands; recovery depended on the patient establishing through his sickness a new and better relationship with divine will. Repentance was an essential part of the cure. The physician was merely an intermediary in the patient's sacramental relationship; modern medicine, in contrast, is formulated on positivistic reasoning.

Generally, each technical advance has been invasive; reducing the medical significance of the outward signs of the body (like facial expressions) and giving less credence to the patient's interpretation of his/her own disease. In Hippocratic medicine, for example, sleeping positions and the appearance of the eyes were significant. If the white showed when the eyes were closed, this was a serious symptom. From Laennec's introduction of the stethoscope in the nineteenth century to computerised axial tomography (three dimensional pictures of internal sections), the biological and internal constituents of the body have been enhanced. The stethoscope projected the patient as a pattern of sounds. While X-rays, developed at the beginning of this century, played down hearing, they transformed the patient into a visual abstraction. From a film patients could now be inspected, discussed and have diagnostic decisions taken about them in their absence. Doctors who had never seen the patient could participate in the collective medical debate.

The biological/anatomical concept of disease and the spread of medical technology worked in symbiotic partnership. Medical technology, however, cannot be totally accredited with patient 'dehumanisation'. One feature of a modern diagnosis is the frequency with which symptoms and parts of the body are referred to by the impersonal 'the', or by 'it'. Doctors often open a consultation by asking: 'what is "it" that has been bothering you?'. Cassell (1976) has noted that reference to disease as an independent entity is found in other cultures. In the *Charmides*, the Platonic dialogue dealing with the relationship between health and the soul, we find Socrates discussing his companion's headache as 'the' headache. However, cosmopolitan medicine tends to treat the scientifically derived medical data in a manner which is divorced from the patient's general well-being.

MEDICAL SPECIALISATION

Technical development brought a decline in the generalist's approach to medicine. New specialisms were devised around discrete organs, body processes, disease types and new techniques, both diagnostic and therapeutic. Reiser (1978) has charted this multiplication. In 1875 the International Medical Congress had only eight sections. Today it runs into the hundreds. Medical techniques demanded longer training. Medical specialisation was associated with urban growth, with its new medical schools and, of course, with the concentration of potential clients. Generalist medicine soon became regarded as 'inferior medicine': leading American surgeons, like Mayo, in 1918 warned of the harm that generalists were likely to inflict on their patients. From the end of the nineteenth century hospitals began to be regarded as 'safe places' and they grew to accommodate the new specialisms. Formerly, hospitals had a bad reputation, fit mainly for the destitute; complaints against nurses' drunkenness and lack of discipline were frequent. Florence Nightingale's reform of nurse training coincided with the rise in the prestige of hospitals and with an increased technological division of labour. Teaching hospitals with combined medical schools rank highest, because of the rapidity of their technological innovations. In the medical hierarchy geriatrics ranks lowly. It experiences little technical diffusion; 'wonder cures' are out of the question. Yet the demands of the elderly on medical resources are increasing more rapidly than for any other group.

The rise in prestige and income of British GPs over the past decade was partly based on the government's expectation that their concentration in health centres would encourage more specialisation. In the United States, with its commercial medicine, hospitals are in vicious competition; new technology is emblematic of their 'efficiency' and they advertise their latest hardware to draw in clients. Technological competition accelerates the cost of health care. It also produces a differential mortality according to the frequency with which a medical procedure is used. The variability in mortality from gastrectomies (Wolf and Berle 1982) was directly related to the number performed; being highest for the small hospitals with fewest operations. Technical specialisation has also meant that an increasing number of patients find their multi-disciplinary condition is being shared between more medical specialisms. The overall responsibility for a patient becomes blurred. The drug regime proffered by one specialism can interact deleteriously with that of another. Technical specialisation has encouraged an increase in the rates of referral, to utilise these medical foci. In the United States, with their fee-for-service treatment, an additional thousand cardiologists each year are released into an already saturated medical market. Unnecessary coronary angiographs are performed, subjecting many to medical risks. The criteria for referral are being continuously adjusted to keep specialists in work.

TECHNICAL DIFFUSION

Although medical technology claims to be predicated on scientific principles, its effectiveness is often not immediately evaluated. Peer evaluation by doctors as a check can be a myth. Organised consumer criticism, as against the high technology of maternity units and surging costs, have focused sharp attention on this issue. There have been, of course, many non-controversial innovations: hip replacements, automated blood counting and pacemakers. However, the disasters have been horrendous; e.g. insulin coma treatment for schizophrenia and retrolental fibrophasia (blindness in young babies). It was normal in the 1940s to treat immature babies with a high concentration of oxygen, to give them a 'healthy' pink complexion. It was not until Lanman's controlled trials in 1954 that it was shown that this caused irreversible blindness (also no general benefits of oxygen therapy on prematurity were found); in fact retrolental fibrophasia had become in the United States the primary cause of children's blindness.

Unlike the production of new drugs, which are to some extent controlled by government sponsored 'watchdogs', it was only in the 1970s that a similar filter was placed on technologically based treatment with the setting up in the United States of the Office of Technological Assessment (an offspring of the Professional Standards Review Organization legislation, 1972). The UK has no comparable body. Many reasons have been posited for the rapid introduction of medical technologies. As men dominate the medical hierarchies, new technologies serve to boost the masculine qualities of power and domination. Many techniques are developed outside the clinical setting and are absorbed because of the lack of full understanding of their potential by specialists wanting to keep abreast of new discoveries. Once a technological culture has been created, it develops its own momentum. Some technological contexts are actually created to solve the problems of previous technological interventions.

An apposite example comes from the maternity services. From 1970 it became British obstetric policy to aim for a hundred per cent hospital delivery with modern technology, to reduce the perinatal mortality rates to those on a par with Holland and Sweden (approximately eight per thousand). Induction was widely practised by administering the hormone oxytocin to stimulate uterine contractions. The perceived advantage was to prevent pregnancies extending beyond the fortieth week, reducing foetal complications. But induction was applied indiscriminately (to approximately 36 per cent of all births in England and Wales in 1974) to non-risk cases (Davis and Kitzinger 1978), primarily for administrative convenience. The 'daylight baby syndrome' arrived; induction was used to reduce night, weekend and holiday deliveries, so reducing staff costs. Births were induced before full term, the latter is difficult to assess accurately, causing babies to be born jaundiced (severe cases can result in brain damage). Oxytocin causes powerful contractions; mothers cannot always control them. Epidural anaesthesia was introduced for relief. Mothers lost control of the birth process, leading to active management with forceps – a 'deadly' instrument in untutored hands of junior doctors who may be 'clocking up' a quota of births, before exposure to another specialism. Drugs administered to the mother rapidly cross the placenta; more babies were born 'flat', in need of resuscitation. Foetal monitoring was also introduced to reduce foetal distress. During labour electrodes were attached to the foetus's scalp to monitor critical functions. The rate of uterine contractions were also monitored. It is calculated that less than 2 babies per 1,000 benefited from this. In the 1960s Special Care Units were set up for low weight babies (less than 2.5 kg), but a decade later they were dealing with the 'casualties' of high tech delivery. In 1977 17 per cent of all deliveries spent some time in these units (three times the rate of 1964). These mothers were deprived of the psychological advantages of early intimacy with their new born.

The ritualistic prescriptiveness of technical use sustains the medical aura of certainty in the face of the unknown. In a 1972 survey, United States surgeons admitted that half their tests and procedures were made defensively, anticipating future malpractice suits. Two billion tests were carried out in 1971, by 1976 this reached 4.5 billion. The same trend is present in the UK, with litigation much less a threat. Automatic analysers do multiple tests on the same specimen, whether requested or not. X-rays have become routine, increasing by over 50 per cent between 1960 and 1970 in England and Wales. The public have been conditioned, too, into the expectation that more tests signify more accurate diagnosis and better treatment. In the United States in the first quarter of this century Diagnostic Societies, formed by syndicates of doctors, flourished, offering the public reduced priced offers of blood counts, heart rhythm etc. Owning one's personalised X-ray photograph was a status symbol. The danger from radioactivity was unknown then. The X-ray craze encouraged one London firm to advertise X-ray-proof underclothing for ladies.

Research shows that doctors can experience data overload from all the tests performed, reducing the significance of personal history taking. In 1984 of the 52 million chest X-rays taken in the United States, 30 million yielded data which could be got from history taking. There are subjective errors of interpretation of all test results; from 10 to 20 per cent (Wolf and Berle 1982). Only in the 1950s did variations in reading X-rays surface as a medical problem. Prior to its mass screening campaign, the Danish government set up the experiment of radiologists reviewing independently the same batch of two thousand films. Each missed about a third of the lesions displayed (Reiser 1978). Stilwell (1984), commenting that diagnostic services are only 10 per cent of patient care cost (they are 36 per cent in the United States) also notes that there is much variable use between hospitals and regions, which has no measurable effect on patient outcomes. Tests are ordered which have no direct relationship on the patient's condition. On the other occasions results are just 'ignored'. Experiments done to educate senior doctors to think seriously about the number of tests to be requested have no lasting effect; so effective was their prior medical socialisation in technical routines.

Technical diffusion has two other characteristics. Firstly, many diagnostic procedures have been introduced before effective treatments for the condition under investigation are known. Mass miniature radiography screening for chest tuberculosis was introduced in 1942. Effective treatment came in 1948, when antibacteriological drugs became available. Taylor (1981) and others have cast similar doubts on the latest innovation, CAT (computerised axial tomography), each costing over half a million pounds. This takes multiple X-rays; details can be amplified and restructured with great clarity. There has been little research attempted to assess treatment outcomes for the problems (for brain tumours, head injuries, etc.) it was designed to analyse. Secondly, some medical technology has been focused on the 'inappropriate' stage of illness. For example, coronary care units were devised in the 1960s to combat the rising tide of this western 'plague'. The type of patient best suited for them was never defined. A decade later their effectiveness was assessed. Patients who would have survived without them had been admitted. This quota helped to produce the favourable statistics indicating the unit's success. But most people die from heart attacks before reaching CCUs – 40 per cent within the first hour. It would have made more sense to concentrate the life support technology in the hands of non-medical emergency services outside the hospital; professional dominance until recently inhibited this.

MEDICINE AS A PATRIARCHAL RELIGION

This is a common thesis of the women's movement. Raymond (1982) has produced perhaps the most pungent version. Men misappropriated the healing secrets, once the possession of women (often witches). Medicine then reconstituted itself to perpetuate male myths. Doctors are performing medical rites, in their covert role of minister, over women who are now the main users. Male doctors thus become the definers of women's 'nature'. Modern technology is used to reassemble women; by cosmetic surgery breasts can be perfected and even virginity 'restored'. The technical fix produces transcendental expectations: hormone replacement therapy (HRT) forestalls the menopause. Patriarchal medicine evokes all the powerful imagery of the sacraments. The gynaecologist 'confirms' the adolescent girl into puberty. Penance occurs when women are given a 'clean bill of health'. More controversially, Raymond maintains that the Holy Eucharist (symbolically participating in the body and blood of Christ) is enacted by medical cannibalism on women – operating unnecessarily. Cosmopolitan medicine, by prohibiting unlicensed practitioners (women's groups) to offer alternative versions, is pronouncing the monopolistic doctrine of no salvation outside the true faith.

There is much that is seductive in Raymond. However, some unnecessary operations have occurred on both sexes (e.g. tonsilectomies). There are more women for example in mental institutions, partly because they live longer, and not necessarily to satisfy a male doctor's urges to control women. The medical profession pursues vigorously what it considers 'quack practitioners', irrespective of gender. The version of obstetricians seeking to express their power over women has many variants. Lomas (1978), a man, using Freudianism (this is also denounced by feminists) has argued that modern obstetrics has developed into its present form because men suffer from the Zeus complex. Zeus was the Greek god who swallowed stones to simulate childbirth – men's incapacity to give birth being a major flaw. Technologically dominated obstetrics rectifies this powerlessness. However, some male obstetricians, like Leboyer, have pioneered birth contexts to fit women's aspirations for 'natural' childbirth. Critical feminists, however, may interpret these moves as only a more subtle form of patriarchal control!

MEDICAL TECHNOLOGY AND ETHICAL ISSUES

The practice of medicine has always involved moral judgements on the parts of practitioner and patient. Ethics sets out to relate moral actions to the broader, essential principles 'underpinning' society – mainly how life should be lived. Morality is much narrower; examining the choices our 'free' will permits in deciding the goodness of specific activities. In one way all human action involves notions of morality, because the social world is an interpersonal and value laden one. The restorative function of medicine is geared towards enabling the sick to return to degrees of everyday 'normality'. In their training, doctors have tended to treat medical ethics in an *ad hoc* way, as opposed to the teaching of their other interests – e.g. the detailed and laborious courses in anatomy and physiology. Technical progress has been its totem. Now, the direction of the innovations has become the concern of the broader society; for instance some techniques, like IVF (*in vitro* fertilisation), have legal implications for the 'family'. The latter is a major institution of social order.

However, the current debates revolving around the question of what is life and death and how this affects the duty of the doctor, are merely replays. The Hippocratic writings of the fifth and fourth centuries BC made them their central concern. Restraint was always urged. Medicine was then an 'art', whose success lay in knowing the *limitations* of its influence to effect a cure. With those 'overpowered' by their disease, doctors were under no obligation to sustain them. Doctors would be guilty of the sin of pride and of insulting the gods if they extended their art beyond the 'normal' limits. Until the twentieth century, medical technology was mainly confined to surgery on bones and some organs like the stomach. (There are exceptions. Some eighteenth century doctors experimentally linked up patients with the circulatory system of ewes.) The major medical therapies were bloodletting, herbs, massage, exercise, diets, prayers and douching.

Current debates on medical ethics have been intensified by three factors. Firstly, medical technology has advanced rapidly on so many human fronts that it is not possible to construct a comprehensive moral frame to cover all. The stance of the transplant surgeon can differ from that of the doctor who is sustaining a 'life' (a potential donor of useful organs) on a support system. Secondly, medicine has permeated social areas where the disease/cure model is inapplicable. Infertility is not necessarily a disease. The notion of care and its accompanying quality of life is also becoming more prominent. Manual methods of artificial respiration used in 1907 were inappropriate for long term care, but since the invention of Drinker's iron lung in 1928 (for a polio victim) technical improvements in resuscitation and support systems can considerably delay death, even with no chance of recovery. This entails considerable resources, which might be more profitably used elsewhere. Who is worthy of such extensions of life? National leaders, like Franco and Tito, all 'benefited' from a prolonged terminal stage. Thirdly, it may not be possible to arrive at a consensus on some emergent moral issues. In a dynamic class society, with opposed interest groups, this may prove impossible. Also, before commencing any ethical debate, it is essential that the full complexity of the disputed medical processes is understood by moral philosophers and other 'outsiders'. Detailed knowledge of genetic engineering may be a prerequisite for a meaningful exploration of its potential eugenic and social consequences. Greek philosophers did not have this problem; medicine was open with no internal mysteries. Some of the tried and trusted yardsticks used by moral philosophers may be difficult to apply today. For instance, utilitarianism (the greatest good for the greatest number) may be used to justify investment in reproductive technology, as 10–15 per cent of couples in this country can experience a problem in conceiving. However this perspective ignores the global dimension. People in the less developed world are being urged, as part of western aid, to *restrict* their families. Reproductive technology mainly at the service of white people can smack of racism.

Some related ethical rationales, the concern of the *Warnock Report* (Report of the Committee of Inquiry into Human Fertilisation and Embryology 1984), will now be outlined. It is interesting to note that the Committee was not composed of any (potential) beneficiaries of reproductive technology. The interested organisations submitting evidence were very diverse: Science Fiction Foundation, South London Islamic Mission, Trades Union Congress, Action for Lesbian Parents, as well of the multiplicity of legal, religious, medical and family pressure groups. Indicatively, the Committee was not unanimous on salient points; especially whether research should be permitted on 'spare embryos' – those not returned to the womb.

Warnock readily admitted that it was making decisions in an area of fertility and birth rights lacking firm data; and where the law was either non-existent or, if present, had been designed for other purposes. The precise number of involuntary fertile couples is not known, nor is the general level of their associated unhappiness. What is certain is that there are now far fewer babies offered for adoption, the stigma on unmarried mothers being very much diminished. There is only one child available for every eight prospective adopting couples. More childless couples are adopting from less developed countries. Warnock completely compartmentalises its deliberations from the 'abortion issue'; since the 1967 Abortion Act there have been 2 million abortions. Warnock also deliberated on the known and 'future' extrapolations of reproductive technology. In June 1978 at Oldham General Hospital the first IVF child was produced. The co-researchers, Edwards and Steptoe then moved their research to the private institute, Bourn Hall. Sperm banks were established; one at Los Angeles claimed donations by Nobel prize winners. Techniques for early determination of sex typing foetuses were available. The vista of a planned and engineered human species was on the horizon; human cloning (which occurs naturally with identical twins) was also theoretically feasible. Firestone (1971), an influential voice on women's rights, had argued, extremely, that women's inequality was rooted in the differences between male and female reproduction roles. Pregnancy made women dependent on men, thus perpetuating an unequal division of labour. A Marxist revolution to alter solely the economic mode of relationships would be inadequate. Firestone's solution (then in the realm of science fiction) was ectogenesis (development of the foetus outside a womb) which would liberate women from the enslavement of their reproductive biology.

The less controversial section of Warnock covers artificial insemination. There are two types: by the 'husband' (AIH) and by donor (AID). AIH has been used when the husband cannot ejaculate (e.g. the physically disabled). If he has had medical treatment resulting in sterilisation (from radiotherapy), his sperm may be frozen and stored beforehand (some vasectomised men also do this). AID is used when the man is infertile, or the carrier of a chronic hereditary disorder. Women not wishing to have a relationship with a male are increasingly using AID, some self-administered. Opinion since 1960 has been turning in favour of AID; the British Medical Association, under the chairmanship of Sir John Peel, recommended its availability on the NHS at 'accredited' centres but these were never set up. Between 2,000 and 4,000 births a year in the UK result from AID and AIH (Council for Science and Society Report 1984).

Warnock recommended: that the AID service should be licensed and under appropriate control (presumably medical); that the 'semen donor' should have no parental rights (although he is the genitor); that prospective parents should be discouraged from seeking a full biography of the donor (only basic information should be available – ethnicity and genetic health); that the law should be changed so that the husband of the women receiving AID would be registered as the father; that there should be a limit of 10 children fathered by one donor; that the donor should not be paid a fee, only expenses, for his services; that on reaching 18 an AID child should have access to 'basic' information about the donor. The latter was not qualified.

The ethical decisions of Warnock are premised on an 'appropriate' version of the British family, based on the heterosexual relationships of husband and wife, within a privatised marriage. Warnock offers no evidence of why other versions should be disbarred, despite the increasing diversity of British family life. Also, cross-cultural variations are not held up for inspection. In matrilineal societies a third person, the mother's brother, is involved in his sister's family; nephews inherit his property. Patriarchal property rights are sustained by Warnock. Warnock admits, however, that domestic arrangements, e.g. from a donor brother, are uncontrollable; with the third party's identity known. Although Britain is a capitalist society, Warnock eschews the determination of market forces. Couples should not bid for the sperm of a favoured donor; nor should the donor gain financially. The assumption being that the 'wrong' type would be attracted. Altruism supersedes that of rational calculability and 'free' choice. The exchange model Warnock adopts is that of the 'free gift', favoured by Titmuss (1970) for blood transfusions. A free gift demands no counter-obligation on the part of the recipient; it is a supremely virtuous act. Titmuss argued that the example of free gifts would morally temper the excesses of capitalism. Warnock does not explicate this view. However, the report was interested in the French system of AID: AID users in France are requested to recruit married couples from their acquaintance so that the male partner will be encouraged to contribute anonymously to the sperm bank. Donation is then an open decision by the couple.

The French also restrict the number of semen samples given by each donor (to five or six, all given within one month). Warnock recommended, too, a limit of 10 children for each donor, reducing the risk of offspring unknowingly entering into incestuous relationships. How the exact figure of 10 was derived, we are not informed. Although the incest taboo, varying as it does between societies, has some genetic consequences, its entrenchment is mainly cultural. The range of 'forbidden' relationships in England has reduced over the last thousand years, reflecting the rise of the state, changes in political control and industrialisation. The Church at one time forbade marriage between third cousins.

Considerations of IVF proved more complex. The fertilisation of extracted eggs outside the womb is 'simple'. The major technical problem is the correct timing of their implantation within a womb. There are many permutations of IVF. One occurs when for some reason a woman cannot conceive (e.g. damaged Fallopian tubes). Ripened eggs can be extracted from the ovary by laparoscopy, fertilised with her partner's sperm and then implanted. Another possibility is that a woman is infertile or has a hereditary disease (or is a carrier of one), so that it is unwise to conceive. She could receive eggs donated by a genetically sound woman, which will be fertilised by her husband's sperm and then implanted in her. The technique of 'lavage' accomplishes the same. The donor can be artificially/naturally fertilised and the embryo is 'washed out', then transferred to the uterus of the infertile/genetically defective woman. This technique contains the risk of the donor having an unwanted pregnancy. There is also 'womb leasing'. A woman unable to bear a child could have her eggs fertilised *in vitro* by her husband and then transferred to a surrogate mother. After birth the child is then given to the genetic parents. Womb leasing usually involves a fee for the service.

Surrogacy is increasing. A woman agrees to conceive a child for a couple, after being artificially or naturally inseminated by the barren woman's partner. Private agency fees for this service in the United States are approximately £20,000. Legislation, following Warnock's recommendation, proposes to ban commercial agencies. Summary imprisonment of three months, with fines of £2,000, are to be the penalty. Surrogacy agreements at present are unenforceable in the courts and they contravene the common law on 'baby selling'. In 1978 an English prostitute, who was paid £3,000 to bear a child by AID, refused to hand it over to the sponsor-couple. The courts upheld the (surrogate) mother's rights to her child. Warnock admitted the impossibility of preventing private surrogacy agreements, as between sisters.

Warnock was very much aware of the litigious minefield posed by surrogacy cases in the United States. Mrs Stiver, who entered into a surrogacy agreement, gave birth to a microcephalic baby. The commissioning party refused to accept the child and told the hospital to withhold treatment. They also sued Mrs Stiver for not producing a 'perfect' child. Mrs Stiver sued those involved in the surrogacy programme – doctors, lawyer and psychiatrist – claiming that the abnormal baby was due to a virus transmitted by AID. The results of blood tests were disclosed to all the interested parties on the Phil Donahue TV show. The baby was actually Mr and Mrs Stiver's, who had not abstained from sexual intercourse after AID.

The ownership of 'spare' embryos and research on them also raised major ethical issues. Warnock recommended that there should be no right of 'ownership' (or duties) in an embryo, when donated to benefit another; the same principle as applied to AID. (In Sweden a child conceived by AID now has legal claims on the donor. The supply of donors has rapidly diminished.) Also, embryos should be stored for a maximum of ten years, with rights to their use/disposal then being granted to the 'storage authority'. The latter would also apply if a couple storing their own embryos died within that period. Research on embryos for genetic disorder was recognised as valuable, but embryos were not to be exploited. The 'dignity' of the embryo was to be accorded *some* legal protection as a human species. It was therefore recommended that research on *in vitro* embryos should only be permitted under licence and that they should be kept alive for a maximum of 14 days after fertilisation. Anticipating future developments, Warnock demanded that the transference of a human embryo to the uterus of another species should be made illegal. These proposals follow those of the United States National Ethics Advisory Board.

What are the ethical justifications for these recommendations? The time limit on embryo storage acknowledges existing family property rights. It is possible for an embryo to be replanted after the death of the husband. The child would be posthumously born. Warnock recommended that a child even born by AIH, who was not *in utero* before the father's death, should be legally disbarred from inheritance. Once there is confusion over family property, this ambiguity could spread to wider property relationships. Marxists would argue that this uncertainty would undermine one of the major pillars of capitalism.

'Ghost marriages', allowing a woman to marry and conceive in the name of a deceased, are known in other cultures, as among the pastoral Nuer. The bride price of cattle is given in the name of the deceased and a genitor (AID) is used. Technologically simple tribal societies generate complex family permutations; operating in this example on the basic principle that cattle beget children – he who gives the cattle owns the womb. Ghost marriages enable a childless (unmarried deceased) male to have children to honour genealogically his name. Warnock, wedded to the status quo, never explored cross-cultural or historical precedents. Yet ethics claim authority from the universality of human kind.

Embryo 'ownership' added to Warnock's dilemmas. While recognising that parents should not 'own' their embyos (sell them) the notion of ownership, as a set of rights, is still present. A couple's permission has to be sought before disposal of, or experimentation on, their surplus embryos. Of 'parents' divorced/separated it remains undecided what rights each have in the embryo. It is also not clear what the limits of the storage authority's rights would be. The Australian state of Victoria has faced this problem (1984). Embryos can be donated there if their natural parents die or 'disappear', rather than be destroyed. An IVF clinic in Melbourne was left with the embryos from wealthy USA parents, Elsa and Mario Rios, who died in an air crash.

The 'human' status of the embryo caused much debate. Warnock did not want to expose embryos to commercial exploitation by their mass-production for routine testing of drugs; even if the donors so desired. Also, limiting the development of the embryo *in vitro* to 14 days, Warnock was confronting an eternal question: when does life actually begin? It simplified its position when it hived off the question of abortion in a footnote (p. 64). The law allows the use of aborted foetal material well beyond 14 days for experimental purposes. There is one dominant view that declares no experiments should be conducted on embryos: they need total protection. A Mori poll (September 1984) conducted for the Order of Christian Unity (with a vested interest) suggests that just over 70 per cent of those questioned consider that all embryo research should be banned. This percentage is more pronounced in the over 55 age group. The Queen's former gynaecologist, Sir John Peel, thinks that by experimentation, a cross-species human born to a chimpanzee would result within 20 years. (At present hamster eggs are used for testing male sperm. They penetrate but do not cause egg division.)

Mr Powell's private members Bill (1985), forbidding all embryo research, is based on the assumption that 'all' life is sacred. There is an inconsistency when the law permits intra-uterine devices (coils) to be used as a contraceptive/abortifacient.

Historical precedents for embryo sanctity stem, paradoxically, from past attitudes towards abortion – from Hebrew tradition, percolating through Greek thought and then into early Christianity. Penalties for causing a miscarriage were determined by the harm done to the mother and the stage of development of the foetus. If the foetus was without visible image (aneikon, or incomplete human child) the compensation was in goods, but if the miscarriage was caused when the foetus had a complete image, then another child (often from a slave) must be given as recompense. Christian theorising on foetal humanisation pivoted on whether the soul had been formed. St Thomas Aquinas in the thirteenth century arbitrarily differentiated on the basis of sex: allowing 40 days for a male foetus and 90 for a female. Later, theologians reduced this period and English law followed. In the eighteenth century life commenced with a 'quickening' in the womb. Women would not be executed at this stage, for the law would have unjustly taken a human (baby) life.

Although current theological debate on 'life' is full of imponderables (for example, with identical twins does the same single soul divide equally?), scientific knowledge is also arbitrary. What physiological conditions of the embryo correspond to 'meaningful' life, as opposed to viable life? The Royal College of Obstetricians and Gynaecologists wanted a 17-day limit on IV development based on early neural structures. Another principle considered was whether the embryo could feel pain, which would be still later. Can pain be distinguished from other embryo sensations? Only 'primitive' brain neurons, with few interconnections, develop before the sixth month of pregnancy.

While granting donated embryos legal protection (even though they may not be aware of it at the time), Warnock did not offer the 'complete' human product a most fundamental right – one which might pose a future, identity crisis – namely the right to know one's genetic originator. It also never penetrated another legal minefield: parents suing for preconceptual damage, if faulty embryos are negligently implanted. There are precedents, especially American, for actions against doctors (and pharmaceutical companies) for birth errors caused by faulty genetic screening and failed sterilisation.

DIALYSIS

Procedures for treating kidney failure, known as end-stage renal disease (ESRD), are now routine, but the moral reverberations are still extremely powerful. The patient usually undergoes hemodialysis in a hospital, but also at home. Blood is filtered through an artificial kidney machine to restore 'normal' fluid and chemical balance. Usually three sessions a week, each varying between six and twelve hours, may be required. The patient is immobile during the treatment. There is also the little used peritoneal dialysis; the dialysate fluid is cycled into the abdominal cavity. Kidney transplantation from a cadaver (often a road victim), or from a live donor, usually a close relative, offers a more satisfactory solution. As long as the grafted kidney functions, rejection being the main problem, the patient can live normally. In the United States the commercial selling of kidneys (the donor can exist with one) occurs. The poor are the sellers; sometimes they originate from the less developed countries in Latin America. This practice has surfaced in a British private clinic, whose clients are wealthy, overseas Arabs. Transplant surgeons are now obliged to ascertain whether the donor, who participates in a simultaneous operation, had sold his organ. If yes, the surgeon is to refuse the operation on moral grounds. But 'realistic' proof is very difficult to obtain.

Prior to 1960 dialysis was only a temporary intervention. Doctors initially hoped that the kidney machine would extract the 'poisons' causing renal failure, allowing the kidneys to revive. American renal research was based on the ideas of Kolff, a Dutch doctor who, in occupied Holland during the Second World War, made the first model from scrap parts, including a bath tub. When a dialysand was treated, surgery was required to insert the tubes into veins and arteries. These lines could only be used once, thus restricting the occasions on the machine. It was only when Schreiner, at a Seattle hospital, overcame this limitation that the issue of 'suitability' for dialysis burst upon the moral horizon. Life could now be sustained without the promise of a cure. The major consideration was originally framed in terms of cost. In England (1984) it is estimated that it costs £14,000 annually to maintain one dialysand. Who is worthy then of being saved? Should doctors alone make this critical decision? The American experience succinctly charted by Fox and Swazey (1978) has its counterpart here.

The first-come, first-saved criteria of the early experimentation period soon vanished. The incidence of failed kidneys is still not fully known. It is often a slow process, sometimes commencing unbeknown in childhood. High blood pressure and diabetes can be associated with it. But the 'key' cause is unknown. Severe kidney failure is manifest with chronic pain, nose-bleeding and vomiting. The less pronounced the failure (with few complicating conditions, like heart disease) the more successful is dialysis – measured in terms of survival. But also significant is the psychological response of the dialysand to the dictatorial regimen of dialysis. A strict diet has to be maintained: no salt or potassium to prevent heart failure; little protein, for its breakdown accumulates in the blood; most onerous is the very reduced liquid intake (from all sources), equivalent to about two cups of fluid a day. Dialysands dream of going on binges of beer and steak. The life-saving machinery takes over their existence. Zaner (1983) has explicated the phenomenological tie. Non-conformity, frequently expressed by suicide (the suicide rate for home dialysis is lower) is a supreme strategy for proclaiming one's individuality and freedom from the machine. To the staff, this is a mark of selfishness; a valuable dialysis place denied others has been wasted. Nursing staff can be exposed, like dialysands, to the danger of hepatitis. Anaemia, infection, marital breakdown, depression, psychosis and 'dialysis dementia' – a newly recognised syndrome with often fatal consequence leading to the disintegration of the central nervous system – can accompany prolonged dialysis.

To understand how the favoured few were chosen the history of the Northwest Kidney Centre (formerly the Seattle Artificial Kidney Centre), one of the technical and moral pioneers, is indicative. It set up a Patient Admission Committee of doctors and lay members to screen applicants, using agreed criteria. The view projected was that its decisions were 'community' sanctioned, and not the prerogative of the medical team. However, the lay members (who insisted that their identities be kept secret) were mainly middle class, biasing the deliberations. Lawyers, ministers of religion, 'housewives', business-men and trade union officials were often members. Professional moral experts were soon drafted in to service the committee – social workers and psychologists supplied evidence about the prospective dialysand's intelligence, likely commitment to the strict medical regime and supportive social networks. Candidates for home dialysis undergo a role reversal; their wives who operate the machinery now control their partners' total existence.

The initial criteria for admission to the programme were: value to the 'community', emotional maturity, age limit of 17 to 50 years, potential for rehabilitation, slow deterioration of renal function, residency qualification of six months in the five states around Seattle. Each item was itself problematic. Value to the community was translated into a question of financial means and a 'good' job. The poor applied directly to the centre and were also disadvantaged by not having a local doctor/advocate who could vigorously present their case. The selectors were influenced by the 'Crowfeather' case. A poor Indian was dialysed and given a transplant, but then attempted to rob the Hilton Hotel by claiming he had planted bombs. On his death there were 280,000 dollars owing in medical costs. The affair was a complex one. Other dialysands commit 'suicide' to provide for their families. When Crowfeather was selected he had the approved personality characteristics advantageous for treatment. His selection was also a liberal gesture towards disadvantaged minorities. The exclusion criteria were dramatically revealed in England (1985), when dialysis was stopped for a homeless man living in a hostel, who was deemed by the Oxford Health Authority to be unco-operative. He created unpleasant conditions for the staff (by allegedly soiling himself during treatment) and was psychiatrically ill.

The lower age limit was reduced after much debate to five years. The moral argument in opposition not only considered economics (children are unproductive and will survive longer on dialysis than those over 50 years), but also the impact of a potential child death on the morale of the nursing staff. Moral issues soon became political ones. Dialysis raised the spectre of the bourgeoisie saving their own kind. The non-egalitarian procedures were also emphasised when various associations financed their own members. The Veterans' Administration for Dialysis funded their own members. After electoral pressure in 1972 the Federal Government, by extending Medicare, made itself responsible for paying the cost of dialysis and transplants for those treated. In 1975 over 20,000 patients received dialysis. Fundamental questions were now posed. Why does the government support one disease but not another? The question of selection remains, because of the shortage of dialysis machinery and kidney donors. Can the government under its law PL92-603 maintain indefinitely a blank cheque with rising medical costs? Treatment on the NHS is also a lottery, often depending on location. Merseyside takes 14 new patients per million of the population. The rate for Northeast Thames is double. However, if the existing units operated round-the-clock shifts, the number of dialysands could double.

COMPUTERS IN MEDICINE

The most significant technological change to shape medicine, as a set of beliefs and practices, will be computerisation. As information technology, it is already contouring medical administration: providing immediate feedback on comparative costings of treatment, bed occupancy, staff deployment and rates of referral, etc. Computer systems are built into clinical monitoring (e.g. CCUs), CATs and laboratory testing procedure. The potential for variegation in doctor/patient relationship is great. Patients at home with self monitoring electronics can feed the data into the hospital's mainframe computer and be diagnosed at a distance. Patients already check their pacemakers by the telephone link.

Patients can interact with microcomputers and present their medical histories, or undergo psychological testing. Carr and Ancill

(1983), reviewing the literature, suggest that the computer could be more effective in extracting certain types of information. Alcoholics disclose higher levels (more accurate?) of consumption. Some psychiatric patients reveal suicidal ideas only to a computer. Computers have been used to build up patterns of communications with autistic children. Allen (1984) has used a computer as play therapy with disturbed children. Working with dreams and stories are the traditional means of exploring inner personal conflicts. Computer fantasy games allow the operator to identify with themes and characters. Allen used Ultima (a Dungeons and Dragons adventure), which encourages the child to play with characters of his own making. Timid children learn risk-taking, within the safety of the fantasy programme and gain confidence. Kurlychek and Glang (1984) have pointed to the potentials of the microcomputer in rehabilitating brain injured people (strokes and head injuries). These survivors often suffer from impairment of memory and loss of other cognitive functions. Such deficits need accurate measurement and necessary remedial education. The computer is able to give immediate feedback and offer appropriate repetitions to reinforce the survivor's pattern of recognition. For example, the Searching for Shapes (SEARCH) programme diagnoses the capacity to match different shapes. The Sequence Recall (SEQREC) programme offers a flow of work and picture items. The patient's listing performance is a corrective to frontal lobe impairments.

Computer usage, concerning access, storage and retrieval, has sharpened the ethical debate on confidentiality and patients' rights. The makers and professional users of test-related software are worried on a number of counts. If the programme and scoring schemes are made accessible to the public (by 'hacking') then the future validity of the programme becomes suspect. Interpretative reports based on these tests can also be vulnerable if security fails. Illicit disclosure of mental illness could prejudice employment prospects. The ethical complexity of computerised records is frequently played out in the United States courts. English law on data protection/privacy is still in its infancy. Kemna's (1984) summary of the United States Head case is illustrative. William Head was a young leukaemia victim, whose only hope of survival was a bone marrow transplant. In 1982 he requested the University of Iowa hospital to search its bone marrow register for a suitable donor. A possible donor was found, a Mrs X, who without her knowledge, had her name placed on the register. She had previously been tissue typed as a possible donor for a relative. Mrs X was contacted, but refused to be a donor. The university refused to contact her a second time, in accordance with its ethical code – not desiring to harass. Head then asked the court to disclose Mrs X's name, claiming that the bone-marrow register was a 'public record', because it did not contain 'confidential' patient records, and Mrs X was not a patient. The university argued, however, that Mrs X, the potential donor, was in fact a 'patient' for she relied on the clinical judgement of doctors and therefore a doctor–patient relationship existed. The court had to balance the rights of Mrs X to her privacy and the saving of a human life. The Appeal Court did not agree that a second letter should be sent to Mrs X, informing her of Mr Head's plight.

Computer diagnosis has accentuated the central, epistemological dilemma in medicine – what is a 'diagnosis'? Before this puzzle of clinical reasoning is resolved, a computer programme simulating it cannot be formulated. Unless dealing with a clearly defined disease, it can be uncertain when the diagnostic process begins and ends. Additional data is always being accreted from other clinical and nursing staff, outside the doctor–patient consultation. Blois (1983) actively addresses this problem by differentiating the activities covered by this collective term. Diagnosis can be the application of a label, like 'middle ear infection', but the latter does not explain the illness process. It can also be the discovery of a body malfunction, missing part, or chemical, as in phenylketonuria. Diagnosis can also be the discrimination of the external agent, as in a whiplash-syndrome, neck injury in a car accident.

Most medical symptoms can be described by their outer appearances and internal constituents; the latter comprising chemical properties, etc. Blois argues that there is a discontinuous zone between these two 'levels'. The internal, or residual level, can only be described by natural science principles. Appearance-symptoms are described in everyday subjective language of the patient and doctor. The patient may say she felt a 'sharp pain', or was 'nervous', or her fingers were not 'right'. In constructing a diagnostic programme a number of urgent methodological issues are therefore posed. How many 'levels', each with their own explanatory laws, should be included? Can the subjectivity of appearance explanations be synthesised with the laws of physics/chemistry prevailing at the internal levels? Simply, can a patient's feelings, expressed as 'depression', be reduced to a chemical enzyme? Chemical composition need not always correspond with personal awareness, as in 'asymptomatic' hypertension. With diabetes, sugar content and behaviour only correspond at the extremes. To build a diagnostic programme for multiple diseases is an added complication.

There are two methods of reconciliation. First, to build a diagnostic programme based on a collation of the known 'facts' about a given disease: the 'textbook' data (reconstructed method) taught to students. Then get the patients to tick off their symptoms. Second, the programme can simulate the procedures, or practical reasoning, actually undertaken by the diagnostician unravelling the presenting symptoms. This approach is more apt for dealing with loosely defined disease. The question still remains, of course, of deciding which physician to use as the model for the programme. Physicians differ in diagnostic style. Blois recounts the interesting story of how a programme called INTERNIST (later called CADUCEUS) was built replicating the diagnostic reasoning of Dr Jack Myers, the professor of medicine at the University of Pittsburgh. Myers had to provide a commentary of his methods. After the programme was finished, Myers had altered his original style. Explicating his tacit reasoning had changed his behaviour!

CONCLUSION

It has been stressed that technology, whether in medicine or elsewhere, is not a neutral scientific fact. It embodies values about restructuring the world and human experience. The notions of patient and doctor have accordingly varied. Although medical technology has grown more complex, it still confronts the same, old moral predicaments and is challenged by the supreme, metaphysical baseline – what is 'natural'?

REFERENCES

Allen D H 1984 The use of computer fantasy games in clinical therapy, in Schwartz M D (ed) *Using Computers in Clinical Practice, Psychotherapy and Mental Health Applications*. The Hawarth Press, New York

Blois M S 1983 Conceptual issues in computer-aided diagnosis and the hierarchial nature of medical knowledge. *Journal of Medicine and Philosophy* 8: 29–50

Braverman H 1975 *Labour and Monopoly Capital: the Degradation of Work in the Twentieth Century*. Monthly Review Press, New York

Carr A C, Ancill R J 1983 Computers in psychiatry. *Acta Psychiatrica Scandinavia* 67: 137–43

Cassell E J 1976 Disease as an 'it' concept of disease revealed by patients' presentation of symptoms. *Social Science and Medicine* **10**: 143–6

Council for Science and Society Research 1984 *Human Procreation, Ethical Aspects of the New Techniques.* Oxford University Press

Davis J, Kitzinger S 1978 *Place of Birth.* Oxford University Press

Firestone S 1971 *Dialectics of Sex.* Bantam, New York

Fox R C, Swazey J P 1978 *The Courage to Fail: A Social View of Organ Transplants and Dialysis.* University of Chicago Press

Hawkins A 1984 Two pathologies: A study in illness and literature. *Journal of Medicine and Philosophy* **9**: 231–52

Kemna D J 1984 Confidentiality of organ donor registry records versus the interest in preserving human life. *Journal of Legal Medicine* **5**: 117–45

Kerr C, Dunlop J T, Harbison F H, Myers C A 1973 *Industrialisation and Industrial Man.* Penguin, London

Kurlychek R T, Glang A E 1984 The use of microcomputers in the cognitive rehabilitation of brain injured persons. In Schwartz M D (ed) *Using computers in clinical practice, psychotherapy and mental health applications.* The Howarth Press, New York

Lomas P 1978 An interpretation of modern obstetric practice. In Davis J, Kitzinger S (ed) 1978 *Place of Birth.* Oxford University Press

Marcuse M 1969 *Essay on Liberation.* Allen Lane, London

McDermott W 1972 Health care experiments in many forms. *Science* **175**: 23–31

Raymond J 1982 Medicine as a patriarchal religion. *Journal of Medicine and Philosophy* **7**: 197–216

Reiser J 1978 *Medicine and the Reign of Technology.* Cambridge University Press

Stilwell J 1984 Diagnostic procedures in the NHS. In Harris A, Gretton J (ed) *Health Care UK, an economic, social and policy audit.* CIPFA.

Taylor R 1981 *Medicine Out of Control: an Anatomy of Malignant Technology.* Sun Books, Melbourne

Titmuss R M 1970 *The Gift Relationship: from Human Blood to Social Policy.* Allen and Unwin, London

Wolf S, Berle S 1982 *The Technological Imperative in Medicine.* Plenum, New York

Zaner R M 1983 Chance and morality the dialysis phenomenon. In Kestenbaum V (ed) *Humanity of the ill, phenomenological perspective.* University of Tennessee

Illness is all around us. Half the population of USA is suffering from a chronic illness. America is one of the richest nations, but its major demographic trend, like all advanced industrial societies, is towards an ageing population, devouring health resources. For example, blindness is increasing, though generally decreasing in the less-developed world. One in ten of the UK population is likely to be an inpatient, at some time, for mental illness. Health invigorating activities even produce their own casualties – aerobic-back and jogger's ankle.

It is appropriate that any discussion of illness begins with Parsons (1951a and b). Although much maligned today (often by those who have never read his words), he made the first major attempt at constructing a sociological framework connecting the multi-dimensional aspects of illness, especially focusing on the sick role – patients' responses to their medically assigned conditions. In the 1940s, the one-sided medical view predominated: illness was primarily biologically rooted, and patients were socially and psychologically invisible in their relationships to medicine and the wider society. The history of medicine was written as the heroic struggle of doctors fighting disease on behalf of amorphous mankind. Parsons also marked the transition of swinging sociology away from being the handmaiden of doctors, studying issues medically delimited for them as being important, to a position where there could be a genuine sociology of medicine and not, as Straus (1957) called it, a sociology 'in' medicine.

Parsons' originality and political commitment have been questioned. Some comment is needed. His professor at Harvard, Sorokin, for whom Parsons once worked as a tutor, has argued that his model of the social system was only a pastiche of the structural principles of Durkheim, Pareto and Weber, etc. But the use of systems reasoning, or social mechanics, long antedates sociology's founding fathers. Parsons used 'few' footnotes in his writings to dignify his sources. At Harvard in the 1930s he had attended Henderson's seminars on Pareto's systems-thinking. Parsons (1951a) does invite the reader to compare his version of the doctor–patient relationship with Henderson's (1935). He also acknowledges Freud's contribution to the notion of sick role, the incumbent being legitimately exempted from fulfilling role obligation.

It must be remembered that Parsons was a model builder, in the tradition of grand theory. His depiction of the doctor–patient encounter was offered as an 'ideal-type', reflecting the structural rules governing his model of society. Ideal-types are not empirical entities; they cannot capture the subtleties of everyday interaction. They are heuristic and methodological tools for analysis. One line critics have taken is to elaborate variations in doctor–patient relationships not 'seen' by Parsons. Discussion on the sick role is complicated by Parsons peppering his account with observations and variations of his own. Parsons was an armchair theorist. One of his rare pieces of fieldwork was of medical practice in the Boston area, but it remained unfinished (for unexplained reasons). His ideas were not static; his final version of doctor–patient relationships was a replication of the stages of a psychotherapeutic relationship.

Summarising Parsons: medicine is an important mechanism and sub-system of society neutralising a major source of deviance, i.e. illness, and thereby being an important 'stabiliser'. Illness incapacitates, causing social deficits in role obligations to others. He cites the example of premature death providing only a partial return for others' role investments. Social order is maintained by all fulfilling their reciprocal roles. Parsons relies heavily on a version of the fully socialised individual, who has successfully internalised all society's values. Reality is different: goals can be conflicting, or even unknown to some. Medicine, he goes on, is one form of institutionalised science, making it superior to patients' knowledge. Parsons does recognise that medical knowledge can produce different interpretations of the same illness and has been wrong, grounded in superstition, as when the French Academy of Medicine, believing in 'laudable pus', opposed Pasteur's discovery. Doctors must be affectively neutral and detached, like scientists: also because they have privileged access to others' bodies, sexual eroticism involving women patients must be eliminated. The latter point he took over from Freud. The value of the nurse/chaperone is acknowledged, but not built into his doctor-patient dyad. Doctors must also be 'collectively orientated' and not narrowly profit-orientated like businessmen. Parsons knows this ideal is not completely possible, but underplays the pull of the USA market economy. He also distinguishes, however, between independent practitioners and those remunerated differently within organisations. The last principle prompting doctor behaviour is technical-specificity: doctors must become experts.

Patients have their obligations. Those allocated the privileged sick role must recognise that illness is a temporary, undesirable condition and must follow doctors' orders for recovery. When ill, there is a duty to seek out expert help; families must also assist in this direction. The patient is in a child-like dependence, paralleling the format of the psychiatrist as father figure. Sickness also immobilises, as the patient is cut off from others. Parsons notes that there are a diversity of illnesses, with different severities (e.g. comas), modifying his sick role. But it is not his purpose to work out the permutations. He does describe, however, patients' tactics for shopping around, testing one doctor's diagnosis against another and how surgeons, as culture heroes, are biased towards operating in the face of uncertainty, while other doctors are more cautious. Parsons astutely questions the official statistics registering the increase in mental illness; suggesting they may represent changing fashions in diagnosis. More people adopting this sick role could mean, he argues, that less are adopting other types of deviance. This will be for the 'good', for the sick role is less harmful for society than many other types of deviance. The 'later' Parsons offers individuals more free will and personal choice. The sick do not form antagonistic sub-cultures, like criminals. He predicts that the position of doctors, in balancing 'society's tensions', will become more strategic.

Although critically dismissed, many have debated with the ghost of Parsons, embroidering the clues he littered around. In that way his work was a valuable stimulant in the future development of medical sociology. We go on to signpost these trends and examine how others have tested the sick role by filling in extra variables; especially comparative medical settings, about which Parsons is generally mute. Perceptions of health and illness are important, being often the trigger for embarking on the sick role. The impact of a sick member on families will also be explored; not only for nudging its members towards medical help, as Parsons suggests. Some roles, like pregnancy, have become ambiguous because of their medicalisation, as we shall see. The sick role takes on new emphases when analysed within a religious context: another important Parsonian subsystem for controlling behaviour.

REVERSING THE PARSONIAN TRADITION

Freidson (1961) produced the first comprehensive critique of Parsons and precipitated other major lines of enquiry into doctor–patient relationships and illness behaviour. Szasz and Hollender (1956), for example, had previously chided Parsons for producing the one type of doctor–patient relationship in which much depended on the illness trajectory. The Szasz and Hollender critique covered various types of doctor–patient relationship. For serious injury and coma the (doctor) *activity*–(patient) *passivity* model would prevail, forced on to comatose patients. For acute illness (especially infectious) the *guidance-co-operation* model fitted, with the patient being willingly compliant with instructions. For long-term and chronic cases the *mutual-participation* model was deemed appropriate with the doctor promoting the patient towards self-help. The Parsonian version embraced the second type (sharing also a little of the first). Szasz and Hollender were, however, still exploiting ideal-types and, like Parsons, were searching for the 'best fit' in relationships, from the doctor's point of view. They also failed to distinguish the consultation from treatment regime.

Freidson reversed the Parsonian tradition. His methodology was different, using *symbolic interactionism* which emphasised the participants' meanings as the basis for interaction. Reality was now a matter for negotiation and not heavily prescribed as in the systems model. The researcher was now where the action was. Freidson combined symbolic interactionism with a realistic appraisal of the market position of medicine; questioning seriously Parsons' assumptions about its altruism.

Freidson made a comparative study of three different medical settings in New York: an interprofessional team (group practice) working pre-paid; individual paediatricians within the pre-paid team; and solo practitioners charging fee-for-item service, operating from their own scattered premises. In all these settings his focus was the patient. Consultations never went smoothly, as Parsons suggested; conflict and bargaining occurred over the significance of symptoms and treatment. The solo practitioner was found to be preferred overall, with patients assuming that he displayed a greater interest in their welfare, although the team was preferred in the narrower context of greater technical expertise. Patients had no 'objective' criteria for their evaluations, but their sentiments were found to affect their behaviour. The method of referral also influenced the patient's response. Parsons has suggested that referral was primarily a family affair; Freidson showed that it was far more complex – lay experts, both kin and non-kin, were important. Whereas Parsons argued that the sick role was clearly defined and acceptable, Freidson demonstrated that its medical imposition could cause role confusion and be resisted. Freidson observes how medicine provides the opportunities for *acting* sick. Parsons had however already planted the seed for this argument in the discussion on how more people may be choosing sick roles in preference to other forms of deviance. Freidson's achievement was to generate new sets of hypotheses derived from observation, giving joint weighting to both doctor and patient roles.

That the setting and timing of illness preconditions patients for the sick role, had been noted prior to Parsons' and Freidson's formulations. Schneider (1947) had shown that there were legitimate and illegitimate sick roles, according to the *stage of army training*. If recruits developed 'minor' illness, not requiring hospitalisation, at the *beginning* of basic training, this was legitimate – caused by the transition from civilian life. If however recruits *lingered* in the sick role, this was regarded as deviant and malingering. These soldiers were gradually isolated from their training group, to protect its cohesiveness and fighting spirit. During *combat*, it is made virtually impossible to achieve a sick role other than by being wounded in action. Other illness is treated as shirking and cowardice. 'Catch 22' portrayed vividly the difficulties of mental illness symptoms being accepted as sufficient evidence of a sick role in order to escape flying missions. Despite all his machinations at gender bending, Klinger never got discharged from MASH. To escape the butchery of trench warfare in World War I soldiers would shoot themselves in the foot, and open up minor wounds. The setting where wounded combatants are treated has also been shown to be important. Those doctored near the front line have less feelings of guilt about their deceased comrades.

Casualty Departments (CD) are another setting where the staff divide morally the great mixture of help-seeking clients, into those more deserving and less deserving of the sick role. Roth (1972) shows how the main users of the USA public urban CDs are mainly from the bottom of the class hierarchy, and non-white. In England there is also a tendency for the lower working-class to make greater use of CDs, often as quick substitutes for GPs, whose appointment system restricts access for their illness crises, and because of high rates of children's accidents. Jeffrey (1979) has argued that CDs are one of the most problematic areas of the NHS. Until recently CDs lacked a comparable career structure for doctors; however consultants are now being appointed, especially where CDs serve major motorways. The low prestige of CDs is partly due to their open access. Staff frequently remark that 'anyone' can walk in. There is little or no professional filtration in the CD, in contrast to other specialisms. In the USA armed police patrol CDs. Staff in England are now also demanding protection from physical attack. Roth points out that drunks (usually men) are treated only for their obvious lacerations without full examinations. A pejorative label for women is PID (Pelvic Inflammatory Disease), with black, unmarried women commonly being ascribed this label when they exhibit fever or abdominal pains which are difficult to diagnose. These symptoms are often attributed to venereal disease, or to the aftermath of illegal operations. Surgical cases resulting from industrial injuries, car accidents and stabbings (victims) are however regarded as more worthy of the sick role; so are children, for they are not responsible for their condition.

Jeffrey's classification replicates the USA experience. He uses the typification of 'good case', for head injuries or cardiac arrest. Casualty officers can then practise their skills on them, including a thorough professional examination. In contrast 'rubbish' covers not only drunks who flood in at weekends, but 'overdosers' and tramps seeking shelter. A slightly higher status is ascribed to overdosers who made a 'genuine' suicide attempt; other overdosers are merely regulars seeking attention. The ambiguity of the CD is reinforced by the lack of agreement on a satisfactory term covering attempted suicide. Deliberate self-harm and parasuicide jostle for official acceptance.

Efforts are made to train unnecessary users into the etiquette of good medical clientship, by attempting to deny them the sick role. Staff will ignore some and shunt others out; or may use public ridicule, revealing their personal details to overhearers. Overdosers can be 'roughly' lavaged (pumped out). Jeffrey follows Parsons' explanation for the staff responses. Most 'rubbish' violate the norms of the sick role: i.e. that illness should be regarded as undesirable and that there should be co-operation with doctors and nurses. With staff being ever more conscious of the effects of health cuts, illegitimate seekers of the sick role are now considered 'criminal' wasters of valuable health resources. Roth argues that staff have very much overestimated the *misuse* of CDs, calculating that only 25 per cent of cases fall into this category, and not the 70–90 per cent calculated by the staff. Jeffrey offers no similar comparisons.

Segall (1976) set out to explore how far the duties which Parsons stipulated for the sick role corresponded to lay expectations, and how the latter might be modified by socio-cultural differences. These were important in influencing, for example, the reactions to pain. Segall chose two groups: Jewish and Anglo-Saxon Protestants in Canada.

Restricting his variables further, he only included for interview married housewives between eighteen and seventy years of age, matched for family size and income – a sample of seventy. Segall's results agreed with one of Parsons' criteria: 84 per cent accepted that the sick had an obligation to get better, and that illness was undesirable. Being absolved from other obligations when sick, required a variety of conditions to be fulfilled, and depended particularly on the perceived severity of the illness. Many emphasised that attempts should still be made to do some housework and to look after children. Segall never tells us whether this view to keep the house going was shared equally between those in 'outside' employment and others. Sixty-five per cent were in agreement that sick persons should seek expert help and would willingly accept doctors' treatment for getting better.

Although both groups tended to share the same views on the sick role, the Anglo-Saxons conformed more closely to the Parsonian ideal, except in respect of being exempted from other role obligations. The Jewish sample were more in agreement with exemption; they also displayed a greater willingness to consult doctors more frequently. Segall shows that the sick role, once the 'limiting clauses' are added, is not a unitary concept.

There are other groups for whom the sick role can be problematic. The aged create a special problem. Geriatrics is probably at the same stage of development that paediatrics was in the 1930s: attempting to work out scales of 'normal development' and incidence of disease. 'Aged' is a social definition. It is uncertain which symptoms are the physiological product of ageing *per se*. For these there is no escape from the sick role, no matter how medically co-operative. Society does not offer effective role models for the aged; being old is something which just creeps up on you, or must be fought off.

Adopting the sick role is the only strategy left to many aged for making sense of their predicament and for manipulating others over whom they are losing control. Hanson's (1985) study of an Ontario nursing home points up this dilemma. Entering the home, no matter how home-like, means a further de-statusing, often involving the relinquishing of property and the loss of control over income. Nurses and aides primarily direct the flow of medical information about residents to the doctor, which further reduces their significance. Treatments (sedatives and laxatives, etc.) are left as standing orders for the staff to administer as necessary. Staff discretion can be influenced by how much the resident is regarded as being a nuisance. This may not correspond to the resident's own definition. Making a loud noise indicates to the resident that he or she is alive, whereas to the staff, this is unruly behaviour. Hanson elaborates the pay-off for residents in adopting the sick role. Relatives may offer more attention, and bring gifts. Their unpleasant public behaviour (e.g. incontinence) becomes more intelligible and acceptable to others. Residents prefer to think of themselves as patients; they could pretend that treatment would end in a cure. To carry your own medication was a status symbol and offered 'magical' security. Many died after about two years' admission.

Alcoholism presents an interesting challenge to the sick role. Alcoholism has always been with us, but it was only after Parsons' formulation that it was fully medicalised. The French doctor, Gabriel, in the 1860s, had actually promoted the *disease* version, but the popular, Victorian, image of the alcoholic as immoral, weak-willed and debased, was then too powerful to permit its adoption. Increased living standards between 1950 and 1970 were accompanied by a doubling of alcohol consumption. The American Medical Association captured the new 'liberal' mood with its 1956 resolution requesting hospitals to admit alcoholics as ill people, having a special allergy or genetic predisposition towards 'drink'. The disease model offered a respectable platform from which to make claims for medical resources for treatment. With doctors (often psychiatrists) responsible for treatment, alcoholism was 'normalised'. Jellinek's *Disease Concept of Alcoholism* (1960) was an influential work urging this approach. No-one was immune; given the right circumstances, we are all potential alcoholics. The executive under stress and the poor with restricted opportunities were fellow victims.

How do alcoholics themselves respond to the sick role? Blaxter and Cyster (1984) investigated this when probing (by mail questionnaire) why over 70 per cent with liver disease continued to drink. One answer was that the symptoms for which they had sought medical assistance had cleared, so that the enforced sick role had now become incomprehensible. Any remaining alcoholic symptoms – stomach pain or gastric troubles – could be accounted for by appealing to other common causes. Alcoholics could even disclaim that they *were* heavy drinkers, or might argue that alcohol never affected *them* as it did others – they themselves having a 'different' immunity. Some alcoholics operated with the *moral debasement* model; since they supported their families, without conflict, alcoholism did not therefore exist! The Parsonian sick role was thus inappropriate. Its major advantage was absent, i.e. exemption from other duties. Alcoholics were expected to soldier on, but without alcohol, which was often the key benchmark for everyday activities.

The passage of some illnesses into death is so rapid that the sick role is evoked posthumously. Parsons hints at, but gives no substance, to these critical conditions. The sudden infant death syndrome (SID), commonly called 'cot death', is a recent candidate. The Office of Population Censuses and Surveys has recognised these unexpected deaths since 1971. Very few occur after one year of age. The figures rose to a maximum in 1982; reaching 2.13 SIDs per one thousand live births. The increase may be due to greater medical interest. Although specific conditions in ten per cent of SIDs have been recorded as the 'mechanism' of death (e.g. bronchiolitis and 'upper respiratory infection', tracheitis and even 'birth trauma'), research has failed to isolate the 'cause'. Most deaths occur within the first five months. There may be some genetic base; SIDs have reoccurred in the same family. New research is focusing on the failure of the 'breathing reflex'. It has also been suggested that some SIDs may actually be infanticide. The SID rate fell between 1983 and 1984, due to a 14 per cent decrease in the male post neonatal (i.e. after four weeks) SID rate. No-one knows why. The absence of a sick role leaves parents unprepared for bereavement and grief.

PERCEPTIONS OF HEALTH

It is a truism that how one perceives health will influence initiation into the sick role. Health is a multi-dimensional concept. One important facet is recognition of the body's internal structures. Alcoholics often cannot conceptualise liver dysfunction. Hearts, lungs and brains have more emotional impact on consciousness than spleens.

Data from Goldthorp and Richman (1975) concerning 250 gynaecological patients' body knowledge, revealed abysmal ignorance. Sixty per cent of the sample were under 40 years of age; 50 per cent had one or more children still under the age of 12; 80 per cent were married or in equivalent relationships. Classified by both their own and their husbands' occupations, there was a clustering of the sample in the skilled-manual and lower white-collar stratas. Assessing biological knowledge of their reproductive organs, they were asked to name seven common parts from a diagram (spelling was ignored) – two distinct groups emerged. Women were either well-informed or knew very little. Fifty-three per cent could correctly recognise five to seven anatomical parts, but 38 per cent knew only two or less. Some expressed hostility at the suggestion they should be anatomically aware. A 41 year old mother of three children undergoing a major operation commented: 'If I had been interested in my body, I would have gone in for nursing or St John's'. A common error was to regard the biological and lay term for the same part as two different organs: uterus and womb; front passage and vagina; and cervix and neck of the womb. Reproductive knowledge was not necessarily a function of age or class; there was a tendency for those between 21 and 30 years to be more aware. Body 'focus' offered a greater 'illness awareness'. Eighty-six per cent of those 'well informed' about the biological functions could also identify the condition hospitalising them. The study confirmed other studies: namely that well informed patients are the most critical of information received from doctors.

Johnson and Snow (1982) show, in a related study, how the reproductive knowledge of women influences their contraceptive practices. (Studies on women's body knowledge far outweigh similar studies on men!) The research was on poor, black women with little education, attending a Detroit inner-city prenatal clinic, who were 'high risk' for pregnancy. Sixty per cent reported at least one unwanted pregnancy; about the same percentage used no contraception. There was general ignorance on menstruation. Many thought it was a purification/cleansing activity. Few knew its correspondence with fertility; 79 per cent could not explain the 'safe period'. Although 63 per cent knew the purpose of a cervical smear, the rest were confused: suggesting tests for pregnancy, VD and 'infection'.

Since Koos's (1954) classic study of Regionville, a small community of 500 families in upper New York State, others have gone on to seek associations between social class, symptom recognition, illness behaviour and utilisation of medical services. Following the footsteps of pioneering, urban sociologists, like Lloyd Warner and the Lynds, Koos put the community's health under the microscope. He probed in depth for a year the health of his respondents' families. As it was a rural community, the range of industrial classes was absent. Koos recognised three classes: class I, middle-class, was mixed containing bankers, schoolteachers and ministers; class II, was a skilled manual and home-owning group; class III, was the least skilled, containing many with seasonal jobs and with the highest proportion of working wives.

Koos asked his respondents to *rate* 17 symptoms in need of medical attention. The class gradient was confirmed. There was only one symptom (persistent coughing) which class II rated (by one per cent) higher than class I. Although 94 per cent of class I rated a lump in the breast as a serious symptom, only 44 per cent of class III did the same. The highest symptom recognition by class III, 69 per cent, was blood in urine; a hundred per cent of class I rated its medical significance.

Only a quarter of the lowest class recognised 10 or more symptoms as in need of medical attention.

Pain has been singled out as a major reference symptom for seeking the sick role. Zborowski's (1952) work set the compass for showing how reactions to pain can only be understood by knowing its cultural matrix. Jews are more likely to concentrate on specifying the symptomatic character of their pain. Italians will elicit sympathy for their anguish. Old Americans (Anglo-Saxons) are worried about possible incapacitation, though remaining optimistic, and having confidence in the skill of their doctors.

To recognise a body change, or symptom, as necessitating medical assistance, depends on an individual's health awareness. Official definitions of general well-being rarely illuminate. Much depends on how people structure their experience and on their use of inter-pretative rules for making sense of that experience. All societies welcome and desire health. Andean Indians recognise the virtues of 'ayni' (health) being in balance and the carrying out of reciprocal duties; although they have never heard of, let alone read, Parsons analysis of the sick role. Their cultural translation will, of course, differ from the Mancunian one. Andean decoding of health has greater cosmological penetration – their gods must not be kept hungry, nor must the members for whom they have responsibility. After expending much effort on other themes, medical sociology is now homing in on the meanings of health. The invigoration of health education has also encouraged research into health meanings, in order to target more accurately its media message. Paradoxically, this was often the starting point for anthropological studies of traditional society. Many everyday activities are public tests of one's health status. The Azande frequently poke sticks into 'termite oracles' at the village entrance, in full view of others, to make an initial self-diagnosis of a suspected affliction.

Williams (1983) has unravelled the lay logic of health held by elderly Aberdonians (over 60 years old) in a middle-class area and in a working-class estate. Health had three main constituents. 'Strength' was one important constituent: a prominent property being that it could be stored for future use, thereby minimising the effects of impending illness. If it was dissipated, then the power for quick recovery would be lost. This 'banking' notion of health has possible links with religion, a tack not pursued by Williams. Religiosity increases with age, with frequent appeals being made to God for strength to overcome daily troubles. The Protestant ethic, too, emphasises conservation, rather than flippant 'social expenditure'.

'Fitness' was a second important constituent of health. You could carry out obligations if fit. Fitness determines ones' capacity to perform tasks, whether paid employment or activities which substitute for work – e.g. errands and gardening. To be in very good health is captured in the saying, 'fit for anything', a condition more appropriate to the young, with their super reservoir of health. Even the process of getting older, with its associated disabilities, necessitates being 'fit' for specified and limited activities; such as being able to walk upstairs, or to make a meal, etc. A third constituent of health was the 'absence of disease'. As Williams explains, there was often ambiguity in how far 'pain' was a clear indicator of the presence or absence of disease. Pain was amorphous, covering many things: a disruptor of sleep, the aftermath of fainting, as well as being the obvious hurt from severe arthritis.

Lay meanings of health rarely explain their origins. Are these concepts derived from childhood and later made malleable to fit old age? Or was ageing the great 'health leveller', generating the same meanings? It was significant that class was not a discriminator. Williams forges interesting links with a French study, of middle-aged, middle-class Parisians. Health as the relative absence of disease and the continuum of strength, have their French counterparts. The greater psychosomatic theorising by the French is attributed to differences in general practice. French GPs, paid on a fee-for-service basis, are heavy prescribers, especially of vitamins and tonics, when patients are slightly off-colour: this reinforces the awareness of psychosomatic symptoms. Class differences could also be an input. The middle class were found to make more reference to psychological explanations – being more 'sophisticated theorisers' – as these are more in keeping with their status.

In researching the relationship between social class, health perceptions and a new dimension, namely *personal vulnerability*, Calnan and Johnson (1985) chose a sample of women, age 21–55 years. Not possessing a complete class range, they divided the women into middle and lower working-class groups. Their findings are offered as exploratory. There are no class differences in basic perceptions of health, although the middle class offered more elaborations. More middle-class women referred to adequate exercise and eating the right foods, for sustaining health, but the numbers were not significant. The researchers expected class to be a discriminator, because of the prevalence of illness in the lower working class. But the prior medical histories of the two groups were not revealed, and this raised questions about the representativeness of the sample.

Vulnerability proved more difficult to pin down, and no close relationship with health emerged. Calnan and Johnson argue that the lay explanation of its interconnectedness with disease demonstrate the powerful projection of the medical model in shaping lay theorising. Professional women felt more vulnerable, the middle class generally having greater longitudinal temporal frameworks; i.e. they have a greater tendency and ability to project into the future. Professionalism itself allows the prediction of career stages, with an associated calculation of the preconditions success or otherwise. The working class are more 'present orientators'; to them the strategies for survival are the more important. It is possible that these temporal frames carry through into calculations of future health risks.

SICK ROLE AND PREGNANCY

The history of the 'capture' of pregnancy from midwives and its medicalisation in the nineteenth century by the burgeoning, male-dominated profession is well-known. Pregnancy as a medical activity curtailed 'outside' competition. Middle-class women were the first to be forced into this sick role; as part of the pattern of conspicuous consumption by their *nouveau riche* husbands, they were shunted into the arms of doctors. The cult of invalidism and frailty was fostered as a strategy for passing time by women denied opportunities both outside and inside the home, which was run by an army of servants. A mixture of vinegar and arsenic could also be taken for creating the 'pale look'. Childbirth therefore became a pathological condition. The uterus and ovaries also became dangerous organs; dictating women's temperaments. The working class were considered a separate 'species', being fit for manual work, having a different 'genetic' constitution.

With the pull of mass medication and hospitalisation after World War II, the sick role for all pregnancies was the medical rule, usually in the name of safety. In the 1960s obstetric research investigated the reasons for variations in labour and pregnancy, some women being recognised as having more difficult births. The explanatory value of the biological model was shown to be deficient. Social factors began to be scoured. Rosengren (1962) was instrumental in showing how women who indulged in the sick role, usually producing a more difficult birth, were those enmeshed in a series of problematic social values. Their husbands tended to be socially mobile in the class hierarchy, pulling them into unfamiliar settings. Other associated conditions were having a husband whose education was inferior to theirs, or having an overly close mother–daughter relationship, the husband then being perceived as unsupportive. Quarrelling with their doctor in the antenatal period was also a factor.

Imposing the sick role on pregnancy cut across a range of social investments made in the birth. Some births were intended to bring couples closer together, or to add gender balance to the family, or to be a finality to reproduction, if followed by a post-partum sterilisation. The hospital sick role was geared to role specificity, i.e. solely to giving birth; it was not intended to encapsulate any extra meanings. Occasionally the sick role would only become emphasised during delivery. Women intending 'natural' childbirth (e.g. using the Lamaze method) may become disorientated in featureless labour rooms. Doctors then insist on the sick role, negating the prior labour training, leading to guilt and a sense of failure.

That fathers also have pregnancy careers is now established, but the sick role is withheld from them. Male pregnancy careers are opaque, lacking the biological and cultural markers of women's. They are also more resonant with their other careers, especially work, where performances can be affected by accidents. The term 'pregnant fathers' and 'fathers in labour' have no currency; medically, men are peripheral to women's pregnancy careers. Freudianism has long recognised that birth can precipitate a mental crisis, reactivating the Oedipus complex; the unborn male becoming a phallic competitor. Zilboorg (1931) was the first to indicate post-partum depression in men. Afterman (1955) at the Veterans' Administration Hospital of Palo Alto, California, located their psychosis (causing some to attempt infanticide) in the structure of their marriage. They regarded their dominant wives as mother-sister-confidantes, pregnancy was therefore a betrayal.

Pregnancy by women other than one's partner (e.g. sister) can also produce male illness. Lipkin and Lamb (1982), at an antenatal clinic in New York State, found that 22 per cent of the partners of pregnant women had some treatment for gastro-intestinal symptoms, including vomiting. No 'objective' causes were discovered and the symptoms vanished six months after birth. It is clear that most doctors do not relate these symptoms with pregnancy.

Male pregnancy illness is sometimes called *couvade symptoms*. The couvade was a male birth ritual common in the Ancient World (Strabo commented on its occurrence in Greece) and tribal societies, but usually absent from Africa. The couvade had two parts: dietary and location restrictions. Some foods were not propitious for birth. The expectant father had to freeze his activities and remain within the village; if he exerted himself, hunted and sweated, it was assumed the pregnancy would be difficult. An early anthropological explanation was that the couvade was a magical-protective rite for the unborn. It has been argued that the lack of couvade rituals today does not make the pregnant father's role culturally explicit. Lacking this public significance some men therefore develop privatised rituals for coping with the uncertainty of birth – an obvious outlet is an 'escape' into mental illness.

The 'purpose' of the couvade still remains unclear. In matrilineal society it emphasised the father's role, counterbalancing genealogical descent through women. The couvade was also present in patrilineal societies, where this emphasis was not needed. Richman (1982) recognised four contemporary pregnancy careers: the birth disavowed; the instrumental approach (birth is nothing unusual, it's the woman's responsibility); birth as a joint activity; and attempts at takeover of birth (socially sterilising the woman). It is likely that extreme psychiatric symptoms typify the first career; with the most 'physical' symptoms being associated with the sympathetic rapport of birth as a joint enterprise.

If it was medically acknowledged that men become vulnerable by pregnancy, then the male obstetricians' claim to 'look after' women would be undermined. Rights to other types of 'men's work', because of greater 'stamina', would likewise collapse. Medicine now recognises that men can play a supportive role. The role of unpaid comforter at birth relieves staff shortages. Male pregnancy symptoms are still not regarded as real, being transient and psychosomatic.

SICK ROLE AND ILLNESS CAREERS

Another way in which the missing gaps in the Parsonian jigsaw have been completed, is by examining the biographical progress through specific illnesses, emphasising their distinctiveness. Parsons offers the short, generalised journey of illness, full of optimism for recovery. *Multiple sclerosis* (MS) and *breast cancer* have been well documented and are useful examples.

MS is little understood; its physical onset often appearing in those in their thirties. The degenerative effects of the nervous system affect speech, vision, physical co-ordination, bladder and bowel functions. Periods of spontaneous remission, unpredictably spliced, occur. The initial symptoms are often problematic – tiredness, numbness, occasional dizziness and difficulty with vision. MS is distinguished by a long period of 'pre-diagnosis'. Doctors may ascribe these symptoms to overwork, to stress or to a 'virus'.

How patients respond to the indeterminacy of a pre-diagnostic stage, which can average five years, is the subject of Stewart and Sullivan's (1982) study. It was made in San Francisco with 60 patients, whose average experience of MS was 14 years. The sample was slanted towards women: 20 white and 20 black women, with 20 white men. They divided the pre-sick role period into three stages. In the *nonserious phase*, symptoms are relegated to minor complaints, or ignored. Doctors are not seriously involved – numbness, for example, was easily explained as poor circulation. Self-medication would be applied. Doctors frequently accepted patients' self-diagnosis in this phase. The *serious phase* occurs when symptoms worsen. Patients become dissatisfied with their 'diagnosis' and frequently switch doctors: confusion exacerbates their condition. Misdiagnosis resulted in prescriptions for tranquillisers and painkillers; some underwent surgery and traction! Only a quarter were correctly diagnosed. It is interesting that 17 per cent of patients correctly diagnosed their symptoms as MS. The medical confusion caused friend and kin support to fall away, as the patients were regarded as hypochondriacs. The *diagnostic phase* was a relief, the patients knowing that they now had an accurate label; most psychiatric symptoms then reduced.

Stewart's findings point to an additional facet of the sick role – that of 'pseudo-illness', bestraddling health and illness. During diagnostic turmoil, patients could be active and accurate with self-diagnosis. This could have been a product of education and income, since the sample was primarily white-collar and skilled manual and almost all had completed high school as a minimum qualification. The cost of frequent doctor switching in the serious phase is only possible at a given income level.

MS provides no opportunity for discarding the sick role. To follow doctors' orders and recover is meaningless. The question is posed by Brooks and Matson (1982): how do patients adjust to a permanent sick role and what criteria are valuable in evaluating this adjustment? To capture changes over time necessitates a longitudinal study and a matched control group without MS. By using the mailing list from two branches of the USA National Multiple Sclerosis Society they logged the progress of MS sufferers between 1974 and 1981. The mean duration of MS, from diagnosis, was about 17 years, about 45 per cent were immobile.

Males are more psychologically affected; their self-concept falls, while women's rises. Autonomy and higher income are also relevant variables, increasing esteem. To be nursed in a home is an obvious reminder of disablement. An increase in disease episodes also lowers the self-concept. Men are more de-statused by giving up full-time employment (as they are at retirement), or by slipping into an inferior job. MS women are more 'at home' within the house. It was interesting to note that although the self-concept of the MS group was lower than the control, it was not appreciably so. Reduction in physical mobility over the period did not predict the expected loss of self-esteem. With a non-response rate of 40 per cent to the mail questionnaire, it is possible that those affected most did not reply.

There are many types of *cancer*, hence a generic cause is ruled out. Skin cancers have one of the highest rates of treatment success. 'Environmental' factors are said to cause-precipitate 75 per cent of all cancers. The medical philosophy is maintained that early detection and treatment leads to more successful outcomes (survival rate). With breast cancer it is more appropriate to talk of control, rather than final cure. Current research is retreading a path laid down in the 1930s, relating the onset of cancer to family crises. Peller in 1940 sifted the statistics of cancer deaths between 1930 and 1932 and found that widows of all ages had a higher mortality than married or unmarried women.

Breast cancer strikes at a woman's femininity; research emphasises the delay in seeking medical assistance, despite 'obvious' physical signs. Many sufferers believe their condition is a sentence of death; others a challenge for survival. Their cancer career is punctuated with 'shock stages', as critical medical information is revealed and decisions are made. Periods of normlessness, which some describe as 'unreal', dominate. This contrasts with the rationality and determinancy of the Parsonian model, which also emphasises the stable personalities of patients, openly facing sickness.

Gyllenskold (1982), who described the responses of patients she researched in a Stockholm hospital, reveals the psychological mechanisms they brought into play. The defence mechanisms of repression, denial, displacement and suppression can figure at all stages, e.g. from first recognising the symptoms, receiving the diagnosis, during treatment and even at hospital discharge. About half the women did not seek medical advice on first discovering cancer signs. The beliefs that if cancer comes it will also go away, or that it was a fatty tissue, often held sway. Patients with serious illness always build their own explanatory models. Some believed that it they had a previous illness in one organ, then that would be immune from cancer. The loss of a breast, by operation, was described in terms of grief, like suffering a bereavement. Western culture has no appropriate mourning rites for the loss of critical body appendages. The Chinese used to preserve dismembered parts; burying them with the deceased. Two years after the operation, patients still queried the doctors' justification for the necessity for mastectomy; and wondered whether they really had cancer.

The sick role for these women over two years was an oscillation of unfinished crises. The critical psychological dimensions were not in the medical remit, although they had a determining effect. Defence mechanisms for managing uncertainty took over. By using suppression, information was not requested about the whereabouts of the amputated breast. Nor did doctors think it appropriate to raise the topic. Grieving for it was an individual act, being 'ragged' and with no public stylistic form, others being excluded from the experience. Medical expectations of illness behaviour do not embrace grief for parts of the self.

CHILDREN'S PERCEPTIONS OF HEALTH

Children are large consumers of medical resources; being the most medically screened section of the population – partly due to statutory requirement. Health cuts fall more gently on them. By seven years of age over 40 per cent have been hospitalised; children from class V having the highest rate of *admission* with their greater proneness to accidents, especially from vehicles. The position is reversed as regards *consultations*. In 1976, in a two-week period, the *consultation* rate for boys 5–14 years was 113 per thousand in class I, and one-third less in class V. Illness reporting in class V was much less, often obscuring the real position. General Household Surveys indicate that there are more GP consultations for boys than girls. The classical sick role was predicted on the notional, 'mature' adult, with his/her subsequent regression to child-like dependency during medical care.

Researching children's *own* perceptions of health is now being confirmed as an independent activity. Children's views had previously been gleaned from parents and other adults. The mountain of epidemiological studies on rates of child morbidity still outweighs those traversing health through children's eyes. Studies of hospitalisation of children have tended to centre on the problem of interrupted child development, family separation and educational retardation. The psychologists' investment in children's perceptions have frequently been subordinated to the task of testing Piaget's stages of cognitive development, using children's health reasoning as an indicator.

Neuhauser and others (1978) provide a typical example. Piaget specified four stages: *sensori-motor* (0–2 years), with understanding of the environment through the infant's bodily senses; *preoperational* (2–7 years), where language is geared to 'egocentric' thinking; *concrete-operational* (7–11 years), where established classifications and causal reasoning are used, primarily concerned with 'immediate' concrete objects and defined experiences; and *formal operational thinking* (over 12 years), in which abstractions can now be grasped, developing a range of possibilities. Their sample consisted of 24 white middle-class offsprings; 12 in the 8–9 years age range and 12 in the 4–5 years range. The stage of cognitive development was important when children considered how much control they had over 'healing'. Those at the *concrete operational* stage felt they had more control. However, older children were *used* to doing more for themselves and this fact may have determined the findings. Older children were able to handle better the abstract concept of illness, when it did not rely on external clues, like cuts or bruises. The researchers concluded that the personality factor becomes important when asking children to perform at the upper range of their developmental ability. The obvious class bias of the sample – the children also lived in a Californian university town – must be recognised when interpreting developmental relationships concerning health meanings.

Early research concentrated on discovering how far parental influences determined children's attitude to health. Paediatricians recognise that children's visits may be structured by a mother's anxiety about her own situation, or may reflect other household stress. Some have used children's symptom and illness recognition as an explanatory variable in distinguishing patterns of socialisation. Mechanic (1964), taking his clues from Zborowski (1952) on cultural differences and responses to pain, explored the influence of mothers on children's health behaviour. Zborowski had shown that over-protective mothers help explain the readiness of Jews and Italians to express their feelings on pain.

For testing his thesis, Mechanic chose 350 mother–child pairs, of a representative sample, living in Madison, Wisconsin. Some relationship was found between children's readiness to report symptoms, the format of their illness behaviour and the degree of interest their mother showed; but the degree of relationship was less than anticipated. The many inconsistencies in health behaviour (e.g. the denial of pain and health risk taking) were best accounted for by differences in age and sex. There are of course many other influences shaping children's health perceptions, such as peer group, mass media and teachers. Mechanic actually overlooked an important family member – the father, whose influence on gender differences for symptom significance could have been important. Fathers expect sons to be brave, and engage in risk-taking activities, but tend to over-protect their daughters. Although they less frequently accompany children on visits to doctors, their health decisions are still important.

Joint parental socialisation based on the use of 'reason', the supplying of health information and the granting of autonomy have been found to be associated with 'positive' health behaviour in children. Discipline-centred child rearing produces the reverse. To show this, Platt (1973) constructed an index of the child's overall health-care practices; this was derived by combining seven items, including nutritional habits, smoking frequency, exercise, cleanliness, etc. It is uncertain however, whether these activities were performed to please 'liberal' parents, or because children had conceptualised good health practices as being beneficial. The study rated only one child in each family, but socialisation varies according to the age distribution of children.

British research into children's health perceptions is closing the gap with the USA. It is still debatable whether children, moving in and out of sick roles, or locked into a chronic illness, would have different perceptions and be more knowledgeable, having learned directly from experience. Eiser and others (1984) made a comparative study of a group of diabetic children and a control group of healthy children; the mean chronological age was 12 years. Their definitions of health were similar, with a tendency for more of the control group to regard 'not ill' as being healthy. Although the study does not comment, the children's criteria of health approximated to that of adults (as described, for example, by Calnan and Johnson): eating good food, not fat, fit, exercise, body working properly, etc.

In offering lay explanations of illness (colds, whooping cough, nits, cancer, diabetes, heart attacks and chickenpox), the only discriminator was that diabetics knew more about their own illness. Eiser concludes that although the knowledge levels of the groups were the same, there could still be untapped differences regarding children's feelings about illness. Diabetes may not however be an appropriate chronic illness; doctors teach children to regard themselves as normal and to take responsibility for its management.

THE SICK ROLE WITHIN THE FAMILY

As Parsons noted, illness is also a family affair; the family prompts its sick member to seek help and oversees the passivity requirement of the sick role. The effects of illness on family dynamics were not in Parsons' brief. With increased medicalisation the burden of a sick member on the family has multiplied and become more complex. Members are made responsible for often complicated medical regimes and faulted for their mismanagement by supervisory paramedics, etc. Home patients are surviving longer with malignancies. The life expectancy for cystic fibrosis now averages 12 years; before 1940 most patients died within one year. A laborious hand process of pulmonary evacuation has to be used daily. The socio-psychological structure of the family can be radically changed by such activities.

One of the first, major explorations of this theme was Davis's (1963) two-year study of 14 children with spinal paralytic poliomyelitis, contracted in 1954 prior to the Salk vaccine. Families are categorised by the new challenges confronting them. Using the Parsonian frame, Davis translates the strategies for pattern maintenance (stability) into 'emergence' and shows how they are deployed in attempts at solving each family's identity crisis. The first crisis period was confirmation of polio, after the period of diagnostic uncertainty. The family felt stigmatised and alienated from a world it previously held to be normal and orderly. Hospitalisation and the absent child impacted family roles, causing indecisiveness and changes in the distribution of rewards and punishments for other siblings. The return of the child with hospital-induced behavioural changes was the next crisis. Contradictory descriptions were offered; the child being labelled either 'mature', too 'possessive' or 'aggressive'. The family had to decide, too, on its external appearance. Some chose normalisation, insisting their crippled child was like others. In one example, despite the great inconvenience, the child staggered on and off public transport journeying to school. Others chose disassociation, avoiding contacts which would show up the child's limitations and would emphasise the handicap.

The type of illness, its severity and trajectory, as well as the organisational competence of the family, must be considered. For example, childhood cancer is more distressing for siblings than parents. It was not only the fear of 'catching' cancer which upset them, but the 'lavish' parental attention given to the sufferer, even after the life-threatening episode. Siblings are steered into positions of emotional isolation, yet may still be requested to participate in the family's anticipatory mourning for their sibling. Serious illnesses can often have their indeterminancy, side effects of treatment not being warned about. Radiation treatment causes growth retardation and delayed puberty – all additional childhood stigmas. Unanticipated side effects are considered differently in adults. Even survival can precipitate its own crisis: crucial dates – birthdays, anniversaries of major treatment, discharge, periodic check-ups and deaths of fellow sufferers – becoming hurdles to be faced with trepidation. Some develop avoidance taboos and freeze their activities prior to their occurrence.

Not least of the family's troubles are financial, especially for those already on the breadline: special diets, extra transport costs and presents to cheer up the sick. When ex-cancer patients resume formal the educational deficit. When home nursing 'fails', resulting in death, the educational deficit. When home nursing fails, resulting in death, the medical links which may have been long cultivated, are abruptly severed, causing additional anomie. Long after the child's death the family may still be recasting itself, in an attempt to accommodate the loss.

It is difficult to generalise about the impact of a spouse's illness. Much depends on the age, sex and occupational status of the helper. Chronic illness, like multiple sclerosis, produces above average separation and divorce rates which are highest where the husband is the carer. Husbands frequently refuse to 'sacrifice' their careers and seek 'normal' sexual satisfaction elsewhere. The timing of the illness is also important. When a spouse has married a physically handicapped partner the condition has usually been explored in great detail by experts, and the commitment is made. The sexual element is to the fore; prosthetic aids are familiar resources. Disablement can also realign the political forces of a family. Wives of USA business executives are often de-statused on marriage; although highly educated, they discontinue their careers to serve their organisational man. They can develop the Mrs Hillside Syndrome – depression, boredom, neuroticism and heavy drinking. If their husband becomes incapacitated and they 'take over', these symptoms are alleviated.

The suddenness of a severe head injury, or a cerebrovascular accident (CVA, e.g. stroke), have different consequences compared with the slow deterioration of a chronic disease, like Alzheimer's. The frequency of strokes increases with age: it is four per thousand for the age group 55–64, but over five times this rate for those aged 75–84. The caring spouse is therefore near, or of, pensionable age. Newman (1984) has produced a model containing the stages through which a spouse, and the immediate family of a stroke patient, may proceed: 1) crisis and shock with sudden hospitalisation; 2) hope when signs of survival appear; 3) expectations pinned on further treatment; 4) hopes for full recovery if improvement discernible; 5) homecoming, generating future optimism for recovery; 6) expectations maintained if progress of recovery discernible; 7) doubts mount when recovery unfulfilled; 8) realisation that patient's uncompleted recovery is permanent.

This trajectory is sometimes curtailed and modified; over 20 per cent of stroke patients die within the first month of hospitalisation. Those in a vegetative state may never leave hospital. Families often routinise this condition by having a rota for token visits. Others symbolise their attachment by insisting on washing the patient's bedwear at home. Regular attenders who stay for long visits will be built into the staff's nursing programme. Others recover sufficiently to re-engage in employment. Newman cites evidence to show that over a third of spouses with a mean age of 60 years, caring for stroke patients, are themselves in sick roles, having treatment for depression. With the cessation of sexual activity (possibly with loss of sensation, or effects of anti-hypertensive drugs), there is a tendency for the carer to adopt a custodial attitude.

RELIGIOUS AFFLICTION AND THE SICK ROLE

Religions have long expressed health concepts, known by 'grace', 'spiritual well-being' and 'purity'. They have also been the prototype for secular models of medicine (see Chapter two for patriarchalism in medicine), especially psychiatry, where moral 'affliction' and 'possession' have their direct counterparts. Jung's interpretation of the psyche is firmly anchored in religiosity. Spero (1983) has also drawn attention to the coincidence of modern psychotherapy and the Halakhic (Jewish ethics) healing model. Psychological disorders are easily translated into spiritual impropriety, for which ethical rebuke (hokhadah) is a corrective device.

The religious sick role is the closest fit to the Parsonian ideal. Salvation (complete cure) is achievable. The religious prescriptions are accessible to all; and can be publicly affirmed. Submissiveness to the greater spiritual power is the path to recovery. The congregation (the greater family) has the moral duty to detect moral turpitude and to direct the deviant to the path of righteousness.

The role of the healer will vary according to the amount of formal structure and religious specialisation. Informal structures tend to place greater emphasis on the healing aspect of religion. Csordas (1983) reports that 19 per cent of adult Americans call themselves Pentecostal or Charismatic Christians, a great number being involved in healing. His study of a Catholic Pentecostal Group listed four major kinds of healing. Physical healing practised by popular evangelists;

spiritual healing, such as treating the soul by confession; 'healing of memories', i.e. treating distressing thoughts still lingering from the past; deliverance, i.e. the expulsion of evil spirits, distorting the personality and behaviour. There has even been a recent addition, the 'healing of relationships', for dealing with interpersonal stresses.

By healing the whole person – soul, psyche, body and interpersonal – Pentecostalists believe they are fulfilling God's will. The diktat of the Parsonian social system also necessitates that equilibrium of the parts be maintained. Illness is a disruption of the biological, personality, structural and functional dimensions.

The medical analogy can be further extended. Pentecostalists accept that even if 'physical healing' is not possible, 'spiritual healing' still is. If medical science provides no cure, then care programmes can be successively arranged for patients. In the healing of memories the member's past is reconstructed by attention, with new insights being directed to painful episodes, especially the installation of Christ to successfully guide the supplicant to the present. A parallel between the erosion of painful memories and psychotherapy is self-evident. The goal is reintegration with Christ and the charismatic movement – i.e. normality. Cosmopolitan medicine's criterion of treatment effectiveness is symptom relief. But Pentecostalists recognise a *transitional* state, a qualitative overlap between sin and purity. This liminal status is played down in cosmopolitan medicine, because of the scientific propensity for categorisation and the pigeon-holing of all conditions.

CONCLUSION

The Parsonian sick role, derived from an antiquated sociological period (when consensus was fashionable), has been the catalyst for many later studies. As an 'ideal-type', lacking spatio-temporal and cultural dimensions, it has obvious limitations as an empirical referent. Its value as an irritant to the sociological imagination is however unquestionable. This chapter has used the sick role as Parsons would have intended, i.e. as a vehicle for navigating the many diverse tracks, focusing on health/sickness. Perhaps the concept of sick role is now expendable. Some prefer 'illness behaviour', and many sick people are still able to carry out a variety of other roles.

But Parsons is correct in the basics. Illness *is* an undesirable condition. Illness as an imbalance characterises all medical belief systems. Parsons would have found it ironic that phenomenologists have been prominent in 'rounding off' his technical principle of patient incapacitation. Their stance is that illness is an assault on our humanity; mutilating the self and distorting its being in the world. This loss of control reduces sensate freedom. Just as we should not blame Weber for not incorporating the organisational principles of the NHS into his ideal-type of bureaucracy, we should not blame Parsons for not seeing what we can today. Most of us can see further, only as it were because we are pygmies standing on the shoulders of past giants.

REFERENCES

Afterman J, Towne R D 1955 Psychosis in males related to parenthood. *Bulletin of the Menninger Clinic* 64: 19–26

Blaxter M, Cyster R 1984 Compliance and risk-taking: the case of the alcoholic liver disease. *Sociology of Health and Illness* 6: 290–310

Brooks N A, Matson R P 1982 Social psychological adjustment to multiple sclerosis. *Social Science and Medicine* 16: 2129–35

Calnan M, Johnson B 1985 Health, health risks and inequalities: an exploratory study of women's perceptions. *Sociology of Health and Illness* 7: 55–76

Csordas T J 1983 The rhetoric of transformation in ritual healing. *Culture, Medicine and Psychiatry* 7: 333–75

Davis F 1963 *Passage Through Crisis: Polio Victims and Their Families.* Bobbs-Merrill, New York

Eiser C, Patterson D, Tripp J H 1984 Illness experience and children's concepts of health and illness. *Child: Care, Health and Development* 10: 157–62

Freidson E 1961 *Patient View of Medical Practice.* Russell Sage Foundation, New York

Goldthorp W O, Richman J 1975 Medical knowledge of gynaecological patients – a study of patients' understanding of their illness and treatment (Tameside hospital research paper). Summaries produced in *British Journal of Sexual Medicine.* Dec. 1975 and Feb. 1976

Gyllenskold K 1982 *Breast Cancer: The Psychological Effects of the Disease and its Treatment.* Tavistock, London

Hanson B G 1985 Negotiation of self and setting to advantage: an interactionist consideration of nursing home data. *Sociology of Health and Illness* 7: 21–35

Henderson L J 1935 Physician and patient as a social system. *New England Journal of Medicine* 212: 819–23

Jeffrey R 1979 Deviant patients in casualty departments. *Sociology of Health and Illness* 1: 90–108

Johnson S M, Snow L F 1982 Assessment of reproductive knowledge in an inner-city clinic. *Social Science and Medicine* 16: 1657–62

Koos E L 1954 *The Health of Regionville*. Columbia University Press, New York

Lipkin M and Lamb G 1982 The couvade syndrome: an epidemiologic study. *Annals of Internal Medicine* **96**: 509–11

Mechanic D 1964 The influence of mothers on their children's health attitudes and behaviour. *Pediatrics* **33**: 444–53

Neuhauser C, Amsterdam B, Hines P, Steward M 1978 Children's concepts of healing: cognitive development and locus of control factors. *American Journal of Orthopsychiatry* **48**: 335–41

Newman S 1984 The social and emotional consequences of head injury and stroke. *International Review of Applied Psychology* **33**: 427–55

Parsons T 1951a Social structures and dynamic process: the case of modern medical practice (Ch. X) *The Social System. Outlines of a Conceptual Scheme for the Analysis of Structure and Process in Social Systems*. Tavistock, London

Parsons T 1951b Illness and the role of the physician: a sociological perspective. *American Journal of Orthopsychiatry* **21**: 454–60

Peller S 1940 Cancer and its relation to pregnancy, to delivery and to marital and social status: cancer of the breast and genital organs. *Surgery, Gynaecology and Obstetrics* **77**: 1–8

Platt L 1973 Child rearing methods and children's health behaviour. *Journal of Health and Social Behaviour* **14**: 61–9

Richman J 1982 Men's experience of pregnancy and childbirth. In McKee L, O'Brien M (eds) *The Father Figure*. Tavistock, London

Rosengren W R 1962 Social sources of pregnancy as illness or normality. *Social Forces* **9**: 260–7

Roth J 1972 Some contingencies of the moral evaluation and control of clientele. The case of the hospital emergency service. *American Journal of Sociology* **77**: 839–55

Schneider D M 1947 The social dynamics of physical disability in army basic training. *Psychiatry* **10**: 323–33

Segall A 1976 Sociocultural variation in sick role behavioural expectations. *Social Science and Medicine* **10**: 47–51

Spero M H 1983 Modern psychotherapy and halakhic values: an approach towards consensus in values and practice. *Journal of Medicine and Philosophy* **8**: 287–316

Stewart D C, Sullivan T J 1982 Illness behaviour and the sick role in chronic disease, the case of multiple sclerosis. *Social Science and Medicine* **16**: 1397–1404

Straus R 1957 The nature and status of medical sociology. *American Sociological Review* **22**: 200–4

Szasz T S, Hollender M H 1956 A contribution to the philosophy of medicine: the basic models of the doctor–patient relationship. *American Medical Association Archives of Internal Medicine* **97**: 585–92

Williams R 1983 Concepts of Health: an analysis of lay logic. *Sociology* **17**: 185–205

Zborowski M 1952 Cultural components in responses to pain. *Journal of Social Issues* **8**: 16–30

Zilboorg G 1931 Depressive reactions related to parenthood. *American Journal of Psychiatry* **10**: 926–62

Chapter four
PATIENTS AND DOCTORS

Under the impact of the social sciences, especially sociology and psychology, the doctor–patient relationship has 'returned' to its rightful position at the hub of medicine. Researchers have trampled over the secret garden of clinical practice; the consultation, the microcosm of medicine, has been reconstructed in ways often unfavourable to doctors. Their mass of data elaborates the minutiae of communication, with forms of talk and styles of diagnosis very much to the fore. Many of the findings resulting from consultation have been found to be contradictory and expressed pedantically, adding to the doctor's chagrin with the social sciences.

Consultations have often been shown to be undemocratic, with patient participation a charade. Doctors on videos often appear unsympathetic and poor listeners. Randomising, Byrne and Long (1976), after analysing over 900 consultations made by over 60 GPs, concluded that the doctor–patient interview can be expressed on a continuum, ranging from doctor-centred to patient-centred styles. The doctor-centred style predominated: here information-gathering was central, with little attempt at open dialogue, denying the patient any opportunity for expression of feelings. The 'analysing and probing' style also prevented patients from challenging the doctor's control of themes. Richman and others (1974), commenting on gynaecologists, had previously referred to symptom-centred and patient-centred styles. The former restricted the consultation to the strictly-medical, usually kept the woman lying down and made the doctor's exit simple at the end of the consultation. The patient-centred approach was deemed 'inappropriate' for hospitals under siege with long waiting and clinic lists. After being made 'important' in the consultation, women expect immediate treatment. It was anti-climactic to be told of long delays.

Psychologists have tended to concentrate more on stress and on the cognitive processes involved in communication, while sociologists have examined speech strategies. Speech conventions offered, for example, by Richman and Goldthorp (1977) are 'just talk' and 'ceremonial talk'. 'Just talk' is used by the nurse when a gynaecological patient utters 'unlinked' words during a painful examination. The nurse 'cocoons' the patient: goes through the routine of offering praise; indicates a fabricated time scale of the 'almost' completed examination, or gives breathing instructions – irrespective of what the patient is saying. The patient's words are not allowed to 'hang'. Gynaecologists use 'just talk' during the rapid rounds of routine antenatal examinations – to 'fill' the spatio-temporal slot, when no more information is needed. 'Ceremonial talk' is used at the end of a consultation, when the prognosis is offered. The findings are presented as the natural consequences of the 'joint', patient-gynaecologist endeavour.

Such revealments contribute unintentionally to the anti-doctor thesis. However, the bulk of social science findings are silent on one major point – was the doctor 'medically effective'? That is a different question from: was the patient's social expectation satisfied and the encounter 'effective'? The medical and social sciences need not however be perpetual combatants. Much of their methodology is in common. Clinical observation is only a variant of ethnography. The statistics of 'controlled' trials (with all the pitfalls of representative sampling) are also in the positivist tradition supporting sociology – Durkheim's comparative study of suicide last century was a model. The themes propounded by sociologists are not alien to all doctors. Despite its natural science veneer, medicine has always had a fallback position, namely that practice remains an 'art'; the doctor's self and intuitive perception being the key resources for healing. For example, Balint and Norell (1973) emphasised the humanistic philosophising underpinning the 'purpose' of the doctor–patient encounter, i.e. his wishing to avoid illness-centred diagnoses. He trained other doctors in the 'flash technique' (mutual intuitive apperception) – a therapeutic interview, meeting the limited time available in general practice. Other sociologists have built on his foundations of the different time considerations prevailing in consultations.

The aim here is to extend systematically the opening comments. First, by detailing the social processes impinging on the GP's activity – the latter being the lynchpin for patient contact with medicine. Although 'wider' social factors may not have been the primary calculation in building their roles, GPs are not, however, immune from the forces of social change. Second, an exposé of the 'internal' intricacies of the doctor–patient interview will be made. Third, we shall summarise the clients' evaluations of their medical encounter. Finally, one major client group, i.e. women, will be focused upon; this will return us to the theme of patriarchalism in medicine, touched upon in Chapter two.

GENERAL PRACTITIONER AND SOCIAL CHANGE

The work of GPs resembles housework: it is often ill-defined, can be boundless, and is usually taken for granted. The GP is the first port of call for those needing to penetrate further into the health service, although most go no further than the GP service. GPs are involved in over 80 per cent of all 'illness' coming within the frontiers of the NHS. Their involvement varies: it includes 'direct' treatment, screening, partial diagnosis and referral, post-hospitalisation 'surveillance', vaccination, etc. Much depends on the medical role created for him/herself from the array of health/illness opportunities. There are obvious parameters which circumscribe the exercise, e.g. age of the practitioner, recentness of qualification, working arrangements (usually in partnerships), medical interests, and so on. The health needs of the area (of the practice) are rarely systematically researched; client feedback and participation in GP planning is the exception. Thus the GP's role is geared more to his own 'personal' circumstances. The official brief in NHS Regulations 1974 encourages this open-ended licence: in summary, GPs are to provide the 'appropriate' medical services that are usually provided by GPs!

Their work overlaps the shifting moral frontier of society. This is not a new occurrence. The period prior to the NHS may often be eulogised as a golden age, when patients were 'respectful' and showed gratitude, but GPs were still faced with the issue of 'role creation'. Honigsbaum's (1979) detailed history of the relationships this century between general practice and hospital care emphasises their role dilemmas. The First World War saw the drafting of half of the doctors in the country. On returning they had great difficulty commencing practices, the remaining doctors having greedily enlarged their lists. Some GPs called for a state-salaried service to cope with the uncertainty; in fact many became 'servile' members of established practices.

Between the wars their relationships with consultants were far more complex and conflict-ridden. Consultants took political measures to exclude them from hospitals, despite having relied on GPs during the

First World War to alleviate shortages. The GPs' medical skills were very much questioned. When, during the 1920s, road accidents with vehicles increased dramatically (the death toll in 1939, with less road traffic, was as high as in 1984, though advances in surgical techniques were responsible for saving proportionately more lives), orthopaedic consultants resented the GPs performing emergency surgery in cottage hospitals, lest their expertise be devalued. Likewise, obstetricians disliked GPs in their wards. By 1930 consultants were even opposing GP entry to low status Poor Law Infirmaries.

Until 1935 the British Medical Association was consultant dominated. GPs then formed their own committee, after the consultants had restricted membership of their own specialist group to 'real' consultants. GPs dispersed into many community niches: private schemes, National Health Insurance Work, Poor Law medicine, tuberculosis services, infant welfare clinics (where they came under additional competition from the new group of 'medical officers') and occupational health schemes, etc.

The Second World War did not see a repeat influx of GPs into hospitals; rather the wounded from the battlefields were dispersed world-wide. The hospitals dealt essentially with civilian air-raid casualties, who were directly admitted without reference to GPs. Consultants often refused to sanction the relocation of GPs within hospitals, although many were medically understaffed. Consultants were the key advisers on the committees for regional planning and deployment of medical services.

The inter-war gulf between GPs and hospital based consultants was not just a matter of the former lacking specialised skills. As Honigsbaum explains, there was also a social class divide. Consultants originated from a higher stratum; they had to be wealthy to survive the lengthy and often unpaid hospital training. The rivalry had unfortunate results. GPs were often reluctant to refer their patients, especially for TB treatment, for fear of losing their clients' fees.

With the foundation of the NHS the GP's status has become firmly anchored, and conflict with consultants has subsided. GPs are no longer in direct competition with each other. The Medical Practices Committee controls their distribution. It seriously encourages GPs to settle in 'open' and 'designated areas', where existing doctors have large lists, usually over 2,500. There are 31,132 GPs in the UK; over 90 per cent are 'unrestricted principals' – the technical term for what most people mean by 'GP'. The rest are *GP assistants*, who are directly paid by the employing GP and do not contribute to the partnership's capital, and *restricted principals*, who provide a narrow range of services, e.g. a company's own doctor, and *trainees*, who, although medically qualified, have to complete three years' training with GPs before being admitted to the register.

Two major trends are visible. First, the movement towards group practices. Between 1959 and 1971, the number of GPs in partnerships of four or more at least doubled. In 1985 only some ten per cent of GPs operated single-handed, many of these being older doctors practising in inner-city areas. The Green paper (1986) has recommended compulsory retirement at 70 years. Over 12 per cent of GPs practising in London's inner areas are over that limit. Second, general practice is no longer the Cinderella subject in medical schools, being the declared preference of most students. The curriculum has been restructured, according general practice more significance.

It is important to note the financial considerations. The income differential between GPs and senior consultants has significantly narrowed since 1975. Consultants now earn only a fifth more than GPs from the NHS. Straight comparisons are of course difficult, and are complicated by the greater capacity (e.g. in gynaecology and orthopaedics) of some consultants' to boost their incomes from private medicine. However in geriatrics this source of extra income is very limited.

Although GPs are on the front line of primary care, there is little official data revealing their cost-effectiveness. Compared with their hospital counterparts, they have experienced few 'monitoring' exercises, yet they consume almost a quarter of the NHS budget for England. The survey of general practice by Dowson and Maynard (1985) was laboriously compiled, and even then only after much badgering of DHSS departments and medical associations. They showed that in the decade from 1974, the average size of lists has declined, from 2,320 to 2,081. Support for GPs – secretarial, nursing, health visiting and financial (e.g. cheap loans from the General Practice Finance Corporation), etc. – has continued to increase. No one knows whether these favourable resource trends have been translated into more effective health delivery, because neither the DHSS nor the Royal College of General Practitioners have bothered to find out. There is no national data on the breakdown of the GP's working day, yet they are legally required to provide comprehensive cover for those on their list. There are many idealistic statements about their roles, but no operational definitions which allow measurement of performance.

The profession has concluded that a list of 1,700 should be the norm (the Review Body on Doctors' and Dentists' Remuneration concurs), without a reduction of income. No objective rationale has been offered, it simply being assumed that patients will get 'longer' consultations and 'better' service. There was little or no discussion on the delegation of health tasks to nursing and social work members of the health team. Butler (1980), reviewing the available evidence, opines that the average consultation lasts between 5 and 6.5 minutes, *irrespective of the length of the GP's list.*

One background consideration is the profession's worry that it will be moving in the foreseeable future into a GP 'surplus', in that it will be unable to absorb the projected output from medical schools. The British Medical Association is now making the validating examination more difficult for overseas doctors coming here to practise. GPs claim that their workload is increasing, and point to the growth in the numbers of the elderly. The DHSS counter this argument by explaining that this factor is balanced by the shedding of some onerous work – e.g. via the introduction of the self-certification of sickness for the first seven days and via the increased use of district nurses and geriatric visitors for home visits.

Lack of an agreed set of rules of accountability perpetuates these moves and counter moves, with the resource game lacking an end stage. Bowers' (1984) study exemplifies but one implication of these endless manoeuvres. She studied the uptake of the six week post-natal examination by puerperal women in Oldham. Her research was hindered by the inaccessibility of basic statistics on such examinations when carried out by GPs. Hospital statistics of uptake were readily accessible, yet covered only nine per cent of mothers. GPs received payment of £6.75 per mother, irrespective of the quality of the examination. Details of childbirth-related morbidity revealed by the examination were similarly obscure.

Even without cash limits circumscribing their performance (hospital departments have fixed budgets and should a renal unit overspend, for example, then it could be forced to reduce its intake), GPs complain that doctoring has become more 'difficult'. The social context is certainly changing, and GPs often view their current situation and patient intake unfavourably against some mythical benchmark of the ideal patient. Problems of sexual morality and identity are certainly more prevalent. The Gillick ruling initially made it illegal to prescribe contraception for the under-sixteens, without first consulting parents, and was a new complication for the 'liberal' GP, until overruled by a higher court in 1986. The child-centred pattern of education has encouraged a new assertiveness from teenagers. The greater emphasis during the 1970s on individual legal rights, generated by the multiplication of local pressure groups and trade union activity, has clearly fed into the consultation. Feminism is a prime example. Again ethnicity, with its selective urban concentration, can radically transform some practices. It can bring communication difficulties, and cultural misunderstandings on child-rearing, and on the meanings of death and family dynamics.

Residual unemployment has brought another wave of clients to the GP's shore. The sick role is one way of establishing a 'meaningful' identity, as meagre compensation for the loss of status. Prescriptions for tranquillisers are no solution to the distress caused by bad housing, low income and no employment prospects. Reluctantly GPs are sucked into local politics. The medical profession has always been a political animal, protecting its own rights; but invisibly performed in the corridors of state power. A few GPs, historically, have always sided with the underdog; those in mining areas between the wars campaigned with trade unions for healthier working conditions and for claims for workers under the Workmen's Compensation Act (the Medical Research Council in fact resisted the addition of pneumoconiosis to the coal industry's list of industrial diseases until 1943). Those in the welfare culture/underclass rely on the doctors' validation of their needs for increased benefits. Mobility allowances, or extra points on the housing list for a new flat, may only be gained when GPs 'take on' the 'authorities' and favourably pursue their clients' cases. GPs may now however share many clients with other agencies, especially the social services, and so may face new interprofessional entanglements. These can be hostile, e.g. from social workers keen to emphasise their new professional expertise or radical intent. At case conferences the primary health care team may dispute the GP's claim for 'natural' leadership and the alleged superiority of the medical definition.

To evaluate the effects of different catchment areas on general practice, Horobin and McIntosh (1983) reviewed a sample of fifty GPs in north-east Scotland, Highlands and Islands, representing urban/rural differences. They were interested in how medical risk-taking varied with availability of time. How similar the urban practices were to their English counterparts is not made clear. Scotland is also the best doctored country in the UK; with 59 GPs per hundred thousand population – a ratio 16 per cent more favourable than England. The *rural practices* operated with a 'time surplus'; many GPs' visits were social events with the elderly and chronic. There was the danger of unsupported diagnosis, without the proximity of consultants. Referral could involve laborious journeys, disrupting home life. The GP's errors were visible to the whole community, which could threaten his reputation. GPs in *urban practices* operated with 'time deficits', having to make quicker diagnoses, but had the advantage of easier referral.

In offering community care to certain clients, GPs experience severe role strain. The care of cancer patients, as discussed by Rosser and Maguire (1982), is notable. Cancer represents both a threat to the patient's life and to the credibility of the GP's skills. Many GPs are still reluctant to discuss openly all the ramifications. Essentially, medical knowledge cannot answer the question frequently asked by patients: 'why me?'. There are patients with lung cancer who have never smoked. (One major Japanese survey does show that non-smoking wives of smokers do have higher rates of cancer than non-smoking wives of non-smokers.) The prognosis, for 'no apparent reason', can suddenly worsen.

GPs are still disease orientated, despite nominal changes in treatment philosophy to holism. Seventy-five per cent of Rosser's GPs expressed some reservations about the use of cytotoxic drugs. The hospital convinces patients that they can produce optimistic results, and GPs are left to 'explain' (and justify) the awful side effects. To become personally involved with patients, dropping the professional facade, presents an emotional challenge few GPs will risk. The tendency for most general practices is to filter client access via organisational and management procedures. GPs are aware of the patient's anomie, but that aspect can be compartmentalised as a 'social problem', the province of the caring semi-professionals. All this makes the doctor's visit problematic – for what? Byrne and Long (1976) have shown that doctors are not critical of their own performances, because they rarely evaluated them. GPs also disregarded any subject that resembled 'psychology', thinking that it was more to do with animal behaviour.

Todd and Still (1984) re-emphasised the above when they explored communication between GPs and patients dying at home. They interviewed both GPs and their patients. The theme was so sensitive, that the initial seven doctors chosen at random from the list registered with the Durham Family Practitioner Committee, refused to participate. No representativeness can be offered for the four doctors found for the study. Doctors are the patients' key informants. Other studies had indicated that the majority wished to be told openly, if they were dying. Yet two out of Todd's four doctors confirmed a policy of 'not telling' terminally ill patients. Even when patients discovered the fact for themselves, these doctors avoided confirmation. It is hypothesised that death-denying doctors are maintaining the 'traditional' doctor–patient healing relationship, bringing comfort and offering a cure; admission of death would undercut this. By 'traditional', Todd and Still presumably mean 'scientific', for other traditional (pre-scientific) healers openly faced the question of death with their patients.

Not least among the 'external' factors impacting general practice is the knowledge explosion in medicine. Although generalists, GPs are expected to keep up to date. One advantage put forward for the move towards health centres was that group practice would permit internal specialisation and more attendance at refresher/training conferences. The level of interpretative knowledge often determined the type of test a GP would request for a patient from the hospital. Dowie (1983) shows that GPs in health centres used more biochemistry tests. Pathological results are expressed in numerical sequences and ECGs in wave patterns. Solo practitioners were more likely to have limited interpretative skills, but there were exceptions with some group practices making little use of hospital tests. Doctors in such 'low-use' practices were often young and recently qualified. It could mean, as Dowie suggests, that these doctors had failed to assimilate interpretative skills during training, or, that they did not wish to display their expertise for fear of exposing (to patients) the limitations of their older partners in the practice. Some GPs could be test orientated, even with low interpretative skill, provided they could draw on knowledgeable partners and friendly consultants for advice.

Little is known about how GPs make the decisions to introduce new drugs. Trials paid for by drug companies are one way. There are no studies which rate the accuracy of these GPs' recordings of the results. Often there is considerable advertising pressure to prescribe branded drugs.

More GPs are introducing computers into the consultation, e.g. for record searches and for the updating of details of treatment. Professional bodies (e.g. Royal College of General Practitioners) have given a cautious welcome, uncertain of the influence on doctor–patient relationships. In one controlled trial by Herzmark and others (1984), two Sheffield practices were linked to the IBM Sheffield Primary Care System computer. Few doctors (one out of four) co-operated with the monitoring project at the middle-class practice; but five out of six for the working-class practice. No reasons were offered for this difference.

It is difficult to draw firm conclusions. The doctors still maintained their hand-written note taking, which took twice as long again when using the computer. In a longer trial their proficiency may have improved. Doctors experienced more stress with computerisation.

They were divided as to its effects on the consultation. (One doctor decided not to use the computer with patients present.) Brownbridge and others (1985) comments that patients' ratings of their GPs' information provision and rapport, and of their own stress, were modified little, although there were variations between GPs.

For those GPs whose careers started *before* the shift towards health centres, there have been substantial organisational changes. The shift has been likened to the move from the cottage industry to the factory. The GP formerly worked at home, with family help readily available: wives were secretaries cum chaperones cum unofficial medical advisers and visitors to chronic patients. Financial incentives were the major encouragement for change; 70 per cent of the cost of employing support is directly reimbursed, the rest allowed for in expenses. The health centre, as an asset, also brings tax advantage. The potential for interpersonal conflict between all the staff in a health centre is real. The collectivity of medical skills may have been assembled on criteria other than that of patient need. The GP from the New Commonwealth may resent his ascription as the 'ethnic' doctor. Assuming he/she is from the Punjab, for example, this is hardly a sufficient qualification for 'understanding' Afro-Caribbeans, or Bangladeshi peasants, and in any case doctors have middle-class lifestyles.

Partnerships are essentially commercial transactions. The Inspector of Taxes assesses the *partnership's* liability to tax, not that of the individual doctors. Accountants work out each partner's share, according to the contractual formula. This is often where disputes arise. The problem of defining a fair day's work is present, and workloads change over time. Management issues mingle with those of patient care. Medical education, which keeps the torch of learning bright, gives little attention to the financial context of medicine.

Most group practices now employ a manager, a crucial appointment since office maintenance, fire regulations, cleaning, building design, appointments all have significance. A recent text on management in general practice, by Pritchard and others (1984), finds a need to caution GPs against trying to outsmart the Inland Revenue! The frontier between 'NHS' and 'private' medicine is becoming increasingly blurred in terms of what a GP can charge for.

New health initiatives, planned 'on high', have their inevitable consequences for general practice. One of the latest, *Healthier Children – Thinking Prevention* (1982), recommends that all preventive services concerning children should be located in primary care supervised by GPs, who are judged the best people to discover and alleviate potential risks on their home visits. That these visits are decreasing and that economic deprivation is the major threat to children's (and others) health, is given scant significance in the Report, written by a group of GPs.

There are a number of strategies adopted by GPs for consolidating their position amid change.

First, the handing over of their 'dirty work' (e.g. chronic and elderly bedridden) to supporting semi-professionals, e.g district nurses. Health visitors often complain that GPs do not always understand and fully recognise their occupational skills.

Second, by referrals to hospitals. Dowie's study revealed no animosity between GPs and consultants, who are often valued for their educative role, which takes place via hospital correspondence and via formal meetings. Some of the GPs in Dowie's study had clinical assistantships. GPs are in a position to boost a consultant's income by requests for home visits, since up to a given number they receive additional payment. The pattern of referral varies between GPs, being a product of their style, medical interest and relationship with consultants.

Third, by organisational screening. Cartwright (1967) found about a third of GPs operated an appointment system: today it is the general rule. Complaints against receptionists have increased. Their delegated authority varies according to practice policy. Jeffreys and Sacks (1983) give examples of their preventing 'undesirables' (e.g. hippies and drug addicts) from joining the list by being told it was 'full', and of their persuading those requesting home visits to attend the practice. They often made value judgements regarding the severity of the illness when constructing appointment lists. Further evidence of reduced accessibility was provided by the study of the London Health Planning Consortium (1981), which randomly rang a number of inner and outer London practices between 11 a.m. and 3 p.m. and 8 p.m. and 9.30 p.m. on Mondays to Fridays and Saturday 10 a.m. and 12 noon. Forty-seven per cent of calls were answered by an answering agency or machine. In the Inner London area six per cent of the callers were told that there was no GP present, nor could one be contacted.

The interprofessional relationship between GP and nurse is ambiguous. Although GPs complain that much of their work is 'trivial', there is a reluctance to delegate a clinical load commensurate with the nurse's competence. Bowling's (1985) comprehensive survey of this organisational dilemma also explains that in the USA and Canada doctors do not share the same inhibitions. Interestingly, the pre-1939 nurses (lacking today's professional skills) living locally, were frequently summoned to crises (usually fever and pneumonia) by neighbours, who could not afford doctors. GPs displayed no professional hostility, perhaps partly because there was in any case little prospect of securing a patient's fee!

In health centres GPs frequently extend the nurse's duties into secretarial work. By limiting the clinical functions of nurses, GPs are further consolidating their own autonomy. They perhaps fear that there would be a sound argument, e.g. cost effectiveness, for enlarging their lists, contrary to the present trend, if nurses should operate at the upper limit of their expertise. Recent moves in nursing have staked out the claim for greater recognition of their clinical expertise, as with the emergence of the nursing process and nurse therapists, etc. Nurse subordination, or Kenny Syndrome, in general practice is just one aspect of male supremacy in medicine. [Sister Kenny had discovered a more effective treatment for polio (in Australia) in the 1930s, but was denigrated and excluded from health centres.] GPs could argue that the 'limitations' they place on nurses are on legal grounds, since it is they alone who have liability for all their list members. However list liability only applies if the GP delegates tasks beyond the nurse's competence. The role of the nurse is further complicated by the fact that the DHSS has never promoted a policy on delegation.

Bowling showed that it is likely that a quarter of GPs delegated no clinical duties; while 50 per cent did so 'slightly'. More recent medical graduates in 'better-run' centres delegated most. USA surveys show client satisfaction with nurse practitioners being highest for those who have direct experience of their treatment. However, Bowling discovered no major impetus on the part of nurses for seriously enlarging their roles. This reluctance may have a financial aspect; the extra responsibility of 'doctor's work' deserving higher salaries. Again the GPs' nurses may be less career orientated; many working shorter hours due to family commitments with young children.

To capitalise on nursing skills and sharpen up 'community health' the Cumberlege report (1986) has promoted the new role of neighbourhood teams of nurses, with limited prescribing rights, serving from 10,000 to 25,000 people. Mr Fowler the Social Services secretary, under GP pressure, has already pre-empted this new structure by opposing the recommendation that GP's nurses be phased out by the removal of the GP's employment subsidy for them.

In conclusion there is some confirmation in these studies of the GP's 'need' for defensive strategies in order to regulate the increasing social 'turbulence'. Some differentiation of their client intakes is afforded by the simple categories of 'good' and 'bad' patients. They told Stimson (1976) that the most bothersome ('bad') patients were the over-consulters; those who demanded 'full' explanations, who insisted on their rights, and who did not trust doctors. More preferable were the ('good') patients who consulted least; i.e. only when absolutely necessary and when they had clearly defined physical complaints. Those with 'psychiatric' disorders tended to be perpetual ('bad') patients. They were troublesome in two ways. The GP could not 'cure' them, and their consultations could not be predictably scheduled, often disrupting an 'orderly' appointment list. However, it must be noted that private medicine has always thrived on the 'over-consulters'.

INSIDE THE CONSULTATION

The doctor–patient consultation is no longer the cloistered mystery of medicine. Its 'secrets' have been recorded on video and the action also reconstructed by non-participant observers. Training films of the encounter are now standard educational material in medical schools. Broadening the discussion away from general practice, will help us flesh out some of the interaction touched upon in the discussion of the sick role.

The consultation, though brief (in private practice usually averaging half an hour), contains multiple activities. Patients have stories to tell, want fears alleviating, need confirmation of their lay theories, want favours, need information and so on. Doctors have fewer and specific priorities: namely accurate medical diagnosis and an 'ordered' consultation. There is no disputing the importance of the mutual decipherment of the consultation. For example, the speed of referral to specialists for large bowel cancer depends, as MacArthur (1981) shows, on whether the GP examined the patient at the first visit. GPs refer more rapidly for breast cancer, being less reluctant to make the physical examination for this. Breast cancer patients also admit to a shorter duration of their initial recognition of symptoms than is the case, there perhaps being less risk of appearing 'foolish'. Doctors' records on such patients report fewer symptoms, usually the main reference is to the 'lump'. According to Zola (1972), patients often discontinue treatment when a doctor gives inadequate attention to the topics they raise, which also discourages their return for subsequent checkups.

Doctors attempt to anticipate potentially troublesome patients, and to allocate them to the end of their list. Gynaecological consultations differ according to whether the patient is 'routine' or 'special'. Attempts are made to keep routine patients to the strictly medically-relevant issues. Special patients have 'time out' from the consultation; they can openly 'possess' more of their own everyday experiences, which will be readily acknowledged by the consultant. Routine and special do not necessarily correspond with the medical severity of the condition. Patients with cancer of the cervix are usually routine, being easily diagnosed. They become special when, for example, they become extremely distressed or refuse treatment. Not all 'troublesome' patients are special. Special patients can be designated before the consultation, or emerge as special, as it proceeds.

Richman and Goldthorp (1977) illustrate the above. Repeat/continuous patients are often special. Their long association has given them a medical acumen. The ductility of the relationship engenders a durability capable of 'safely' containing joking and quasi-courtship relationships, temporarily erasing the differences of status. After the first few visits the medical/biological focus becomes exhausted and there is an 'inevitable' gravitation to their everyday experiences. Women then have greater control over the interpretation of this consultation resource. This happens in cases of infertility, when no physical causes are apparent. With ex-cancer patients returning for check ups, this informality is additional proof and reassurance that all is well. It is made obvious that the gynaecologist is not talking to a patient, but to a trusted friend. The opening greeting of these consultations is an invitation to 'tell all' ... 'Well it's four months since we last met. What's been bothering you in the meantime?'

Professional patients have to be 'carefully' listened to. One subdivision of these 'special patients' are those who have circulated widely through a large number of medical specialisms – perhaps originating in gynaecology and returning via psychiatry, general surgery and orthopaedics. The gynaecologist is forewarned by their voluminous casenotes, composed in different medical styles. The telling of their complex history has been well-rehearsed and authenticity is built into it by the way other specialists' names and medical terminology are enlisted. If these patients are 'cut off' abruptly from telling their story, then their co-operation is forfeited. Professional patients are needed for gleaning extra clues about their past treatment, especially the effects of drugs, which may be confusing the current symptoms. These patients become important mediators of what Smith (1974) has called 'document time'. All doctors selectively record what they consider to be the significant facts derived from a consultation. The professional patient can be the key to the unlocking and discovery of 'what really happened'.

One example of patients emerging as 'special' during the consultation is when they are 'mislocated', being referred to the wrong specialism, or its sub-branch. Consultants structure their antenatal clinics differently from their gynaecological ones. Each location has its own inbuilt patient expectancies. Less time is allocated to the patient in the antenatal clinic. Pain is not regarded as a significant and legitimate feature in the gynaecological clinic. Their pro- and anti-natalistic cases are usually separated. The sequencing of a gynaeco-logical clinic was once suspended for 20 minutes in order to convince an emotionally overwhelmed woman, when it was discovered that she was pregnant. A sonic aid had to be brought over, for her to listen to the baby's heart.

Special patients are often those who have their 'external' status acknowledged. Gynaecologists will frequently meet hospital staff, their relatives and prominent people in the community, not necessarily those in powerful positions. Special patients are also recognised in socialist countries. In China, top party officials and survivors of the Long March are medically denoted, the latter had wards reserved for them.

Most patients are linguistically structured into being 'routine'. Their own sense of illness history and theoretical explanations are overridden by medical concepts of time. In the following extract the doctor had reached the *end* of his consultation and was summing up; reassuring that the bleeding was insignificant. The woman was able to interject, by using the title 'doctor' (line 5), eliciting the moral obligation of an acknowledgement. Not only does the gynaecologist re-interpret the theory of her 'fall' – into one of being 'shaken' – but he also subsumes it by switching the initial, medical explanation to a more serious condition, suggesting cancer. If patients are allowed their own explanations, they can make claims to the steering of future treatment regimes.

Gyn.: It's just what we call cervicitis, you know. It's just uncomfortable, I know.

P.: Well. (Cut off.)

Gyn.: It certainly looks all there is to the naked eye.

P.: A good while ago doctor ...

Gyn.: Yes.

P.: I was washing my hair and children in the bathroom you know ...

Gyn.: Yep.

P.: ... and my foot was soapy and it slipped ...

Gyn.: Yep.

P.: ... and I banged myself, you know, and I bled a little bit after. I injured myself there. (Points to her back which had not been examined.) I thought it might have been the shock of falling you know.

Gyn.: No. You may have sort of, er, shaken yourself. Even if it turns out that the smear test shows atypical cells. Right.

P.: Yes.

Gyn.: As opposed to normal cells it could be microscopic and would be a hundred per cent treatable.

Freidson noted (Ch. 2) that bargaining occurs to prevent irreparable breaches in the consultation. Time and medical procedures are the chips. In the USA free drug samples, more convenient times for consultation and cheaper rates are offered. The gynaecologist can promise only tiny scars (below the bikini line), a short circuiting of the waiting list ('If telephoned are you prepared to come in at a moment's notice, if someone drops out?'); the assurance that he, the consultant (and not the 'junior'), will do the operation.

Comaroff (1976) has attempted to pin down the variables accounting for the different strategies used by GPs in communicating information on non-fatal illnesses. Her analysis was derived from interviews with 51 doctors in a large South Wales town. We have no observational confirmation. She concludes that the difference in communication patterns are a *response* to the way GPs define their professional role and to the type of relationship they want to preserve with patients. This depends, of course, on the way they typify patients. Those doctors who offered elaborated strategies (e.g. explaining diagnosis and treatment fully; responding openly to patients' requests for further information; offering diagrammatic information on bodily functions, etc.) did not emphasise their professionalism nor enforce a status gap between themselves and the patient – but aimed for a more egalitarian relationship. This study offers a model for interpreting the doctor–patient relationship, but cannot explain whether, or how, the GP's occupational orientation will change over time.

The concept 'room for the patient' has been introduced by Bensing and Verhaak (1982); this refers to the number of opportunities made available for patients to express their real worries during the consultation. Byrne and Long had shown that longer consultations are more 'effective' than short ones – effective in the sense that doctors and patients are on the same wavelength. In contrast short consultations tend often to result in doctors and patients being at cross purposes. Korsch and Negrete (1972) however claimed that the length of consultation did *not* correlate with client satisfaction. Their sample of consultations ranged from 2 to 45 minutes. Much depends, of course, on whether patients have the desire to express worries. Some may come for a simple procedure – such as a change of dressing or ear syringing.

The researchers used Dutch GPs (the Dutch National Association of General Practitioners, 1977 had declared a policy of 'openness' to patients' problems) for uncovering the factors related to 'room for the patient'. An analysis was made of 273 videos of the consultations of six separate doctors. The average time per consultation (excluding examination time) was about five minutes, with 29 per cent lasting longer than six minutes. It was confirmed that socio-psychological topics tended to feature in the longer consultations. The average number of medical complaints offered by the patient was 2.3; again, the longer consultations were associated with a greater number of complaints being raised. The researchers operationalised 'room for the patient' by fourteen variables (length of consultation, doctor's talking time, patient's talking time, interruption, attention, prompting, elaboration by patient, etc.). These were later collapsed into four factors: conscious control by the doctor; affective behaviour by the doctor; talkativeness of the patient; and relative talking time of doctor and patient. A surprising result was that doctors' affective behaviour (which other studies had emphasised) did *not* discriminate between those consultations which permitted and inhibited the patient's opportunity to express worries. The main discriminator was found to be the degree of *conscious control* exercised by the doctor.

Thus, like members of any other occupation doctors developed strategies and orientations to work, as their particular tools of the trade. The consultation can never be a free floating enterprise. The different styles of consultation are still underpinned by the common purpose, that of maintaining medical control.

THE CLIENT'S VIEW

Studies on the client's view are increasing. Most express favourable and tolerant responses to medical practices. The proliferation of client assessment has been due to: (a) the impetus of the post-Parsonian tradition, which sided with the 'underdog'; (b) the increasing vociferousness of consumer groups, clients' surveys being their main ammunition; (c) hospital services, which now are producing their own feedback (monitoring) – in part to head off external, political criticism; (d) increasing professionalisation of nursing, which has encouraged the development of its own knowledge base, patients being a favourite and accessible source of research; (e) Community Health Councils, which require indicators of 'community' health needs and of their 'satisfaction'; (f) the biological basis of clinical trials, which is incorporating more 'peripheral' personality and social attitude data.

Client studies have to be used with care. Those using 'broad satisfaction' ratings of 'medical experience' making it especially difficult to discover exactly what it is that is being rated. Most clients not only lack knowledge of medical procedures but have no comparable frames for evaluating their own experiences. As a general principle client studies made soon after the medical experience show more favourable ratings than those made later. People are glad to have 'survived', later they can reflect and seek others' views. In some studies 'clients' speak on behalf of other clients – e.g. Korsch 'designated' the mother as patient in the study of children at the Children's Hospital of Los Angeles.

In a study of fathers' attitudes to hospital delivery Richman and Goldthorp (1978) report a 93 per cent favourable response – these fathers said they would be present for the 'next birth'. Observational data and in-depth interviews from a smaller group had revealed a great deal of emotional discontent. Because of the hospital's organisational behaviour towards them, some fathers referred to themselves as the 'third party'; others spoke bitterly of the 'entrance trauma'. They arrive with their wives, who are 'snatched' away by midwives, leaving the men standing there 'lost', with no attention focused on them. Fathers present at birth tended to describe their wives as having 'less pain' than did fathers who were only present during labour. They could not always explain their criteria. Some considered their wives to have less pain by the 'quickness' of birth and less 'anxiety' shown by staff. The study was made in the baby honeymoon period in the hospital, with no birth abnormalities known. Some fathers who 'agreed' to be present for the next birth, may not intend to have future children.

The maternity services were among the first to attract clients' evaluations. Some have been selectively captured. *The Good Birth Guide*, rating hospital units, relies heavily on unsolicited letters of mothers' experiences. Studies attempting to match up doctors' perceptions with their patients' are rare. Bowers (1984) is an interesting exception. The six weeks post-natal examination is an under researched activity. Following childbirth, mother and baby receive care from midwives for at least 10 days, sometimes 28 days; then two weeks or later, GPs usually make their examination. Specified information is scheduled: details of delivery; condition of infant (feeding habits, etc.); mother's condition (return to menstruation etc.); physical examination (of abdomen, vagina, perineum and cervical test, if not done antenatally); discussion on contraception and 'bonding'. The GP can still claim his fee if it can be shown that efforts were made to encourage attendance for the examination.

Out of a random sample of women delivering in August, September and October 1983, 91 per cent (from 210) were interviewed. There were some major discrepancies. According to mothers, GPs paid 'insufficient' attention to feeding, their biggest worry, and 46 per cent said it was not even discussed! Yet 84 per cent of GPs said that they had discussed this topic. Much hinges on respective definitions of 'discussion'. Again, 23 per cent of mothers said they had urine tests, whereas GPs claimed 51 per cent. Bowers concludes that the major expectation of mothers from the examination was help with 'personal' problems. For example, GPs rated episiotomy problems high, and 'depression' low, with the reverse being true for mothers.

Following up their 1967 study of GPs and patients, Cartwright and Anderson (1981) could not discover any relationship between the changing organisation of general practice and patients' attitudes to the consultation – in terms of doctors listening fully to them, explaining things comprehensively, and giving thorough examinations. Whether the GP was a solo practitioner, or a corporate member of an efficient group, had no discernible effect. Patients' views were influenced more by their own social class and age. Women also tend to have a lower regard for hospitals than for GPs; possibly because they are more familiar with the latter.

In their in-depth study of five practices, Jeffreys and Sacks (1983) detected a tendency between 1972 and 1975 for more group-practice patients to be dissatisfied. However, when the demographic composition of the intakes is examined, it turns out that *younger attenders*, especially women, who generally express more critical views, are more characteristic of group practices. Also, those seeing doctors other than their 'own' generally express more discontent, which again occurs more often at group practices.

Clients are rarely critical of doctors' technical competence. Of the 800 mothers questioned by Korsch and Negrete (1972) on the consultation for their children, only 54 raised this. Their main dismay was with doctors disregarding the accounts they gave of their children's symptoms; 149 also reported that they had not been told which illness their children were suffering from.

Segall and Roberts (1980) have reviewed the studies made of doctors' estimations of patients' medical understanding; most under-estimated their level of knowledge. This factor points to the abbreviated and unsatisfactory discussions with patients on symptomology. Segall replicated the Samora and others (1961) study, whose average level of understanding (percentage of correct answers) was then 52 per cent; with Segall it had risen to 79 per cent. Patients had to complete multiple choice questions on common diseases and medical terms (e.g. malignant, swab and sterile, etc.). Caution is offered; Segall's data was derived from the returns of a mail questionnaire posted to respondents at home. It was impossible to confirm that the residents completed the test unaided.

Finally, we turn to the commonest method of patient evaluations – the swapping of stories of personal experiences with others. Stimson and Webb (1975) collected a large repertoire during their study of general practice. Such stories have a serious intent, though at first glance they could be dismissed as exaggeration and gossip. Patients can own stories, accruing prestige with their telling to different audiences. The teller can appear as heroine, reconstituting the consultation to show her contribution in a favourable light, 'correcting' and 'modifying' the doctors' judgements. Thereby psychically readjusting outside the consultation the asymmetrical power relationship between doctor and patient prevailing within. Story-telling can also provide cathartic release for pent up worries.

Some stories have built-in instructions for the perceptions of others, such as explaining how to interpret doctors' questions, elaborating the significance of some symptoms and, above all, explicating criteria by which doctors' performances can be morally and technically evaluated. Good doctors listen well and take 'decisive' action on behalf of their patients, and do not allow discomfort to linger. Some stories are open and cumulative, allowing others to elaborate the themes with their own experiences. From this patchwork a model of the potential health processes and resources of a locality, or hospital, can be offered.

DOCTORS, LABELLING AND WOMEN

The western industrial nations and the USA have health surveys indicating a higher morbidity for women, but with a greater longevity than men. Whether women 'really' have more illness, both physical and mental, is still in dispute. The indicators of utilisation of health resources and morbidity are weighted towards women, but mainly from the age of 16 years. Women make more visits to doctors, declare more symptoms, have more periods of incapacitation, have a greater incidence of acute conditions, and have higher rates of admission to psychiatric beds, etc.

Many explanations have been tendered for this gender difference. The medical view that women have a 'distinctive' biological constitution has long been fashionable. They were flawed by their reproductive anatomy, so their capacity to withstand illness was much reduced – or so ran the argument. A favourite diagnosis offered in the nineteenth century was neurasthenia, a lack of 'nervous strength' in women. The 'surges' of puberty, menstruation and menopause precipitated many illnesses, like manias. Ovariotomies were the remedy. While epilepsy in women was a reflex of the womb, in men it was a 'real' disease. Men's mental illnesses were caused by lesions in the brain. However, women's 'animal-like' reproductive system produced uncontrollable, moral-threatening manias – erotomania, nymphomania and homosexuality. Women's mortality from the White Plague (TB) was twice that of men. Their inherent 'weakness' was used as a justification for denying women the opportunity to train as doctors. Women were weakened, often by multiple pregnancies and their aftermath. These nineteenth century biological arguments have been transposed into those relying on 'personality' differences; making women more susceptible to 'stress'. But the paradox remains: if women are so prone to illness, why do they live longer? They also have greater (biological?) resistance to infectious and degenerative diseases.

Another way of approaching gender differences is by examining men's and women's roles in society and their respective relationships with doctors. Women are more locked into doctors, not only for gynaecological purposes; for instance they usually accompany their sick children to the doctors. If not employed in the labour market, their 'freer' use of time facilitates their 'slipping' into sick roles, as they are less de-statused by so doing. But many other variables intervene; women with young children resort less to sick roles; married women are 'less healthy' than others; 'working women' over 45 years have less 'absenteeism' than others, including men.

The majority of doctors are male (about 80 per cent of gynae-cologists) who have been conditioned to operate with stereotypes of femininity and masculinity. Doctors give different emphases to the 'same' symptoms, according to gender. More credence is given to women's presentation of 'emotional' symptoms, partly because they offer them more freely and openly. Men's 'back troubles' are regarded more seriously, being seen as directly caused by (heavy) work. Women's 'back troubles' are labelled as part of women's general gynaecological condition – intermittent aches and pains.

Macintyre and Oldman (1977), Macintyre, a medical sociologist, in the account of her experience of migraine, describes how its causation and treatment philosophy dramatically changed when she was a university student. Migraine was attributed to her competitiveness, her neuroticism ('typical' of intelligent women) and her exposure to stressful (examination) situations. Her 'personality conflicts' resulted from sublimating the desire (natural) for marriage and children into academic achievement. Her doctor recommended psychiatric therapy as treatment for the deep 'emotional problems' precipitating her migraine.

Doctors operate with many stereotypes, besides those of gender – the typical malingerer, the intelligent patient, the troublemaker and so on. These shorthand caricatures, once established, influence the consultation. The doctors' labelling has powerful consequences. Once labelled mentally ill (then cured), the likelihood is that the person will more easily be so labelled again. Also, patients conform to the expectation of their illness label. Those misdiagnosed as heart-diseased have altered their way of life and perceptions of themselves. Doctors' labelling activity supplements the working of the biomedical model. In psychiatry, especially, women are expected to conform more precisely to the female stereotype; there being greater 'flexibility' with the masculine stereotype. Women tend to be labelled for conditions which are more disturbing *to themselves*, like phobias. Men tend to be labelled when their behaviour disturbs *others*, as in the workplace. Brodsky (1984) presents some evidence to suggest that the psycho-dynamic approaches foster 'self-blame' in women.

Gove (1984) has modified the 'gender labelling' approach by arguing that women do actually have more mental and physical illnesses. He attributes this to differences between the nurturant roles of women and the fixed roles of men. The nurturant role, with its major responsibility for the welfare of children, spouses and elderly kin, has many hidden demands built into it. Women therefore find it more difficult to adopt the sick role, being unable to sever their obligations to others; this impairs their rest and recuperation, 'running them down' physically and mentally.

Fixed and nurturant roles need not be the prerogative of one sex only. Many male managers could be said to occupy nurturant roles, with obligations to the firm. They are often sick in their own time. They frequently try to run the office from the hospital bed, or go back to work too soon. The picture is however more complicated: those with the greatest work satisfaction tend to be healthier – they certainly live the longest.

CONCLUSION

Much of the discussion on the doctor–patient relationship has centred on the GP, justifiably, as he/she sees most of our symptoms. The social sciences have provided a window on the consultation, revealing its social intricacies. Video recordings are now providing a picture of all the action. An examination of non-verbal leakages is opening up an additional dimension of the doctor–patient communication. The availability of this rich texture has posed new methodological problems of interpretation, which we have been unable to explore here. There is a fundamental problem: what is a 'unit' of social action? This does not correspond to a film's still. Quantification of body movement and words does not necessarily equate with the meaning intended by the participants.

The consultation is not an encounter apart, rather it represents a segment of society under change. It is debatable whether GPs are 'sensitive' to these changes, which has an intimacy with the presenting symptoms. The most outstanding criticism of patients in the 13 years between the Cartwright studies has been the failure/reluctance of GPs to visit, when requested; a fourfold increase has been observed. The retreat to the barracks of the health centre has brought personal and financial benefits to the practitioners. Paradoxically, health centres were intended to spearhead 'community care', outside the hospitals. However, by losing contact with patients in their own homes, the GP has forfeited many illness clues, as patients have more control in their own territory, and are freer to speak when at home. To be able to tell one's illness story and be listened to, creates confidence for recovery. With an increasing number of illnesses not being susceptible to 'physical cure', talk (the art and major resource of the pre-scientific doctor) can be the pathway ahead. The increased bureaucratisation of health centres may not be the appropriate setting for this aspect of health care. Hart (1981) optimistically sees a new breed of doctor appearing. One who promotes health, rather than waiting for illness to come to him. This means more active social and political involvement outside the consultation room. Doctors are in a strategic position for these new battles on the part of the weaker and forgotten members of society. If doctors are serious about improving health, then they must make realistic attempts to improve the 'health environments' of their patients.

The majority of psychiatric conditions (especially neuroses) are seen, 'contained' and treated by GPs; only a minority are referred to psychiatrists, and even fewer are admitted to hospital. The main factors which predict the long duration of lesser psychiatric disorders are the environmental pressures of poor housing, poverty and isolation. It is well known that treatment regimes, *per se*, have little association with rates of recovery, personality and social factors often being more crucial. The relationship between urban ecology and types of mental illness is still being explored. The link between schizophrenia and deprived areas could be due to downward social mobility. Those with schizophrenia becoming 'skidders', and then gravitating to poor areas. There is no disputing that poverty is an added burden to the ill. Psychiatric illness is often accompanied by physical illnesses; chest, heart and lung conditions. Whether people with non-responsive physical illnesses worry and become 'depressed', or, whether psychiatric illness 'exposes' the individual to more physical illness, is again not always clear. In any event, the environment, in the broadest sense, remains the 'reservoir of illness'. To attempt to solve these health problems by having more surgery-based GPs will enlarge the diagnostic catchment of illness cases. Though without necessarily affecting the environmental factors underlying the symptoms.

REFERENCES

Balint E, Norell J S 1973 *Six Minutes for the Patient: Interactions in General Practice Consultation*. Tavistock, London

Bensing J, Verhaak P 1982 Room for the patient. *Nederlands Tijdschrift Voor de Psychologie* 37: 19–39

Bowers J 1984 *Uptake of Six Weeks Postnatal Examination of Puerperal Women in Oldham*. BSc Nursing Studies Project, Manchester Polytechnic

Bowling A 1985 Doctors and nurses: delegation and substitution. In Harrison A, Gretton J (eds) *Health care UK; an economic, social policy audit*. CIPFA

Brodsky A M, Hare-Mustin R 1984 Psychotherapy and women: priorities for research. In Widom C (ed) *Sex roles and psychotherapy*. Plenum, New York

Brownbridge G, Herzmark G, Wall T D 1985 Patient reactions to doctors' computer use in general practice consultations. *Social Science and Medicine* 20: 47–52

Butler J R 1980 How many patients? *Occasional Paper on Social Administration*, no. 64. Bedford Square Press, London

Byrne P S, Long B E 1976 *Doctors Talking to Patients*. HMSO

Cartwright A 1967 *Patients and Their Doctors*. Routledge and Kegan Paul, London

Cartwright A, Anderson R 1981 *General Practice Revisited A Second Study of Patients and Their Doctors*. Tavistock, London

Comaroff J 1976 Communicating information about non-fatal illness: the strategies of a group of general practitioners. *Sociological Review* **24**: 269–87

Dowie R 1983 *General Practitioners and Consultants*. King Edward's Hospital Fund for London

Dowson S, Maynard A 1985 General Practice. In Harrison A, Gretton J (eds) *Health care UK; an economic, social and policy audit*. CIPFA

Gove W R 1984 Gender differences in mental and physical illness; the effects of fixed roles and nurturant roles. *Social Science and Medicine* **19**: 77–91

Hart J T 1981 A new kind of doctor. *Journal of the Royal Society of Medicine* **74**: 871–83

Herzmark G, Brownbridge G, Fitter M, Evans A 1984 Consultation use of computer by general practitioners. *Journal of the Royal College of General Practitioners* **34**: 649–54

Honigsbaum F 1979 *The Division in British Medicine*. Kogan Page, London

Horobin G, McIntosh J 1983 Time, risk and routine in general practice. *Sociology of Health and Illness* **5**: 312–32

Jeffreys M, Sacks H 1983 *Rethinking General Practice*. Tavistock, London

Korsch B, Negrete V F 1972 Doctor–patient communication. *Scientific American* **227**: 67–74

London Health Planning Consortium 1981 *Primary Health Care in Inner London*. DHSS, London

MacArthur C 1981 Speed of diagnosis, referral and treatment in cancer of the breast and large bowels, *Report to DHSS*. Department of Epidemiology, University of Manchester

Macintyre S, Oldman D 1977 Coping with migraine. In Davis A, Horobin G (ed) *Medical encounters*. Croom Helm, London

Pritchard P, Low K, Whalen M 1984 *Management in General Practice*. Oxford University Press

Richman J, Bedford J R D, Goldthorp W O 1974 The gynaecologist: friend or foe? *New Society* **30**: 474–6

Richman J, Goldthorp W O 1977 Becoming special: gynaecological ideology, gift exchange and hospital structure. *Social Science and Medicine* **11**: 265–76

Richman J, Goldthorp W O 1977 When was your last period: temporal aspects of gynaecological diagnosis. In Dingwall R, Heath C, Reid M, Stacy M (eds) *Health Theory and Health Knowledge*. Croom Helm, London

Richman J, Goldthorp W O 1978 Fatherhood, the social construction of pregnancy and birth. In Kitzinger S, Davis J A (eds) *The Place of Birth*. Oxford University Press

Rosser J E, Maguire J E 1982 Dilemmas in general practice: the care of the cancer patient. *Social Science and Medicine* 16: 315–22

Royal College of General Practitioners 1982 *Healthier Children – Thinking Prevention*. Report from General Practice, no. 22, Exeter

Samora J, Saunder L, Larson R F 1961 Medical vocabulary knowledge among hospital patients. *Journal of Health and Human Behaviour* 2: 83–92

Segall A, Roberts L W 1980 A comparative analysis of physician estimates and levels of medical knowledge among patients. *Sociology of Health and Illness* 2: 317–34

Smith D E 1974 The sociological construction of documentary reality. *Sociological Inquiry* 44: 257–68

Stimson G V 1976 General practitioners and types of trouble. *Sociological Review Monograph* 22: 43–60

Stimson G V, Webb B 1975 *Going to See the Doctor*. Routledge and Kegan Paul, London

Todd C J, Still A W 1984 Communication between general practitioners and patients dying at home. *Social Science and Medicine* 18: 667–72

Zola I K 1972 Studying the decisions to see a doctor. In Lipowski Z S (ed) *Psychological Aspects of Physical Illness*, vol 8. S Karger, Basel

Chapter five

PROFESSIONALISATION

Professionalisation is the dominant occupational trend. Wilensky (1964) reflects this surge in the title of his paper, *The Professionalisation of Everyone?*, showing how the process is increasingly affecting many forms of work. The declining manual strata, the growth of white collar occupations and the shift towards the knowledge-based 'service society', have all been important trends. A profession claims that its distinctiveness (and its superiority) stems from the ownership of a knowledge-base unique to itself. The greater the professional assertion, the more abstract and theory ridden tends to be its knowledge base, derived from much academic toil, aimed at prising open nature's secrets. The professional enterprise consistently seeks to differentiate itself from 'mundane', everyday reasoning.

To apply 'abstract' knowledge needs both an intellectual mind and a trustworthy character, according to the logic of professionalism. Schooling has long been dichotomised to accommodate the prestige and 'worthiness' of academic knowledge and to downplay manual skills. Routinised work and the authoritarian control of the shop floor have their counterparts in the school organisation and curriculum designed for many working class pupils.

The notion of profession is central to any debate on health and illness. There are many competing interpretations of this phenomenon, aligned along political and methodological axes. There is general agreement, however, that a profession is both a descriptive and an organising concept, representing the ideological and practical framework for medical practices. The medical profession is one of the oldest and most prestigious, and has managed to direct the activities of other occupational and professional groupings (lesser ones are usually called semi-professions) involved in health delivery. This contact has promoted the medical profession to the ideal prototype for emulation by others – it has inadvertently become the catalyst for the explosion of professionalism within and outside the hospital. Professionalism encourages separatism, the rigid guarding of the frontier of the newly staked-out claims to autonomy and expertise, which fragment further patient care and add to the problems of organisational co-ordination. Any study of a profession cannot be made in isolation from the affairs of others. Professions respond to influences far more extensive than those of their clients, in whose name their professional edifice has been constructed.

To simplify matters, we shall discuss the essentials of the medical profession and, to a lesser extent of nursing, under a number of themes. First, the key characteristics often deployed to explain the substance of the profession. Second, the aspects of professional socialisation involved in becoming a doctor. We focus especially on the medical schools, seeking to examine the effects of this long and cloistered educational experience on future practice. Third, the ways in which the medical profession exerts control over segments of society, the settings where doctors work being important in this respect. Finally, we shall consider Illich's (1976) uncompromising critiques of medicine, which he regards, like all professions, as disabling and the enemy of the client.

PROFESSIONAL DETERMINATION

Those engaged on the long haul to professionalism are quite certain of their goal. To them (and others) a profession is defined by a number of favourable attributes, which can be calibrated so that assessments can readily be made. The notion of 'measuring up' to a standard is a major consideration, although agreement is lacking on the total number of professional traits to be incorporated – up to 23 have been identified. However Barber (1963) lists just four essentials: generalised knowledge, dedication to community interests, a code of ethics internalised by all members, and a public recognition which suitably rewards their work endeavours. Each of these imply other supporting aspects: e.g. a code of ethics entails the formation of a standard of personal conduct above that of the 'rest' of society and the presence of internal mechanisms for dealing with breaches. This tape-measure method of delimiting a profession is used to distinguish it from an 'occupation', and to rank other professions. Etzioni (1969) has distinguished two poles – the fully-developed professions and the semi-professions. Semi-professions, like nursing, have a high proportion of female members, who have a shorter period of training. Their specialised knowledge is 'simple', and is often diluted from 'higher' professional sources.

This approach conveys no understanding of *process*, such as the rise and establishment of the profession and the details of its everyday work, and the alleged benefactor, the client, has no place in such an approach. The desirable traits are professional *self-embracements*, with the projected image of a unified body being a mirage. The medical profession in fact consists of overlapping sets of factions and coalitions of interests, delicately cohered under the same flag at a given time, but responding to internal and societal changes. Bucher and Strauss (1961), pioneer field-researchers in medical sociology, gave early recognition to professional diffusion. We have noted the technological fragmentation and colonisation of the body in Chapter two. They record the battles for new specialities. Their analogy with political and religious missions to establish new, professional 'truths' is apt. The professional fracturing of medicine along the lines of research and clinical practice, permeates the whole of medical development. Research, demanding new forms of training, is the power house, generating new types of knowledge for medical innovation. One set of radiologists, for example, are nucleated around *diagnosis*. A later group developed around the *application* of radiation for treatment. High flying researchers and clinicians, working on the frontiers of knowledge, are often 'itinerant' in professional orientation; occupationally mobile, and continuously seeking new medical centres offering better resources for innovation. They are the 'true' cosmopolitans, as depicted in Merton's ethos of science, being addicted to the thrill of discovery.

Bucher offers the term 'alliance' to distinguish cross-professional relationships from internal colleagueship. One professional segment, e.g. experimental pathologists, have more in common with (and often work with) genetic engineers and biochemists – members of other professions. Even within the same profession, colleagueship or peer recognition may in practice be restricted to one's immediate fellows, or to a section of a hospital or to contemporaries who graduated, in tribal, age-grade fashion, at the same time from medical school.

Another view regards the professions as an 'inevitable' consequence of the industrial division of labour: a way of institutionalising important knowledge on behalf of society. The functionalist account offered by Parsons regards them as modern guilds, their members having long, effective training under the control of experts, which guarantees the quality of their work. Their dedication engenders a sacredness, according them a special place within society. Their reward is both honorific, by way of symbols, and by appropriate remuneration, compensating for early sacrifices necessitated by their long training. There are two immediate questions to block this trail of analysis. First, the high salary of doctors is more a product of the monopoly position of their skills, rather than the general will of society. Second, the practicality and effectiveness of the knowledge of doctors can also be questioned: much of its importance arguably being due to its deliberate mystification and to its inaccessibility to outsiders.

Freidson (1970) undercut the functionalist argument that professions were ordained by the 'hidden hand' of society, exposing the power games which must be played for successful professionalisation. While maintaining the link with the division of labour, he adds that the support of powerful status and class groupings is crucial to professionalisation. After the doctors' claims for success had been acknowledged by the middle classes, the 1858 Medical Act followed, giving the General Medical Council power over the registration of doctors and others. An important element in this process was the spread of anaesthetics, making operations 'painless'. Queen Victoria took a 'few drops' of chloroform during the delivery of Prince Leopold, in 1853, thus removing any lingering, religious objections to its use in childbirth. Freidson stopped short of actually accusing the profession of being joint conspirators with the ruling class for controlling the masses and perpetuating capitalism. Nevertheless he stressed that the medical profession, like any other, pursues its own ends in preserving its members' autonomy and privileges. As a closed status group, with caste-like features, it expends much political energy on foreclosing the professional boundaries. The medical profession became a successful organisation towards the end of the nineteenth century, by riding on the prestige of the breakthroughs in scientific/biological discoveries, thereby making its medical monopoly more credible.

The brief history of the rise of the nurse practitioner in the USA is illustrative of the boundary issues in professionalism. The scheme for nurse practitioners originated at the University of Colorado in 1965 while courses for graduate nurses had long been established, nursing skills had not advanced commensurately with academic qualifications. The highly qualified nurse practitioners tended to find outlets in education and administration. In 1970 there were about one thousand nurse practitioners, rising to thirteen thousand active practitioners by 1980. The medical profession was under political pressure during this period to reduce costs and to diminish the hospital's dominance. The Medicare and Medicaid programmes for the elderly and poor were not being adequately met by existing doctors – many had dismissed the programmes as 'creeping socialism'. The nurse practitioner could now fill the gaps caused by the differential shortage of doctors. Doctors made little protest about the breaching of their medical domain, partly because nurse practitioners concentrated on the doctors' non-favoured clients, the chronic, the aged, rural dwellers and the poor. Doctors tend to prefer to be sited in urban affluent areas. The increased risk of being sued for negligence, some USA doctors have given up obstetrics – leaving more opportunities for midwives.

The nurse practitioner, together with doctors, often provided complementary services for mothers and children. Doctors have long recognised the value of the nurses' 'intrinsic' skills with these clients. Legislation was easily pushed through, with 46 states granting nurses the legal mandate for their new tasks. Over 90 per cent of the nurse practitioners' employers and clients have been shown to be satisfied with them. The employers have saved money, and many patients have been the grateful poor – 47 per cent of patients coming from the lower income groups. The impending glut of USA doctors by 1990 might however alter the position, if they are 'forced' to invade the nurse practitioners' territory. The nurses' political base is not as powerful as the doctors', who are now attempting to reassert their authority by insisting on 'partnership' control: e.g. some nurses can only be reimbursed for Medicare work if it is sanctioned by doctors.

Another version of the professions is that they are translations of the privileges of the upper class. Although democratisation has eroded many of their public rights and symbols, the British medical profession embodies the characteristics of the 'gentleman'. The hierarchical authority of medicine is based on traditional rules. The leaders of medicine have been attributed with charisma, since a great deal of learning by students is by informal contact with elders. Nurses fit the scenario of a supporting, service role, further enhancing the status of doctors. Their dress of caps, apron and shawls is more in keeping with domestic servants. The matrons resembled house-keepers, kept a tight rein on all aspects of nursing staff, even restricting their private life with evening curfews. Important vestiges of female service remain – from providing tea after ward rounds to dressing male surgeons for theatre.

In pre-industrial England, physicians did have aristocratic back-grounds. When the Royal College of Physicians was founded in 1518, an Oxford or Cambridge University degree was required for entry. The Universities were only open to Anglicans. Even by 1790 an oral in Latin was the main requirement. Physicians only catered for the wealthy: barber surgeons and apothecaries treated the rest. The medical hierarchy later deemed apothecaries suitable for incorporation.

Light (1975), quoting from *Samhita*, the Hindu book of medicine, shows that the ideal doctor has changed little: born of good family, with character, self control, energy, intellect, good memory and with purity of mind and body. On the latter point, the higher you are in the medical hierarchy, the more you are regarded as being 'germ-free' – junior staff are compelled to wear white, 'protective' coats, consultants can roam at will in everyday attire.

To be accurate, many doctors in the nineteenth century did not have aristocratic origins. Some were from the lower (often impecunious) middle class. Queen Victoria did not recognise as gentlemen and officers army surgeons who had won the Victoria Cross. They were not invited in 1859 to the Royal Ball at Buckingham Palace; nor did she invest them personally. Doctors' status rose towards the latter part of the nineteenth century when, in return for more professional privileges, they agreed to do extra 'social policing' for the state. But the profession has resisted being a servile lackey of state, always leaving its options open to negotiate, like a trade union, the best deal for its members.

The USA context was different. There was no aristocratic model to follow. Up to 1850 doctors faced hostility: some states believing in the virtues of self-help, cancelled the licensing of doctors. Only at the opening of the twentieth century did doctors' status rise remarkably, with the restructuring of the medical schools following the exposure of doctors' inadequate training in the Flexner Report (1910). Their new medical knowledge then became an expensive commodity, much in demand.

Summarising, many explanations are offered for the rise of the professions, and of medicine in particular. They fit into the wider debates on society's division of labour. At one extreme there is the consensus view that they form the basis for coherence and interdependency, with their skills having found their 'rightful' level and reward. Others argue that the division of labour promotes the formation of antagonistic classes and thereby exploitation: therefore medicine culturally embodies the ideas of the dominant class. Following Hughes' advice (1971), the ideology espoused by the profession should not be allowed to rest unquestioned. In many ways it is for external consumption. It is a resource deployed by all occupations claiming the luxury of autonomy for managing their affairs.

BECOMING A DOCTOR

Going to medical school has been likened to fulfilling a calling. The profession argues that it is here that the medical ethic and sense of duty to the patient is instilled. Some sociologists, like Hughes, have concurred. Although university based, the student doctor's education is structured differently from most other courses. It is longer and, in part, medieval; weight is given to the adoption of the 'proper' attitude, to learning by example from the experienced, supported by continuous testing, often by viva. Doctors look back on the medical school as one of their most momentous experiences – laying the foundations of practice. There are sociological disagreements, however, on whether the embryo doctors are passive recipients of their new learning, submitting readily to professional control, or whether their future medical practices are determined elsewhere.

Adult socialisation is different from that of the very young. Personalities have already been shaped and there is an accumulation of life strategies for reality testing. However, medical students are in a dependent position vis-à-vis their superiors; clinical teachers, fathers of the profession, are role-models for the students' development. Merton (1957), using the functionalist approach, adopted the profession's position that medical schools were the guardians of the values and skill norms of medicine. These formed a homogeneous culture which was imparted successfully through the structured controls of the schools. Doctors were set up for professional life on leaving.

Sociological observation within medical schools transformed this picture of idyllic fit. Becker and others (1961) empathised with the students and showed how the roles of 'student', 'junior doctor' and 'professional' were problematic, their definition shifting under continuous negotiation. To survive the competing ideological and academic demands, students formed subcultures for strategic 'retreats'. In these it was possible to experience 'autonomy' – a cherished professional value – away from the dogmatic and authoritarian controls. Professionalism was resisted and could be partly thrown off.

Under the pressures of work and role confusion, the students' initial, professional idealism of wanting to be dedicated doctors may be submerged: only to reappear towards the end of the course. As far as career orientations are concerned – towards research or patient care – other studies note little deviation from the original choice on entry.

This picture, and Merton's, of medical education, produces some ragged corners. It does not make clear what is distinctive about professional values in medicine: trust, respect of more learned colleagues, dedication to learning and respect for life, etc., are shared, in various quotients, by those outside medicine. Values do not exist like lonely sentinels, they exist in context, beset by many limiting clauses. For example, established doctors themselves are divided on whether to save life (whose?) at all 'costs' – the latter involves a discussion of resources. Embryo doctors come to medical school with their own tried and tested morality. How this becomes entwined with professional decision making is not always clear. Doctors can make precise decisions, because it is primarily they who have the authority to make those kinds of decisions.

These studies of medical schools underplay the effects of other influences on professionalisation, namely the pull of the different hospitals where students train. Hospitals are multicultural institutions: administrative, nursing, patient and non-professional streams exist. Mumford (1970) elaborates this with her comparative study of the effects of two hospitals on interns. One, called 'University Hospital', had its own medical school, and was a centre of excellence with leading cosmopolitan researchers. The other, 'Community Hospital', had a mixed intake of patients, with many routine cases. Here, the intern soon establishes the identity of 'real doctor', has greater freedom of clinical judgement and has his status readily acknowledged by patients and referring doctors. He becomes highly sensitive to patients' needs. In the University Hospital, with its rigid medical hierarchy and greater precision of procedures, the intern doctor–patient relationship differs. His actions are governed by how he assumes his superiors will judge him; his role as doctor has no firm contours, always under 'threat' from impending professional scrutiny.

Shuval's (1975) study of Israeli medical students confirms much of the USA descriptions – the move from 'boy' to 'colleague' along the road of professionalisation is not a gradual progression. The first couple of years of academic training are mainly classroom based, often tutored by 'unimportant' graduate students; here there is much in common with their former school experiences. Students have to perform for multiple audiences, each having a rating influence. During clinical training however the professor assumes a powerful authoritarian position. He not only evaluates the students' performance, but is also the potential future employer. Most graduates were found to have a preference for hospital medicine, rather than community medicine.

There were many factors responsible for the oscillation between boy and colleague roles. In small clinics the informality would encourage the doctor-trainer to refer to the student as 'my colleague' in front of patients. But at formal staff meetings the students were frozen out of discussions on hospital decisions, often being relegated to the back of the room. They could be castigated publicly for failures (e.g. lack of preparation, or lateness, etc.); many of their tasks would be menial – collecting samples. Nurses could sabotage the students' attempts to play the professional role, by informally feeding unfavourable comments back to superiors. Patients were important professional evaluators. Some patients would demand an examination by a qualified doctor, not a student. Fellow students could also be censorious if one adopted too freely the role of doctor in inappropriate settings. Yet students would often assume the doctor's role with each other; offering diagnoses for complaints and testing body functions. Professional socialisation for the trainee therefore means being able to reconcile successfully the contradictory 'stimuli', both supportive and negative, to his future role of doctor. Even after qualifying, his past performance as student/doctor can determine his future career. Medical professors have long memories.

The decision to become a doctor is often made when 'very young'. Rogoff (1957), from a retrospective sample of USA students, noted this. One deciding aspect was the pre-professional socialisation of living in a family with medical connections. She discovered that 74 per cent of those bent on a medical career, when younger than 14 years, had a *father* who was a doctor. The comparable figure for those with *no relatives* in medicine was 40 per cent. This trend could be reinforced by the selection procedures. Coming from a medical family is seen as 'indicating' the appropriate, personal qualities to be a doctor. Older students, with no medical background, could be regarded as more 'troublesome' material for socialisation. The emphases on doctoring backgrounds and high income families have been changing since the early 1970s. Nevertheless, the majority of USA surgeons in that period had decided on a medical career under the age of 17 years. Medical graduates, however, from non-medical families, have comparable results with those from doctoring backgrounds. In 1984 21 per cent of UK medical students were still the children of doctors.

There have been few longitudinal studies attempting to gauge the relative importance of the three major influences involved in medical socialisation: the socio-economic origins of students; the impact of the medical school; and the immediate setting where the newly-qualified doctors work. Chappell and Colwill (1982) used a sample of approximately one-third of the students who had entered Canadian medical schools in 1966. (This was part of the follow-up started by others.) The findings on 'career attitudes' refer to 1978: four years after completing medical schools. The attitudes were collapsed into four orientations: prestige, intellectual, patient and pressure (the latter examined the source – marital status, family, type of practice, etc.).

Support for the significance of medical schools in affecting change in career attitude was evident, especially for patient orientation. Although there was a selection bias towards the middle and upper-middle class, not all class attitudes matched future orientations. Irrespective of class background, men entered medical school disposed towards the most prestigious specialisms; while women were anticipatory socialised towards the 'less significant'. The father's professional education, surprisingly, had no predictive value; however the mother's status, ignored by other studies, did – and not just for daughters. The relevance of dual career families in attitude formation is now being appreciated. The importance of present work settings in moulding professional values was found to be of little consequence, with a slight exception for prestige orientation. Chappell makes no judgement concerning the moral appropriateness of the values examined for doctoring.

MEDICAL PROFESSION AND CONTROL

The control medicine can exert varies with its state mandate, its own internal organisation and its format for client relationships. Its potential power is rarely on public display; an exception being when in serious pay dispute – with threats to withdraw its labour. Medicine is intimately closeted in 'advisory' capacities with many of the local and national decision makers. The government's decision not to increase significantly the intakes into the medical schools in the 1950s (based on an unfulfilled projection of a continuous drop in the birth rate) in order to maintain the market position of doctors, and the policy for one hundred per cent hospitalised births, were based on doctors' recommendations. In clinical practice the doctor's authority is buttressed by his control of information. Patients have no access to their medical records, let alone being able to rectify any wrong information they may contain. Medicine's capacity to continuously create and legitimate new illnesses has been likened by Pellegrino (1983) to the actions of a perverse hydra; when one disease has been 'smitten', new ones sprout up. He posits that today's illnesses are more experientially crippling; with so many having been 'vanquished', it is all the more difficult to accept the current burdens. The dependence on medicine is becoming that much greater with the eradication of many previous illnesses. We shall go on to amplify these opening abbreviations.

Johnson (1972) has classified professional control into three types: patronage, collegiate and mediation. Before the nineteenth century, when doctors had few effective cures, they were very dependent on the good will (patronage) of wealthy clients to support them. Doctors' limitations thereby allowed patients much freedom. Collegiate control, synchronised with mature professional status from the mid-nineteenth century onwards, gave doctors greater supremacy over clients. Increased heterogeneity of illness and legal requirements to seek help for some medical conditions weakened the client's position vis-à-vis the more homogeneous medical culture, with its superior scientific knowledge. Mediation control is the new trend. A 'third-party', state-bureaucratic organisation, is 'intervening' in the doctor-patient relationship. Sometimes seeking to reduce the doctor's influence by, for example, giving clients limited rights of appeal, or by reducing the range of drugs available for prescription. But the profession's administrators and legal representatives are skilful navigators of bureaucratic hurdles.

In socialist countries, where state planning is prominent, the profession's mandate is more precise. Medicine mirrors the political and economic structure. In the USSR work norms are established for consultations expected per hour in most specialisms. There are no independent medical associations offering practitioners protection from state directives. In the 1920s these were abolished, as reactionary vestiges from the Czarist days. Doctors are state employees who are directed to work in regions and at posts deemed necessary; in mid-career, doctors do however have more flexibility. The Soviet doctor can join the union of medical workers, which covers all workers in the health field – porters, cooks, administrators, etc.

As direct agents of the state their coercive functions are overt. During the Stalinist push towards collectivisation and heavy industrial production in the 1930s, there were severe shortages of disciplined labour. Doctors were put under severe strain, having to maintain the health of the workforce and, at the same time, to eliminate 'malingering'. Field (1953), from a sample of displaced citizens, discovered that 20 per cent admitted malingering, as a temporary escape from oppressive work. Methods used included: self-inflicted wounds; injections of kerosene (to cause swelling), taking salt water and sugar solutions, etc. The doctors' humanitarian judgements were critically tested: what was a 'tolerable' illness permitting the sufferer to continue working in a steel mill? Doctors were also tested by government *agents provocateurs*. To grant 'too many' certificates of absence would throw doubt on the doctor's commitment to the state. The use of psychiatric treatment to correct the 'improper' thoughts of dissidents is a continuation of the state's use of medicine for political control. Mass executions and purges of the Stalinist era are now unacceptable to world opinion.

Improved health is one of the major emblems for newly founded socialist states. Cuba is a good example. Polio was eliminated by mass vaccination of the population in three days in 1963, well ahead of the USA. Following the Revolution in 1959, half the doctors fled the country, being members of the former elite. Against the trend for comparable socialist states, Cuba heavily slanted its health scheme towards the doctor base; traditional medicine and local midwives have largely been denied and public health workers accorded little prestige. In 1971, 31 per cent of university students were studying medicine, and the state has now reduced the quota to 20 per cent. Cuba's surplus doctors are drafted into active service in other less developed countries which themselves are undergoing socialist revolutions.

The heavy reliance on doctors has amplified the medicalisation of life, creating an over-dependency on technical medicine. Mothers are not taught or encouraged, for example, to treat their own children's diarrhoea. As shown elsewhere, with healthy children, the mothers' immediate intervention is usually most effective. This medical dominance has two contradictory sides. As with cosmopolitan medicine under capitalism, the prestige of hospital specialisms has a magnetic attraction: 80 per cent of doctors apply for them after completing their two years of compulsory work in rural health centres. But the pull of the immediate consumers is also great; for example dissatisfied patients will be supported by 'Popular Power Groups' (based on neighbourhood or factory) in their demands for better treatment, different medication and more tests. Directors of medicine usually side with the people. Cuba can only afford its luxurious doctor service because the economy is heavily subsidised by the USSR.

Let us now focus on the situation at home. Despite modifications in party policies, the medical profession has managed to use its position as an independent and powerful pressure group to mould the health service in its own professional image. The medical mind has always 'known' what is best for the client. The origin of the NHS is familiar history. Doctors successfully resisted the prototype, the Brown Plan of 1943, with its proposals for an all-salaried service and a simple administrative structure based on local and regional control. The then minister of health, Bevan, explained how he finally persuaded doctors to join the scheme, namely by 'stuffing the consultants' mouths with gold'. His oratorial appeals on the primacy of improving the nation's health were not entirely borne out in practice. The resulting fragmentation and maze of health delivery, often defying logical administrative principles, provided doctors with a political moat, behind which they could retreat. Thus 'protected' they had effective freedom of practice, being relatively undisturbed by administrative controls and able at the same time to neutralise consumer initiatives. A consultant's clinic starts when he commences it; the same professional principle that applies with courts and judges.

The professional ideals of service and dedication have been rudely exploded by bouts of militancy. Doctors in Israel and Belgium have downed stethoscopes and walked out. In England it has been sufficient, so far, for doctors to threaten to withdraw their labour. Atkinson and others (1977) presents a detailed case study of the GPs' threatened resignation from the NHS in 1965. In that March, 17,000 undated letters of resignation were sent to the British Medical Guild, the trade union arm of the profession's British Medical Association, to be used if negotiations failed. To keep their professional ethic 'uncontaminated' by financial matters, professional associations usually hive off negotiations on money and related conditions of service to a separate body. Of course it is the profession's skill monopoly which is the vital underpinning of doctors' professional posturing.

In earlier negotiations the GPs had expressed resentment at their status not being commensurately acknowledged by pay awards. Money is widely regarded as the universal measure of professional esteem (rather than patient gratitude). There was an increasing differential between GP salaries and support mechanisms and hospital salaries and resources, aggravated by the research and 'high-tech boom'. The reward of GPs was calculated on the performance of the 'average' GP, from a complicated and fluctuating pooling system. This method was interpreted as an attack on their professional standing, with the counter claim that their work was of such variety and complexity that the concept of a 'typical' GP was meaningless. Professional entrenchment depends in part on sustaining the position that one's tasks are indeterminate and require special judgements, which only come with extensive and dedicated training. To accept the award would have demystified their activities, making them amenable to 'work study', as on the shop floor. The General Medical Services Committee offered the government a 'Charter for the Family Doctor

Service', as a new contract. The government acquiesced since defence of the NHS has strong electoral support. The Charter reaffirmed the GP's 'specialist, clinical expertise' based on the one-to-one relationship with patients. Thus the GPs came out of the pay dispute in the mid-1960s with a greater professional recognition.

The profession has usually been seen as reactive to political and economic policies, rather than proactive – i.e. not being the initiator of change for the benefit of patients and society. With the present health crisis, the profession has focused mainly on issues of resources for medicine. It has never questioned the efficiency of its own internal professional structure, or the future role of medicine in society, the continuation of its own practices being regarded as paramount. There is some significance in Lenin's dictum of a 'state within a state' being applied to the medical profession. The 'cuts' have dramatically exposed the internal segmentation of medicine: each specialism with budget shortfalls, in different health authorities, goes public, pleading the morality of its own professional activity as it seeks extra resources. There is little or no concerted attempt at 'deep' political analysis. The profession maintains its current control by hoping to ride out the economic crisis with minimum professional cost.

This begets another point. How effective are the profession's mechanisms for maintaining standards? What does colleague control entail? Evidence suggests that bad practitioners are concealed rather than publicly revealed. The profession has no committee authorised to *seek out* poor performers. Disciplinary committees hear cases associated more with doctors' standards of personal conduct, e.g. improper relationships with patients. The USA obstetrician, I. W. Potter, was permitted to use his 'internal podalic version' of delivery – the dangerous practice of feet-first birth – and his career spanned over 45 years. The resulting heavy, infant mortality rate and birth damage among the survivors were disapproved of by his colleagues at the 1916 American Association of Obstetricians, but he was never stopped. Freidson and Rhea (1963) noted that USA GPs were aware of incompetent members, but did not denounce them. GPs would put the 'word' around, discouraging referrals to them, and thereby hoping to isolate them.

The profession relies mainly on the individual judgement of each practitioner both in deciding the limits of individual skill, and when best to retire. The mismanagement of the long-stay institutions in England was never revealed by the medical hierarchy, but by other sources, and then often secretly to the press. The inquiry into the Ely hospital (1969) scandal castigated the medical superintendent for failing to bring the unsatisfactory ward conditions, etc., to the notice of the Hospital Management Committee.

Although the profession does not root out incompetence, it *is* able, paradoxically, to evaluate distinguished service. Consultants are annually awarded 'merit money', above that of their salaries. This award was one of the inducements offered to consultants for joining the NHS and forgoing private practice; but part-time consultants in private practice receive also a pro rata award. In 1984 over 40 million pounds was allocated in this way by a secret committee. It is advised by a formal committee including the profession's top echelon – e.g. presidents of the Royal Colleges. The rationale of their rating scheme is not disclosed. There are four scales: the 'top A' are worth nearly 21 thousand pounds, the bottom C awards are worth over 4 thousand pounds. The awards reinforce the profession's internal ratings of prestige: percentage wise, over twice as many men receive awards as women, and the awards are slanted towards the hospital rather than the community. Within the hospital the high tech. areas receive a greater share than do accidents and casuality, and geriatrics. Over half the 'heart surgeons' received merit awards, compared with a quarter of community specialists.

The ineffectuality of consumer feedback into the NHS has been repeatedly illustrated. Pearson (1984) exemplified the pervasiveness of the professional definition. Exeter Community Health Council (CHC) took its brief seriously for ascertaining users' views in the area covered by the Exeter Health District. The latter was simultaneously carrying out its own planning exercise, involving the front line staff of GPs, nurses, social workers and representatives of voluntary organisations, with the CHC excluded from the deliberations. The conclusion of the Health District was that the 'confused elderly' were the main concern, whether on wards, in day hospitals or at home. The CHC, which sampled 168 parish councils, came to a different conclusion. The 'confused elderly' had the lowest consumer priority (6 per cent), with the main problems identified being inadequate public transport to hospitals (39 per cent), getting prescriptions made up, getting to the doctor's, and getting chiropody. Pearson recounts how the 'go-ahead' CHC made 20 recommendations for improving the service, but doubts whether any have been implemented.

There have always been segments of the profession which have worked in unison with coercive agents of control. American doctors 'discovered' that slaves who ran away from their masters suffered from the illness, drapetomania – delusions of freedom! In prisons, the captive audiences have been readily used for medical experimentation.

In the 1930s experiments to test treatments for syphilis left a 'control group' untreated, who were never followed up on release. American prisoners earn remission not only by 'freely' donating blood, but also by taking part in trials to test the effectiveness of new drugs. Between 1930 and 1950 psycho-surgery was in vogue, for improving the behaviour of deviant, psychiatric patients. One estimate puts the number of prefrontal lobotomies at 40,000 in the USA, the patients being reduced to irreversible, cabbage-like existence. Chemical implants are today used to control the urges of sex offenders. In mental hospitals the line between using tranquillisers as treatment, and as a patient-restraint for the convenience of staff, is not always distinguishable. It is noteworthy that the Mental Health Act 1959, which allowed for a compulsory admission of up to one year (Section 26) on the recommendation of two doctors, never defined its key phrases, such as 'in the patient's own interest' and 'mental disorder'. Instead psychiatrists decide, with no obligation to offer reasons.

The criteria doctors apply in accepting or rejecting a client vary between practitioners. Decisions made on the grounds of personality are masked as professional judgement. Following the 1967 Abortion Act, doctors showed their disapproval by using 'delaying tactics', hoping that the applicant would change her mind. The referral process was likened to a game of snakes and ladders. Some approving gynaecologists decided their abortion numbers on a 'hidden' quota, their argument being that they did not want their normal workload distorted by becoming known as an 'abortion doctor'. Some would grant abortions, provided the women agreed to a sterilisation, to be done at the same time. From the mid-1970s the NHS paid consultants an additional fee for sterilisations. The rules of the game were never made public. The effects of delay and choice of method directly affect abortion morbidity. Patterson (1981) quotes figures indicating that dilation and evacuation abortions performed in the 13–20 week interval have a cervical injury rate of 1.16 per hundred.

Alberman and Dennis (1984) report that the women who waited longest between consultation and operation were those aborted between 17 and 19 weeks: over a quarter had not been operated on within a fortnight after the consultation. Some NHS consultants also took the view that if the girl was fit and could afford it, she should go to the private sector. Over 50 per cent of women having private abortions referred themselves, many not wishing to anticipate their doctors' delaying strategies.

Askham (1982) has listed 19 possible criteria used by professionals in deciding to take on or refuse a patient. Some are based on assumed personal characteristics, e.g. an applicant is likely to 'do better' with one doctor and not another. Some hospitals will refuse mentally ill patients with criminal records, fearing their disruptiveness, or the lowering of the institution's image by having the 'wrong' type of patient. The criteria put forward for selection may only be a justification for decisions made on other unexplicated grounds.

Those with disabilities find that they have to conform to the official definitions of the agencies with whom they come in contact. It is the thesis of Scott (1969) that most blind people are made, not born. To be classified as 'blind' has legal implications, for government grants, etc. The blind must have, generally speaking, on the Snellen Chart, a central visual acuity of 20/200 or less in the better eye, even with correcting glasses. This is only a crude measure, and most have some vision. The 'blind' are therefore a heterogenous sighted-group, with visual impairment. To receive benefits they must submit, however, to professional control; this often involves conforming to the philosophy of rehabilitation based on the notion that the blind are helpless and docile, and in need of psychological readjustment for their affliction. Scott contrasts the USA with Sweden. Blind organisations there do not permit fully-sighted people to hold administrative positions and thereby to ideologically shape their blindness.

PROFESSIONAL SETTINGS

The settings where professions work support their roles. A home territory always gives an advantage. With domiciliary births, for example, women are among their familiar everyday objects, conveying intelligible sentiments, which help to normalise the event. However, male gynaecologists are challenged by the potentially disturbing threat of the sexual element of their work. The vaginal examination contravenes deeply-engrained social rules on the exposure and handling of genitalia outside prescribed sexual encounters. Control is maintained by using neutralising techniques. The clinic setting is manipulated to aid the gynaecologist's performance. By the time he sees the woman, she has been transformed into a medical object. Junior staff have already taken a preliminary history. The self has been translated into a narrow focus of limited biological functions, concentrating on the 'regularity' of periods, blood pressure, age and weight, etc. By being tucked into bed (examination couch), there is reversal to infantilism.

Professional control relies heavily on the support of others – especially nurses – who can become faithful lieutenants. We have already referred (Ch. 4) to how the nurse 'takes over' difficult patients, using 'just talk'. The nurse, largely unobtrusive, has a two-pronged role: switching between the technocratic and the emotionally supportive. She assures that the medical equipment is at hand, for taking 'smears', for example, but, above all, she calculates the appropriate size of speculum for the vaginal examination. This saves the consultant from rummaging in the box for the correct one, which would shatter the delicate timing of the examination. The nurse also anticipates potential distress, by holding the patient's hand, and screening her from the doctor's activities. If a patient is a cancer phobic, distrustful of the gynaecologist's findings, the nurse will be used as a prop for managing the verdict. The information will be relayed to her 'first' by the doctor who will ask: 'Come nurse, look at this perfectly healthy cervix.' The nurse's 'confirmation', from her as a woman, validates the doctor's professional competence and trustworthiness. At the end of the consultation, when the doctor has left, the nurse becomes the unofficial (and only) translator of the doctor's deliberations. Few patients will interrupt, to tell the doctor that they don't understand him during the consultation. The doctor's control of the sequencing of the consultation, when he will often talk in dual language codes (using medical terminology to attending junior doctors and nurses and 'everyday' language to the patient) also confuses.

Patients are a major resource for the doctors' evaluation of others' professional standards. A patient can emerge as 'special' if she is 'tagged' with extra information. If an 'interesting' operation scar is revealed, the consultation will be interrupted while details of the performing surgeon are elicited. A woman will also have 'time out' from the consultation, if she has been referred by an 'unknown' GP. She may be prompted to comment on the new practitioner. Should the consultant wish to sever his professional ties with a GP, he will make unfavourable comments about his/her competence ... 'I don't know why your doctor has been treating you for X, you clearly haven't got it.' The news will certainly be transmitted to the GP in question.

Patients are used not only as the medium for reshuffling referral ties, but also as counters in interprofessional politics. Gynaecologists are in a strategic position to receive nurses and other female staff as clients from the rest of the hospital. If a consultant has one of his 'girls' immediately (at a convenient time) examined/treated for a gynaecological condition, the effect on staffing levels will be minimised. With less paid overtime, a consultant, as leader of a theatre team, depends heavily on its good will. The 'receiving' gynaecologist, at another time, will ask for a reciprocal favour, ranging from mutual support in committee struggles for resources, to extra surgical assistance in a complex operation – as when a woman's gynaecological condition crosses the boundary of other disciplines.

The setting and its accompanying medical regime can be transformed into punishment-centred rules for directly controlling patient behaviour considered 'deviant'. Hospitalised treatment for TB caused 'problems' for the professionals. The diagnosis is certain, the prognosis is not. Patients always asked the question: 'When can I leave?' The doctor cannot give a precise response. He attempts to convert the patient to thinking in terms of 'hospital time', so avoiding the difficulty. Medical time is constructed from the sequencing of tests and treatments given. Patients evaluate progress by their stage on the medical trajectory. Each carries its own privileges, such as weekend leave. Roth (1963) noted that those patients who attempted to equate their progress with those at a higher stage, and thereby sought to 'speed up' their recovery and release, would be regressed to earlier tests they had already completed. In this way doctors would convince them of the 'severity' of their condition and of the impossibility of discharge in the 'near future'.

It is obvious that professional expertise alone is inadequate for assuring patient acquiescence. Further, the more unstructured the setting, the less the significance of inter-professional demarcation and professional etiquettes. Medicine practised on the battlefield and in emergency refugee camps in drought-struck Africa, are examples. In war, medical orderlies have performed procedures in crises to save life that final year medical students would not normally attempt in the theatre. The unpredictability of the setting, negates the orderly, hierarchical arrangement of professional rules.

The occupational settings of nurses are being investigated more for testing the effects of professionalisation. In the UK and USA graduate nurses tend to experience more work dissatisfaction than the less qualified. Their professional education demands more critical reasoning and equips them with skills of evaluation. The study of 'open' subjects, such as medical sociology and philosophy, instils a scepticism, and even hostility, towards doctors' and nurses' customary practices. It is unlikely that all their new hospital posts, etc. will accommodate their vibrant skills and their inclinations to innovate in order to bring things, as they see it, more into line with current thinking. Decker (1985) has examined the 'professional rebound' of USA nurses showing, with the use of path analysis for delineating key variables, that the process is more complicated than first formulated.

The effects of their 'more professional' values are often played out in specific role conflicts – mainly with 'head nurses'. Whether they develop job satisfaction within their immediate environment largely determines their tendency to leave, in their quest to keep faith with their new values. Education and ambitions for advancement are only indirectly related to this choice.

In less developed countries, especially outside their urban centres, where doctors are thinner on the ground, nurses have greater autonomy over patient care. Jelley's and Madeley's (1984) discussion, based on one health centre, Machava II, near Maputo, capital of Mozambique, is indicative. Since the former Portuguese colony became independent in 1975, after a struggle by the Frelimo Liberation Movement, many resources have been put into health care even though the country is poor. The enormity of its health problems can be gauged from its 1984 infant mortality rate of 150 per 1,000 live births; England and Wales averaged the same in 1871–75.

Most cases are seen, treated and sifted by the nurse. Almost 80 per cent are given a drug prescription, and only 10 per cent of adults are referred to doctors. Nurses have a wide referral discretion, since no precise criteria have been laid down, with much therefore depending on their variable skill in diagnosis. Patient numbers also prevent nurses from following existing guidelines. They are supposed to make a preliminary survey of the queue of waiting children, and to immediately refer those seriously ill. The researchers noted that nurses spent approximately the same time with all mothers, irrespective of whether their babies were underweight or not. There was no discussion on the causes and remedies to the illnesses. The heavy curative demands of clients, the medical isolation of the health centre and the poor communication about the results of their referrals to urban doctors, allowed nurses to develop their *own* work strategies relatively unimpeded. The official medical ideology of health prevention by the primary health centres was in effect impossible to fulfil.

ILLICH'S ONSLAUGHT

One of the most personal crusades against the professions has been conducted by Illich from his Centre for Intercultural Documentation in Cuernavaca, Mexico. More precisely, his vehemence is directed against the march of industrialism. The professions are considered its chief architects, leading us all to ultimate destruction. He makes no distinction between the merits of industrialisation under different political systems. Illich's concern for saving the less developed countries from 'industrial contamination' is sincere and many (not only the Greens) would agree with the logic behind his promotion of 'intermediate' technology and the preservation of existing craft skills. There are more cost-benefits from bicycles than there are from the parasitic tutelage of motor cars, which soaks up valuable exchange resources with oil imports.

Illich has a ready formula for attacking professional dominance, whether they be educationalists or health experts. We shall restrict his debate to medicine. Citizens, he argues, are incapacitated by the five illusions promoted by the professions. These are summarised in the small book, *Disabling professions* (1977), which he co-authored. First, the professions have misappropriated the faith of religion and resurrected new temples for homage, all aspects of life now coming under their purview. Homes become socially sanitised, made unfit for the human experiences of birth, death or illness. Salvation (personal problem solving) cannot be achieved without the attending expert. Illich warns us that we are not born as consumers. We deny our cultural heritage and humanity by allowing the expert to 'satisfy' needs for which individuals should/could have their own responsibility. Beyond a 'given' level of satisfaction of needs, he sees the benefits as solely those of professional advancement.

The second illusion is that technological advance requires more complex skills, training and trust – the founding trinity of professionalisation. These techniques could be made into consumer-friendly packages, but for the professional monopolies. The third myth is that lay techniques, which have been 'community assessed', are only proper if professionally validated. An example of the latter would be a mother waiting for the paediatrician's or health visitor's ruling before carrying her baby in a body sling. Illich's fourth and fifth disabling illusions are 'repeats'; namely, that societies being socialised into what they require are also informed about what they don't need, and finally, that before self help is valid, it has to receive a professional seal. In the USA there have been medical debates suggesting that only 'fully professionalised' patients should be allowed to practice self-medication. Those 'shown' to be competent, and to have willingly internalised the medical ethos (as good/conformist patients), should be trusted to engage in limited medical activities and receive privileges. Illich refers to proposals that only those certified in self-medication should be permitted to dispense aspirins to children.

The Illich solution to the medically-generated, diseased society is drastic – deprofessionalisation of medicine (and all other professions).

Medicine's licence, the lynchpin of its monopolistic evils, should be removed. The clinical, social and structural iatrogeneses will then fall away. Humanity and culture will reharmonise: individuals will gain the benefits of their restored sensateness; life, pain and death will be accorded equal and exalted recognition. Illness will no longer be a pathology belonging to doctors, but a telescope for exploring the limits of human experience. 'Existential being' will be an everyday topic of discourse with our next door neighbours, as we mend our bicycle punctures, or hoe our potatoes.

Treatments and medical explanations will be sought from those most competent, as validated by community use. It must be said that Illich expects deindustrialisation and deprofessionalisation to be simultaneous. Each medical transaction will impose its own reciprocal obligations on the healed. The expected, health networks resemble O'Neill's (1983) account of Montaigne's relationship with his kidney stone. Montaigne was always on the move, seeking new spas with their distinctive lines in water. He recorded faithfully the effects of each on his constitution. At Aigues-Caudes he could detect no effect of the water, but was free from renal colic for a year. The waters of Bagnères had an immediate effect on the bowels, but after two months Montaigne's condition returned. In all, Montaigne was grateful for the stone's pain, for the accruing moral benefits for the soul – reminding him of his own fallibility, with the periodic attacks of colic. Montaigne experienced his own illness, in his own way, without the 'peverse' technological distortions of modern doctors.

To accept the Illich solution requires an act of faith on the part of his adherents. There are no half measures. The present medical system is too well engrained in all dimensions of life to undergo reform – from individual consciousness to state institutionalisation. To pour more resources into the NHS would engross doctors' and others' dominance. To reinforce client movements would only increase their knowledge of doctors' ways and impel mixed compromises. Socialism, with redistributions of health resources, would only replicate capitalist medicine. The key battle, as Illich sees it, in all industrial societies, is between managerial experts and increasingly dependent consumers.

Deindustrialisation has the same explanatory potency for Illich as has the removal of 'alienation' for Marxists. There is complete vagueness about Illich's new world. What is the mechanism for transformation? Is there to be a revolutionary Luddite uprising, starting in one country and then exporting its message? Perhaps the aftermath of a major ecological catastrophe involving nuclear energy could generate a new consciousness? Repeats of the Chernobyl disaster in the west could provide the momentum. Illich's (1976) finger drifts towards the example of the sub-Saharan Sahel, the prototype for total world disasters. All prophets are critical scrutineers of current evils, but expect their new society to find its own 'natural' level of social conviviality. Details on size of communities, limits of technical development and devices to head off improper skill enlargement, are absent. We are left to ruminate the proposition that a 'healthy' environment will coincide with a healthy population.

Illich's global attack on an undifferentiated model of cosmopolitan medicine can arouse many different supporters. The women's movement will agree with the excesses of technocratic birth. Social medicine will particularly concur with the analysis that major improvements in health have sprung from environmental and public health reforms, and that institutionalised, technocratic medicine is largely ineffective for the mass of current health problems. Marxists will accept Illich's analysis of health exploitation and the multinational's pharmaceutical profits at the expense of human misery, especially in the less developed countries, as the products of capitalism. They will not accept, however, that the same doomsday scenario applies to socialist states, where the health services are 'geared' to social needs. Marxists argue that Illich shows political naivety, confusing the roles of the state in different ideologies, and that there is no universal culture of industrialism, but that under capitalism conflicts over health delivery mirrors the existing class conflict. Further, his final solution – of each seeking personalised solutions to health dilemmas – contains a latent ideology, resembling a free-enterprise *laissez-faire*. The virtue of capitalism's perfect market economy has materialised in a humanistic and utopian guise.

Illich's response would be simple. Socialist societies, like the USSR, are producing similar illness trends to those of the West. The technocratic base of cosmopolitan medicine is also their dominant model. Cuba has now partially admitted this error, and is 'broadening' doctors' training to include psychology, hygiene and ethics. Early in such courses, some time is spent at polyclinics in the rural communities, but the bulk of the doctors' training will remain hospital based. In socialist countries, consumer movements are non-existent, and there are no open platforms for expressing patient discontent.

As Illich adopts a monolithic approach to medicine, he is forced to admit that there are a few possible benefits, such as the usefulness of treatments for malaria and syphilis. He tardily admits that more 'defectives' (handicapped) are surviving, but goes on to add that they are then condemned to a life under institutional care. It is not apparent what course he is advocating for medicine. To let 'nature' have sway and not treat all those with birth defects? There appears also no voice for parents' wishes, or for competing moral perspectives among doctors on the subject. Illich's concern is that the handicapped later become defenceless patients, whose future is medically determined. Again, there is the hint that 'sado-medicine' desires these 'objects' for testing its skills.

Horrobin's (1978) blustering reply to Illich enlarges this criticism. Illich frequently asserts that medical intervention (e.g. for TB) has no statistically significant effect on general life expectancy. However, for those who can now survive, medical intervention was significant for them. To Illich it becomes a pathology to survive with medical assistance. Apparently patients' choices are not to be trusted with matters as important as their own life, cosmopolitan medicine having warped the individual's capacity to think rationally about matters of personal survival. Illich knows what is best for all!

On matters of historical detail, Illich's interpretation is open to doubt. His claim that medicine deliberately contrived to filch the management of death away from the Church, in order to buttress its power over human experience, is inaccurate. Illich's observation, however, that a society's explanation and presentation of death reflects its dominant health belief model is sound. Medicine handles death badly and would rather be without it. Death undercuts medicine's scientific optimism. Rationalism, secularisation and privatisation reduced the significance of the Church, so that death 'gravitated' towards medicine.

In summary, Illich's scatter gun approach on the excesses of professional medicine has many genuine targets. Whether his prophetic mantle is sufficient for others to follow him to the promised land of medieval romanticism, where there will be a fusing of the soul and nature – the fulfilment of the primordial contract – is debatable. To be able to bear one's pain intellectually, or rejoice in the life spirit of the dance of death, may not be sufficient reward for most!

CONCLUSION

Although there are diverse views on the origins of the professions, their template is well established. The medical model has had a contagious effect on others. The professionalisation of nursing is replicating the dominant segmentation between practitioner and researcher. Mystification of its knowledge base has set in. Nursing's 'new' skills, like the 'nursing process', are crude imports of managerial paraphernalia from systems reasoning – namely management by objectives. Salvage (1985) has recently cautioned on the dangers of the professional road. Top nurse managers are soon acculturalised into the dominant logic of cost-effectiveness, and of reinforcing the existing system, stifling essential debates on health delivery.

The rules of the professional game have been well illustrated by Ovretveit's (1985) study of the development of professional autonomy in physiotherapy – a newcomer to professionalisation. In the 1970s physiotherapists fastened on to the Salmon Report (1966), which had developed a management hierarchy for nurses, leading them away from the ward. The 1974 restructuring of the NHS, together with DHSS encouragement, provided the legal remit for physiotherapy managers to represent their own members on the District Management Team and Health Authorities. These manoeuvres coincided with the development of new, 'theoretically orientated' treatments. However, the master player, the medical profession, acquiesced in the physiotherapists' moves, for it still retained control of the key feature of their role – the right to authorise physiotherapy treatment to their patients and, if need be, to have it cease. The physiotherapists sponsored elevation could be also interpreted as an attempted check against nurses' demands for increased autonomy in patient care.

Finally, the professions never test their own sacred proposition, that increased professionalisation causes better patient care. They rest on the 'knowledge' that patients generally express satisfaction with treatment. As the medical dominance is pushed further down the line, i.e. as lesser groups professionalise, patient control intensifies. Psychiatry, for example, has parcelled out some of its skills, such as counselling. This diffusion contributes to the reinforcement of a therapeutic climate, sustaining core psychiatric beliefs.

REFERENCES

Alberman E, Dennis K J 1984 *Late Abortions in England and Wales. Report of a National Confidential Study*. Royal College of Obstetricians and Gynaecologists, London

Askham J 1982 Professional's criteria for accepting people as patients. *Social Science and Medicine* **16**: 2083–9

Atkinson P, Reid M, Sheldrake P 1977 Medical mystique. *Sociology of Work and Occupations* **4**: 243–81

Barber B 1963 Some problems in the sociology of professions. *Daedalus* **92**: 662–73

Becker H, Geer B, Hughes E, Strauss A 1961 *Boys in White, Student Culture in Medical School*. University of Chicago Press

Bucher R, Strauss A 1961 Professions in process. *American Journal of Sociology* **66**: 325–34

Chappell N L, Colwill N L 1981 Medical schools as agents of professional socialisation. *Canadian Review of Sociology and Anthropology* **18**: 67–81

Decker F H 1985 Socialisation and interpersonal environment in nurses' affective reactions to work. *Social Science and Medicine* **20**: 499–509

Etzioni A (ed) 1969 *The Semi-Professions and Their Organisation*. Free Press, New York

Field M G 1953 Structured strain in the role of the Soviet physician. *American Journal of Sociology* **58**: 493–502

Freidson E, Rhea B 1963 The process of control in a company of equals. *Social Problems* **11**: 119–31

Freidson E 1970 *Profession of Medicine*. Dodd Mead, New York

Horrobin D F 1978 *Medical Nemesis: A Reply to Ivan Illich*. Churchill Livingstone, Edinburgh

Hughes E C (ed) 1971 *The Sociological Eye*. Aldine, Chicago

Illich I 1976 *Limits to Medicine, Medical Nemesis: The Expropriation of Health*. Marion Boyars, London

Illich I, Zola I K, McKnight J, Caplan J, Shaiken H 1977 *Disabling Professions*. Marion Boyars, London

Jelley D, Madeley R J 1984 Primary health care in practice: a study in Mozambique. *Social Science and Medicine* **19**: 773–82

Johnson T J 1972 *Professions and Power*. Macmillan, London

Light D 1975 The impact of medical school on future psychiatrists. *American Journal of Psychiatry* **132**: 607–11

Merton R K, Reader G A, Kendall P L (ed) 1957 *The Student Physician*. Harvard University Press, Cambridge

Mumford E 1970 *Interns: From Students to Physicians*. Harvard University Press, Cambridge

O'Neill J 1983 Essaying illness. In Pellegrino E D (ed) *The Humanity of the Ill*

Ovretveit J 1985 Medical dominance and the development of professional autonomy in physiotherapy. *Sociology of Health and Illness* **7**: 76–91

Patterson I 1981 Risks and choice: a review of the complications of abortion. *Medicine in Society* **7**: 20–4

Pearson M 1984 Consumers and the NHS In Harrison A, Gratton J (ed) *Health care UK 1984*, CIPFA

Pellegrino E D 1983 Being ill and being healed. In *The humanity of the ill, phenomenological perspectives*. University of Tennessee Press

Rogoff N 1957 The decision to study medicine. In R Merton (ed)

Student physician. Harvard University Press, Cambridge

Roth J A 1963 *Timetables: Structuring the Passage of Time in Hospital Treatment and Other Careers*. Bobbs-Merrill, Indianapolis

Salvage J 1985 *Politics of Nursing*. Heinemann, London

Scott R A 1969 *The Making of Blind Men*. Russell Sage, New York

Shuval J T 1975 From 'boy' to 'colleague': processes of role transformation in professional socialisation. *Social Science and Medicine* 9: 413–20

Wilensky H L 1964 The professionalisation of everyone? *American Journal of Sociology* 70: 137–58

Chapter six

THE HOSPITAL, ORGANISATIONAL ASPECTS

The hospital, in various forms, has long historical roots. Despite this heritage the hospital perhaps only came of age in the twentieth century, as its structure increasingly converged towards that which already underpinned the large business enterprise. The 'hospital culture' extends well beyond its doors. Most regard hospitals as safe places where 'real' medicine is practised, and life-giving operations are performed. Before admission most pre-patients will engage in anticipatory cleansing-rites at home.

Eiser and Patterson (1984), when studying children's perceptions of hospitals, discovered that most got their information from watching television (and to a lesser extent from books); the current 'soap saga' being a favourite source. Children's knowledge and interests varied. Young ones (5–6 years old) emphasised the physical layout of wards, while others (9–10 years old) noted the social organisation – the interplay of doctors, nurses, visitors and other patients. All connected pain and unpleasantness with hospitalised illness.

Large segments of the population have direct contact (DHSS Bulletin 5/85). In England, in 1984, there were 6.18 million *in-patient* cases (up 2.6 per cent on the previous year). *Day cases*, coming for investigations, treatment and operations but not staying overnight, totalled a further 0.9 million (11 per cent up). *New out-patient attendances* were 8.51 million (2.4 per cent up); and *new accident and emergency* attendances were 10.2 million (up 2.6 per cent).

The word 'hospital' is derived from the Latin, *hospitalis*, pertaining to a guest, and these early antecedents were supportive residences. Among the earliest were the Greek health spas, located usually in coastal areas, swept by health invigorating breezes. They catered for the wealthy and mainly able-bodied, who could make the long journeys. But the Greek example was exceptional. Much hospital development, stretching into the nineteenth century, served as hostels for the sick poor, usually the 'deserving poor'. The bulk of the population were treated and died at home, with the kitchen table often being used for operations. Surgery was of low status until the early 1800s and was performed by 'quacks' and by others having served a rudimentary apprenticeship. Woodward (1974) calculates that in 1801, out of a total population of 10 million in England, Wales and Scotland, there were only 30,000 in-patients in the voluntary hospitals.

Religion has continuously been entwined with the history of hospitals. The Hippocratic Oath was solemnised to the gods, and the doctor's healing was tuned into nature. Monasteries, as a matter of course, frequently had refuges for travellers and the sick. Woodward informs us that the Hospital of Saint Peter was the earliest authenticated hospital in Great Britain, founded in 947 by the canons of York Minster. Some monastery hospitals became famous; for example Palermo became a specialist centre for treating wounded crusaders. Medieval municipalities encouraged the provision of general purpose alms houses. Those at Bruges and Amsterdam catered for the aged, offering besides medicine, their own sheltered accommodation, cloistered gardens and chapels. In 1420 England had 600 alms houses cum hospitals. There was often little distinction between the 'sick' and the 'staff', the former, according to their condition (and relatives), would also help run the place.

The dissolution of the monasteries led to civic petitions for royal charters to originate new hospitals. Guilds and merchants would sponsor their own, dedicated to the patron saint of their respective occupations. The tradition of workers supporting their 'own' local hospital continued until the formation of the NHS, through the Hospital Saturday funds. King William IV granted royal patronage to Salford Royal, whose outpatients was opened in 1831. Patients brought their own linen, and gas and water was donated by local companies, with the Manchester Sewage Authority donating deodorising charcoal. Local ties with hospitals still linger on, and modern hospitals are still streaked with religion/sacredness. At one extreme this is most expressive in hospitals and hospices organised by the Church. Religious iconography, church uniform and ritual are overt representations, and patient death can be openly signalled – some Irish Catholic hospitals ring a bell, as a public invitation to all for private prayer. In secular hospitals, the majority, deceased patients are 'smuggled' from wards, and open access is provided to ministers of all denominations. Here, technological ritualism creates the aura of mysticism.

The conventional wisdom that nineteenth-century urban hospitals were squalid germ pits – those entering having to abandon hope of coming out alive, let alone with a cure – has been questioned. The criticisms and solutions of Florence Nightingale are historically enshrined. She recommended a new design for hospitals. A pavilion structure, radiating from a common administration centre, with each ward distinctly segmented from the rest, preventing the mixing of their 'atmospheres'. Each ward would be positioned to receive the maximum of 'pure', outside air. The surgeon, James Young Simpson, from Edinburgh University, added his own criticisms in the 1860s. He attacked what he called 'hospitalism', including the higher death rates from hospital surgery. From a sample of 2,000 amputees, he claimed that more survived in country practices and among those who had their operations and recovery at home.

Woodward has balanced the account, arguing that hospitals were not the 'gateways to death', as popularly imagined. By modern standards their mortalities were excessive, but the picture was mixed. Many had a policy of selective intakes; for example, some restricted dangerous fever cases. Others specified the occupational background of patients to be admitted, e.g. servicemen under given conditions. Large urban hospitals were more likely to receive the severest (often injury) cases than were their rural counterparts. Some were leaders in 'cleanliness'! even in the 1770s Manchester Infirmary established that patients on admission should receive clean sheets, and that these should be changed every three weeks. The 1860s saw the same hospital responding seriously to the outbreaks of gangrene (and its lesser form, sloughing) on its surgical wards. The Florence Nightingale and Simpson statistics could therefore be severely challenged. Woodward concludes that hospitals did make a contribution to health improvements and that in the nineteenth century their mortality rates were 'generally low', less than 10 per cent of the patient intakes.

The nineteenth century debate on hospital hygiene and mortality has its counterpart today. As organisations, hospitals are still 'mysterious' places, defying the construction of a comprehensive overview. Reviewing the psychiatric hospital scandals over the past fifteen years, Martin (1984) acknowledges the great difficulty administrators have in assessing the quality of care and service provided. They can measure the 'inputs' – drugs, equipment, staff ratios, hotel services, patient turnover, etc. – but cannot be certain of 'effective use' and maintenance of hospital standards. By not being pro-active top administrators are often 'taken by surprise' when clinical crises appear. The stonewalling of patient complaints also reinforces the veil of secrecy.

The language of the modern debate on 'effectiveness' has changed. Talk is now of performance indicators, clinical audit, waste of resources, bed blockage (when a patient's recovery rate takes longer than 'expected', perhaps due to an inappropriate operation), etc. For example, according to the survey commissioned in 1984 by the Social Services Secretary, almost a third of the food served to patients is 'wasted'. Surprisingly it found no difference in catering costs between NHS hospitals and private ones, and high spending hospitals did not necessarily provide better food. Again, by statistically vetting the current waiting lists for admission, a 10 per cent reduction (some 70,000) was immediately achieved at no 'extra cost'. This revision would not only remove those who had moved away or changed their minds, but those having died while waiting for treatment, as well as those compelled in the meantime to have emergency treatment.

The safety aspects of hospitals have come under renewed scrutiny. Salmonella food poisoning and Legionnaires disease make the headlines, but are only the tip of the iceberg. More serious are the range of *nosocomial* infections – diseases that originate within the hospital. There are no accurate figures of death from hospital generated disease in England, but Bennett (1979) states that the annual mortality in the USA is 15,000 patients, with a further 1.6 million patients being infected. Over one billion dollars is thereby added to the annual health costs in providing further hospitalisation. The hospital in-patient total for England is approximately 20 per cent of the USA, and this might be used for extrapolation purposes. Pathogenic strains of bacteria, highly resistant to current drugs, have appeared with the lavish use of antibiotics. Both USA and UK hospitals have Infection Control Nurses, or similar, to monitor and give instruction on infection control programmes. Modern sterilisation equipment can 'lead' to lapses in personal hygiene by all staff, such as doctors wearing their gowns outside operating theatres.

The rest of the chapter goes on to explore three related themes. First, to locate the hospital within the general debate on organisational theory; examining salient, administrative issues on the distribution of status, authority and conflict. Hospitals display many variations according to their size, treatment philosophy and function. They are represented by secure hospitals, cottage hospitals, children's hospitals, private hospitals, teaching hospitals, military hospitals and open psychiatric hospitals, etc. In the NHS one distinguishing variable is the amount spent on food: more was spent on patients in teaching hospitals than on handicapped and mentally ill patients. However, much of the data presented here will centre on the 'general hospital'.

Second, to return to the topic of patient dependency and alienation. Third, to look at some assumptions embedded in the Griffiths proposals to introduce 'real' management and stricter accountability.

IN SEARCH OF THE HOSPITAL STRUCTURE

Much endeavour is now being expended by the government, administrators, management scientists and others in getting the hospital structure 'right'. This political discourse usually assumes that there are agreed definitions of 'health', 'cure', 'care', and 'patient'. The major decisions for restructuring are made at a 'distance' by people who are removed from the day-to-day process of health delivery. They usually deploy the rationality of one-dimensional, formal principles of macro models of organisational design. The tidiness of systems-coherence is to the fore, demanding clear 'lines' of communication to 'solve' problems of status ambiguities, and hoping to raise staff morale by its 'clarification by fiat'.

Sociologists have largely neglected to research hospital organisations in the UK. The USA picture is much rosier. Hospital organisations in the USA are businesses and have attracted greater public concern about treatment costs. Protests about psychiatric abuse were raised earlier and formed part of the general protest movements of the 1960s. Freidson (1963) offered good reasons why social scientists should be more involved. Unlike commercial firms, with a scientific base, hospitals have no trade secrets to conceal – their use of medical science, founded on principles of universalism, is to be disseminated. There was also the belief of the day that medical sociologists, working on doctor-defined problems, would be able to improve the service. However, doctors soon became wary, because of the sharp criticisms made of medical practices. Freidson's own work is noteworthy; especially his attack on the so-called objectivity of the 'clinical mind'.

British hospital research has been piecemeal. Sociologists have frequently examined sets of specific relationships (the doctor–patient one being the favourite) and medical encounters in closely prescribed settings. Psychologists have extracted for study generalised problems, such as stress induced by medical examinations, or ways of improving 'communications'. Ethnographic and other naturalistic methods of investigation are not easily applicable to the study of the major 'organisational frame'. Medical ethnographers are too ready to assert, without supplying the evidence, that their particularistic study is a microcosm of the whole – that is, not only the organisation, but society as a whole. Although hospitals generate mountains of documentation, and not just patient records, historians, to date, have used these primarily in constructing organisational analyses of past administrations.

To illustrate one of the above points. Davis's (1982) study of children in clinics provides a rich flavour of medical work, telling us a great deal about normal childhood, parents' worries and their effects on consultations, inspections for birth damage and discharge, etc. But the administrative frame encapsulating the setting is 'shadowy', mainly referenced in official, prescriptive terms – such as how it should work. When the clinic-schedule becomes 'unregulated', there is little elaboration on the processes of administration. One explanation is that doctors are on the receiving end of decisions made in another part of the 'medical system'. In fairness, Davis's study of an outpatient clinic does offer interesting details on the 'wider' administrative parameters.

Sociologists researching one facet of the hospital very often have to rely on the patronage of the doctors in that speciality. The writer knows from experience how difficult it becomes to branch out elsewhere, after having been closely associated with one group of doctors. Hospitals are segmented on insider/outsider lines. Each specialism, besides being territorially discrete, also has its own medical culture which it wishes to conceal and preserve. The last thing doctors want is for the 'administration' to have a 'complete overview' of all their activities. This is the same posture adopted by the shop floor and by middle management in industry, in the face of 'external' threat.

Other reasons can be posited for sociologists' neglect of hospitals. By reason of political bias, much energy was focused on the industrial enterprise, the major dynamo of capitalism. Organisational theorists wanted to improve its economic performance, while many industrial sociologists wanted to reveal the intricacies and 'evils' of the system. The economic mode of production, as represented by the industrial organisation, was the strategic site for working class initiatives towards restructuring society, particularly by rectifying political and economic inequalities. For the 'left' the hospital never had the same strategic significance. Although there are many studies on the class origins of the captains of industry, comparable details on the social biographies of top hospital administrators are conspicuous by their absence. It is still common to find that texts on organisational theory (see Burrell and Morgan, 1979), do not even reference 'hospital' in the index. It is only over the last decade that the very notion that hospitals have 'management' has gained common currency. The low paid ancillary workers and other staff are now to some extent recognising their common exploitation.

Thus the main body of organisation theory was derived from studies made elsewhere, and not necessarily corresponding with the distinctive culture of hospitals. To illustrate further, Woodward (1970), after much juggling with engineering scales of technology, worked out an organisational classification based on them, ranging from the 'simple' to 'complex' small-batch production (e.g. specialised engineering firms), mass-batch production (e.g. the car industry) and process production (e.g. automated chemical plant). It is very difficult to make this classification fit the 'hospital base'. Although some hospitals can be described as having 'high tech.', how do drugs and rehabilitation, and other regimes fit into an embracing technical scheme?

However, a major impetus towards the bureaucratisation of the USA hospital was the formation of the American College of Surgeons in 1913, shortly after the demands made in the Flexner Report for drastic reform in medical education. As the hospitals then usually kept no records, and many did not possess the requisite technology (e.g. analytical laboratories), surgeons could not fulfil the strict entrance requirements of their College. Consumer demand also forced hospitals to come up to technological and organisational scratch.

Even more general purpose classifications have to be 'contorted' to accommodate hospitals. Blau (1963), using the principle of 'who is the prime beneficiary?', recognised four types of organisation: mutual-benefit associations geared to their membership; commonweal organisations benefiting the public at large; business concerns where the owners are the prime beneficiaries, and service organisations where clients are the prime beneficiaries.

Hospitals are 'covered' by the latter category. While patients may benefit from hospital treatment, there are other prime beneficiaries. Hospitals are also the 'clients' of the state. Their funding is ultimately dependent on government policy, which is increasingly attaching conditions. Unlike a commercial firm, NHS hospitals are not market orientated. They do not go out to seek clients, or attempt to solve client-defined needs. Despite their long existence, hospitals still operate with rudimentary measures of health needs. Professional judgement has always been considered the 'equivalent' of market research. When the Resource Allocation Working Party (RAWP) was set up to redistribute resources according to area need, the only indicator that the new managerialism could agree upon was the available data on mortality rates.

The RAWP formula and assumptions have become more complex.

But it is still assumed that 'similar' populations will make 'similar' health demands. By health promotion one 'similar' population could of course make greater demands! However, there is still no precise definition of the standard level of health demand. When a region under-performs, as judged by the standard health indicators, should the hospitals be awarded more resources to bring them up to standard, or be penalised for incompetence?

Haywood (1983) and others have repeatedly shown how hospital routines (and health structures) are set to satisfy the needs of powerful staff. In other words the hospital can be best viewed as a political organisation, with patient services as the end product of the interplay of different types of power trading – both within and outside the hospital. Any organisation, with scarcity of resources (perceived and real) and with conflicting and ambiguous goals, as found in hospitals as between patient needs and the enhancement of staff careers, becomes dominated by intra-organisational politics.

In 1970–80 there was, for example, a 24 per cent increase in the number of general surgeons; but the discharges per surgeon fell by 27%. We have no measure of knowing whether the 'quality' of these operations improved, but there was clearly a mismatch of resources in terms of this statistical format. At the same time resources allocated to other groups failed to reach their target, as with the provision of geriatric in-patient beds which will only reach 80 per cent of their target by 1990. Between 1974 and 1984 the number of available geriatric beds averaged 50,000 at a time when the number of in-patient cases rose by 85 per cent (to 350,000). The duration of stay fell by 47 per cent – the largest percentage drop of any medical sector.

When management theorists have difficulty in explicating the internal workings of complex organisations, the systems model is usually enlisted. There has been a continuous flirtation between systems-reasoning and hospital processes, the attraction being that systems-reasoning is a self-contained logic, very much like witchcraft, with its own vocabulary dignifying the findings. Although the rules for transforming organisational reality into the systems model are matters of value judgement, nevertheless the main attraction is the manufacture of 'precise findings' – transforming imponderables into the 'coherent'. The surge towards the systems model has been assisted by the mathematicising of health performances in financial terms; permitting further statistical manipulation of large segments of hospital activities – not just bed occupancy and cost of treatment, etc., but also staff development and rates of technical innovation.

The input (resources)/output (treatments) orientation appeals to the crude, balance-sheet mind. However, the social structure and processes of the hospital, as for example translated into nurse–patient relationships, remains firmly hidden within the 'black box' of the system. Definitions of optimisation of 'systems resources', at any given time, depend on the arbitrariness (skill?) of the evaluator to convince those 'powerful others' of the 'reasonableness' of his claim. The planned systems approach leads to all kinds of anomalies. Renal or heart units could maximise their resources over a short period of time by increasing their 'treatment ratios'. This short-term aggrandisement would exhaust fixed resources (unless it got money from other allocations), deleteriously affecting its existing clients, if, for example, some beds were to close until the next financial year. The government is now encouraging hospitals to generate their own finances, like commercial firms, to add more flexibility, to iron out anomalies, or to enlarge existing priorities. In Greater Manchester some are opening their facilities (like opticians, laundry and catering) to the general public.

The 'crazy' patchwork of rules, power and status, constituting the hospital, is the product of former isolation from centralised planning. The privileged traditionalism of patrimonial order has also led one set of analyses to concentrate on unravelling the different bureaucratic mixes. Wessen's (1958) study of a general hospital of 800 beds in New England, disguised as 'Yankee Hospital', is an early research probe. He took the ward to be the 'heart' of the hospital, finding that a typical one frequently had representatives of at least 23 different occupational status-groups – dieticians, nurses, residents, consultants, social workers, physiotherapists, auxiliaries, etc. On a typical British ward the comparable figure today would be around 30, with the increased fragmentation of labour. In explaining the resulting patterns of status and communications, Wessen referred to them as 'almost caste-like segregation'. The highest status had no obligations to interact with the lowest, except in circumstances defined by them. Wessen noticed one major exception. In surgical units, status segregation broke down with the necessity for intense co-operation during operations. During the final stages jokes and free banter are typical, most initiated by the surgeon. At moments of tension they can also negate their status with expletives. As the patient is 'asleep', this is not a violation of the doctor–patient relationship. Wilson (1954) recalls how one surgeon would commence an operation by uttering: 'Brethren, let us spray'.

A dominant sociological tact became to locate the hospital within the post-Weberian debates on bureaucracy. Smith (1964) is typical of this genre. One of his concerns was with the 'duality of control', the lay and the professional, and with 'hybrid areas' where both types of authority overlap. Weber's ideal-type of bureaucracy had specified distinct hierarchies of control and roles with well-defined tasks. The main 'problems' confronting hospitals were with the 'charismatic' authority exerted by doctors. Weber had recognised the possibility that doctors' authority would be charismatically linked, but never constructed his bureaucratic model to incorporate it, having more in mind organisations like the Civil Service. Weber did allow for a 'dash' of charisma at the apex of bureaucracies, for organisational flexibility. However, doctors' authority permeates the major administrative line (and other lesser professionals). For example by claiming medical 'emergency', or that this patient is 'mine', doctors can disrupt established routines. Borrowing from Chester Barnard, the same point can be emphasised in terms of the clash between 'scalar' and 'functional' status. Scalar status is hierarchically ordered; 'functional' status adheres to the task performed, regardless of official ranking. On the grounds of patient safety, a low-ranking doctor can abrogate (temporarily) the directive of a top-ranking administrator.

Smith goes on to analyse the range of hospital settings (like the pharmacy) impinged on by the dual-system of control. Jocularly, he suggests classifying hospitals by a 'weeping index' of the tears shed by administrators and others, whose tasks are far more difficult than those in other organisations. In 1975 the Merrison Committee (inquiring into the regulation of the medical profession) was still arguing that the medical profession should primarily be self-regulated, to maintain its 'dignity'. If hospitals acceded to this principle, the administration would have to be continuously negotiating its way around 'that' deemed to represent doctors' self-esteem!

The residual conflict of values between doctors and the administration is much exaggerated. It becomes pungent only when polarised as clinical autonomy (humanism) versus the universalism (impersonality) of bureaucratic rules. All occupational groups value their own autonomy: by pleading clinical freedom, as a sacred value, doctors themselves obfuscate the unrestrained power-dimension they wish to exert. The doctors' historical claim to clinical freedom was staked when the majority worked outside the hospital. The myth of the solo practitioner is kept alive within the hospital by doctors having their 'own' beds. Doctors may dislike (some) administrators, but their own tasks contain a great deal of administration, not always recognised as such. Goss (1963) noted that USA doctors expressed a great interest in administration. The emphasis of her own study of a teaching hospital was in elaborating the mechanisms of accommodation between the two sides. Many doctors develop a great loyalty towards their hospital and this factor can moderate their hard professional stance. USA doctors took part in fund raising and in community activities, and British doctors have always been well represented on important committees. In 1966 approximately 60 per cent of the membership of Regional Hospital Boards was composed of doctors – nearly all being consultants.

It is noteworthy that the Royal College of Nursing's plan (Administering the Hospital Nursing Service) in 1964 was accepted by the Salmon Report (on Senior Nursing Staff Structure) in 1966. The new administrative structure for nurses would match that of the hospital's administrative frame, allowing it to tap into the available resource points. There were no professional qualms about introducing the new title of 'nurse-manager'. By incorporating administrative techniques, first established in industry, this was seen as a means of invigorating the nursing profession by elevating its line of command and offering new role models of nurses. Salmon went out of its way to criticise senior nurses who rolled up their sleeves to help out on the ward. This projected the 'wrong' image of the profession, by being anchored to patients' beds.

Attempts have also been made to apply Gouldner's (1952) three patterns of bureaucracy, a refinement of Weber: namely representative, mock and punishment-centred. Representative bureaucracy is the product of joint agreements, equally binding on both parties. Mock bureaucracy occurs when an external third party imposes rules on at least two other parties; the latter may pay lip service to the rules, or jointly break them. Punishment-centred bureaucracy is an alternative definition of the Weberian, in which one side imposes its rules on the other and will punish the weaker party if they are transgressed. Gouldner developed his models from studying the management succession at a gypsum mine and factory; he exemplified mock bureaucracy by describing how a manager and a worker will both smoke directly under a 'no-smoking' notice – the sign is an insurance condition. The joint light-up is a token of mutual support.

In a hospital, representative bureaucracy would cover, in theory, the team approach of health workers, but in practice doctors' views in any group decision making tend to carry most weight. Therapeutic communities tend to be moulded on lines of representative bureaucracy, incorporating both patients and staff, with the group agreeing, for example, when a patient is ready for discharge. Mock bureaucracy represents the 'short cuts' in standard procedures which doctors and nurses will jointly make when hurried. Punishment-centred rules are by far the most numerous, weighing heaviest on lower-ranking nurses, who often are even deemed responsible when merely carrying out the prescribing errors of doctors' medications.

The different functions of rules, as described by Gouldner, are also readily seen. The 'screening' function prevents relatives and patients having open access to doctors. The 'remote control' function of some rules allows seniors, from a distance, to control junior staff, for example, by having them phone information at set times.

Goss (1963) noticed a fourth type of hospital bureaucracy: 'advisory bureaucracy', on the obligation of seniors to offer advice to subordinates on how to tackle technical and other related clinical issues. The junior has the responsibility to reflect seriously on such advice. If he errs, when rejecting this advice for his own judgement, then he has to face the informal strictures of colleagues.

In considering the hospital as a political organisation, Haywood (1983) has enlisted Luke's classification of power. The capacity to resist others' attempts to alter one's status and behaviour, is one display of power. As Haywood emphasises, there are more significant manifestations of power, such as control over the philosophy (ideology) of the organisation, which allows the 'guardians' to be the moral arbiters of new developments, and control over the agenda, which gives firm bureaucratic control over what issues are offered for discussion. The complaint from hospital public sector unions is that they are often excluded from crucial discussions on allocating budgets to different specialisms and departments. During the strikes of the 'winter of discontent' in 1979, the unions attempted to modify the medically set agenda by wanting to restrict admissions to only 'serious conditions', and to exclude private patients from NHS hospitals.

The tendency for organisational concepts, derived from 'elsewhere', to be applied to hospitals is paralleled by the imposition of other administrative arrangements. When hospital crises occur, ideas are 'borrowed' out of context. The NHS inherited a peculiar mix of often outdated hospitals, many being inappropriately located for modern needs. The only rationale explaining the dense cluster of London teaching hospitals was that they were formerly in hansom cab distance from doctors' private practices in Harley Street.

Hospitals had generated no architectural tradition of their own, aimed at fusing client and medical needs. Lacking planning skills, they borrowed from current fashion. The tower block design being used lavishly by councils in the 1950s and 60s was one import, being used for some medical schools, like the Royal Liverpool. Then came the 'Lego' stage of design, from the 'Harness Programme' and the

'Nucleus Programme' of the 1970s. The mono-stage, large, expensive hospital was found uneconomical (its construction bedevilled by industrial disputes and delay), whereas the harness and nucleus designs allow flexible expansion, if needed, in the 'future'.

Staff development was influenced by the Lycett Green Report in 1963. Civil Service standard selection procedures and annual staff appraisal were introduced. Hospitals multiplied lavishly the job specifications for middle and top administrative grades, most appointees being 'internal'. Many lacked the immediate skills demanded. This was clearly visible at the outset in areas concerned with industrial relations, planning, monitoring/research and accounting practices. For many years hospitals had luxuriated on the 'topping-up' principle, with money being found from 'somewhere' within the global accounting. The Zuckerman Report 1968, however, was not adopted. Following Scientific Civil Service lines, it had proposed to centralise all technical staff under one career structure. Incipient professionalism and rivalries thwarted the scheme and increased status fragmentation.

The structural upheavals of the 1974 organisational reforms are still seismic. Jaques (1978) refers to the events of 1974 as a 'quantum leap', because of the unique complexity of the organisational issues and the intricacies of interpersonal relations nexused in health delivery. We cannot pursue all the facets of this 'final' reform to get things 'right'. As part of the new order, hospitals were to be run by a 'new mangerialism', deploying techniques of business efficiency. Corporate plans, unit efficiency and throughput were to be the dominant vocabulary conveying the reality. The Secretary of State, in the foreword to the Annual Report (1984), proclaimed that a 19 per cent increase in 'throughput' means 'more and better service to more patients'.

The government did draw upon some social science findings. The Brunel Health Services Organisational Research Unit (under Jaques) had been researching the groundwork for the reorganisation with the Management Steering Committe of the DHSS. The government, however, hurried its scheme before the Brunel findings had been completed, especially those on technical services. A subsequent defect was the lack of a recognised authority to monitor the whole scheme, including hospitals. Knowledge of organisational process therefore remains incomplete, and often contradictory, yet corporate planning demands reliable data and effective mechanisms for following up innovation and for correcting 'failures'. A consequence of undigested change, combined with the frustration of not knowing who is 'actually' responsible for some functions, has lowered morale. The 1974 reorganisation was introduced, ironically, to raise staff morale, with the lesson having been drawn from Revans (1964) research, that poor morale adversely affected patient recovery rates.

Although the unions, nurses and consultants may commune over the principle that hospitals cannot be run like businesses – patients are not commodities – the business imagery has long stalked the hospital. The consultant's team is referred to as the 'firm', with the consultant acting like a managing director, deploying resources and controlling staff. For example it is he who is responsible for the training of junior doctors, and for cultivating his own management style. Like a tribal 'big man' his role is multiplex. Consultants 'own' (have rights over) so many beds, and patients are known by his name. A topic of conversation in the doctors' common room is the current rate of BUPA operations and who is earning what from private practice.

Although there is a tightening of the parameters circumscribing managerial activities concerning size of budget and staffing, within these parameters great flexibility persists in work style. With reduced operating time during one hospital dispute, I have known one consultant phase his list 'accordingly'. Another transformed his theatre schedule into all 'heavy cases'. This put great pressure on the newly-qualified anaesthetist and the junior doctors were denied the exercise of their limited skills. A list is usually mixed, with juniors being given controlled instruction and 'limited' surgery on heavy cases, while the routine ones at the end are 'theirs'.

Since 1974 the number of occupational grades has increased, although it is difficult to be precise. Jaques (1978) expresses this uncertainty by stating that the NHS has some 'forty or fifty different grading schemes'; for example, there are nine hospital technician and ten nursing grades. This multiplication has lengthened the hierarchical line of command for each occupation, leading to a constant refining of job specifications. The top-down line of communication intensifies the mechanistic tendency of hospitals, reducing their flexibility and making it difficult for 'spontaneous', horizontal co-operation across occupations as they will need different hierarchical approvals for these initiatives. The incumbents of each grade resist, in order to prevent the 'favourable' contents of their job being defined away. Jaques explains how health employees 'push' for increased grading on the mistaken grounds that all will benefit from improved career prospects. The new levels actually diminish the status of those lower down and increase the control to which they are subject, heightening their relative deprivation and reducing morale. Holders of new managerial grades may consider themselves as 'co-ordinators' and 'facilitators', further adding to the confusion.

The mechanistic structure, Schulz and Harrison (1983) argue, forces top managers to be reactive, rather than be radical innovators. Their reputation accrues from their ability to dampen organisational conflict, rather than from their ability to improve patient service. To keep the service 'intact' is the dominant goal. The organisational response which Burns and Stalker (1961) first described for mechanistic industrial firms, when challenged by contradictions and change, is replicated by hospitals. The hospital handles this conflict by setting up working parties and additional committees of the involved parties, thereby intensifying the bureaucratic undergrowth, reducing bedside innovation and overloading the organisational head with 'everyday trivia'. The researchers suggest that the power of the top managers can be enhanced if they are given control over 'slack resources' (i.e. resources not earmarked for specific activities) to support new initiatives.

The organisational blueprint of the 1974 reforms had another glaring error; it assumed a conflict-free system would ensue. There was no reference to industrial relations in the Grey Book (1972)! The labour tensions to which the hospital was subject were many. Successive governments used the NHS, as state employees, to spearhead incomes/pay norms' policies, with the low paid suffering the most from a number of fixed percentage increases. Hospitals are unique in that employees, ranging from the highest to lowest in status, come into frequent public and work contact. Self worth is critically sharpened by this status exposure, prompting a leap-frogging of wage claims, based on a mutual evaluation of each other's workload. Inter-union rivalries have also led to recruitment battles, in which a militant posture became equated with effectiveness. There was also an initial uncertainty concerning which level of management was to handle industrial relations.

The diffusion of bargaining bodies increased such problems. Members of the same profession sometimes held dual membership of different unions. For example, the Junior Doctors' Association broke away from the consultant dominated BMA, for inadequately representing their interests. The Medical Practitioners Union is actually a section of the ASTMS and promotes the values of socialist medicine. The British Hospital Doctors Federation now negotiates for about one-third of all hospital doctors.

In summary, the search for 'the' hospital structure continues, the major problem being that hospitals were for a long time beyond the pale of organisational theorising. Consequently they were often acted upon by 'alien' philosophies, mainly political. The internal contradictions, with managers claiming to be administrators, allowed powerful groups to stake out organisational domains. The business ethic is now pervasive, instilling a common, organisational language across the multifarious occupational frontiers.

PATIENT ALIENATION

The chances of becoming an in-patient are increasing. This is due to more people surviving into old age and to the spread of new surgical procedures and treatment regimes. In England, 1979–83, the discharge rates (per 10,000 population) for all operations and procedures rose from 421.8 to 472 (Hospital In-Patient Enquiry, OPCS Monitor MB485/2). There were no discernible differences between sexes. However, the discharge rates in the same period for all in-patients rose more significantly for the over 65s, than it did for the younger age-groups. For those aged 20–24 years it was 692.1 and 710.9; for those 70–74 years, 1613.7 and 1879.7. There are of course disease variations: among the increases are diseases of the circulatory system (from 104.2 to 117.5), cataracts (from 8.4 to 10.6), and malignant neoplasms (75.4 to 84.4). Among those with an almost constant rate of discharge are cystitis (0.8), operations on the gall bladder (7.1), and mastectomy (8.2).

Disease variations have still produced a common and growing concern about hospital regimes and patients' rights. Children were the original focus. The WHO, 1955, produced what amounted to a 'children's charter', after summarising the research, mainly American, which demonstrated the hospital's adverse effects – unstimulating and drab wards, restricted parental contact, no attempt to explain proposed medical interventions, and inappropriate paediatric nurse training. Psychological damage was assumed for the very young à la Bowlby's theory of maternal deprivation. Other researchers, for example Gofman and others (1957), showed that children benefit from pre-hospitalisation preparation, which helps to make them aware of ward routines and medical equipment.

Change was not easy. Hall (1977) reported the social ripples from the introduction of play leaders into children's wards of a British hospital. The play leader's role consisted of three functions: educational, boredom relieving and therapy. The staff restricted medical knowledge, thereby preventing play leaders both from giving therapy and from alleviating anxiety by informing children about their illness. Play leaders became mediators, translating the children's world to nurses and parents because of their more intimate knowledge of child care. The domestics were most aggrieved by the innovation of sand and water, for play materials, on the ward. The crux of the nursing process was that staff had great difficulty in deciding what was a 'normal' response by a child to strange and confusing surroundings: children were expected to cry on admission, but afterwards there was no common agreement about the 'crying rate'. Nurses, too, regarded play as one of their essential duties but, with peaks of work pressure, it was relegated to the lowest priority, though they resented this activity being carried out by non-professional 'strangers'.

The irreversibly comatose patient is one of the latest to be researched. Rolston (1982) stipulates the hospital's moral duty towards these dying patients. For family and doctors the endless waiting appears futile and anomic. From an evolutionary perspective, Rolston argues that natural selection operated on all levels of human life – and not just on consciousness. The primitive encoding of our earliest reptilian brain still exists. Although the patient has no subjective interest in his well-being, objectively life continues – organs function with external nourishment, etc. The objective life, though partial, still has value. Rolston wants to defend the irreversibly comatose from both the 'extremists', i.e. those who defend life at all cost, and from those who renounce biological existence as life.

Exempting psychiatric hospitals, little is known about the social dynamics of ward culture. Psychologists have concentrated on hospital-induced stress and on the adoption of behavioural techniques for neutralising its effects on patients – the central theme of this section. Rosengren and Lefton (1969), from the USA experience, formulated a set of propositions relating 'hospital orientations' to anticipated patient responses. In comparing long- and short-term hospitals, patients in the former are expected to develop their own strategies of group control. There is more medical control of patients in short-stay hospitals. Much depends, too, on the patient's familiarity with hospital routines. In Coser's (1963) classic, comparative study of the social organisation of a medical and surgical ward, the indomitable Mrs Rothstein became a 'special patient'. After repeated hospital-isations and thereby becoming most familiar with the medical setting, she decided that this qualified her as 'hostess'. She greeted and settled down new patients with personally vouched for information. Doctors acknowledged her status by not submitting her to 'unnecessary' tests.

Wilson-Barnett (1984) has summarised the stress ingredients of hospitalisation. Threats are presented by the unknown illness; by loss of liberty and privacy; by the forced dependence on significant other persons, whose style of communication is hierarchically ordered and who refuse to answer the significant patient question about the illness mystery – why me?'. By no means least, there is also the challenge of learning how to be a 'good' patient – there are no hospital rule books to help. The hospital's rites of separation are often effective in inducing 'infantilism', and the symbolic accoutrements of patients being socially anchored to their beds reinforce passivity. A contradiction appears however when it becomes medically appropriate for patients to 'do more' for themselves. Patients then undergo cumulative relearning processes, in an *ad hoc* fashion.

The concept of 'alienation' has complementary, explanatory import and, like stress, has undergone many vagaries of use. Marx, one of the promulgators, did not refine alienation sufficiently to make it easily operational; not wishing to put his head on the chopping block of nineteenth-century English philosophers. The German *Entausserung* (alienation) and *Entfremdung* (estrangement) have come to be used synonymously, causing some 'confusion'. Seeman and Evans (1962) first applied six 'varieties' of alienation to hospitals: powerlessness, meaninglessness, normlessness, cultural estrangement, self-estrangement and social isolation. Although criticised for failing to explicate the actual processes involved in alienation, and for being interested more in introducing measurement scales of the phenomenon in the positivist tradition of USA sociology, Seeman's dimensions remain, nevertheless, useful cultural probes.

It is possible to see how Seeman's varieties will cluster distinctively for patients according to the progression of their medical career. Zerubavel (1979) has reduced the hospital organisation to a mesh of interlocking, multiple time-cycles: staff shifts, theatre time, career stages of staff (e.g. final year intern), temporal boundaries between different activities, admission rounds, medication rounds and so on. Hospital staff only have privileged knowledge of, and access to, some of the temporalising. However, these new and 'strange' timetables are imposed on patients. Becoming dismembered from their everyday temporal reckoning, they become an appendage of the hospital master clock with its different time zones – over which they are powerless and from which they are culturally estranged. Zerubavel proclaims that one of her most fascinating findings was that staff frequently calculated the passage of time by patient numbers – i.e. patients were transformed into units of time.

The major discontent of patients waiting in clinics is that doctors will not specify a fixed clock-time when they are to be seen. To be told, 'the doctor will see you next', is more reliable than being given a precise time in minutes, which may not materialise. The Health Service Commissioner's Report (1985) reveals a temporal conspiracy between nurses and doctors in a casualty department. Duty doctors were not to be disturbed between 7.30 and 9.00 am, if nurses assessed the case as 'unimportant'. A man was admitted at 7.30 am, because of breathing difficulties, and his wife informed by the nurse that the duty doctor would 'soon' see him. The unofficial, one and a half hours' interlude was maintained, and the delay contributed to the man's death by heart failure.

Many medical procedures are beneficial, diagnostic tools, but engender powerlessness, estrangement and normlessness for the recipients. Sigmoidoscopy, for example, is used to detect colon cancer by inserting an instrument through the anal passage to examine bowel mucus and detect pathological growths. Sigmoidoscopy, if used as part of a general screening programme for the over forties, is effective in early detection. It is not the physical discomfort of stretching the bowel which is the major source of worry, for both men and women, but the cultural estrangement of the requirements of the medical setting. Patients are partially nude in the prone position, having no control over the insertion of the scope.

Alienation can exist outside the hospital. Pre-patients, waiting for admission, are full of many doubts. The symptoms of gall-bladder patients may improve by dieting, and they then may suspect the diagnostic authenticity of the condition. Geographical variations in hospital waiting lists for the same condition increase the problematics. The aged wait much longer for hip replacements in the retirement towns of the South Coast, worsening their immobility and isolation. In England and Wales in 1984, about 28,000 urgent cases waited more than one month. Discharge can bring its own problems, with patients given the meagrest of preparation and told to see their own doctor. Women having hysterectomies can feel self-estranged and worry about what has replaced the body space formerly occupied by the womb. Hospital visitors experience spasmodic alienation. Finding their relative's usual bed empty on the ward, they can assume a death unless given prior knowledge of the patient's whereabouts. Asian husbands have also assumed their wives' deaths, when handed their bracelets for safekeeping by nurses. Hospitals are now recognising the ethnic cultural variations in diet and bereavement.

Psychological intervention has been established as the major way of overcoming patient alienation. Many of the initial experiments recorded high success. Janis's (1958) model set the fashion. After being given pre-surgical information, patients coped much better with surgery. They had earlier discharge, required less medication and made less medical complaints. Other studies provided patients with sensation details (of what will be felt) and offered appropriate coping mechanisms – breathing exercises and use of different body posture. Later, information videos were used to show the full pictorial sequences of medical procedures.

Experimentation also moved in the direction of environmental control and patient decision making. Langer and Rodin (1976) demonstrated dramatic results by introducing 'minor' choices into a tightly bound setting. The aged on one floor of a nursing home were given a plant to tend and were allowed to decide for themselves when films were to be shown. The other floor were given plants, but the staff tended them and also decided the film schedules. The staff reported better morale, improved health and lower mortality for the self-participatory floor. Questions remain about whether meaningful decision making by patients could be introduced into general hospitals. The composition of wards fluctuates, with a high patient turnover. Patients are also at different recovery stages. Like most experiments on Human Relations lines the Langer study was not longitudinal. We do not know if the effects of the original innovations wore off, or whether the staff support for the scheme was maintained.

New doubt has been cast on the original, psychological optimism to overcome patient alienation. Shipley and others (1979) have shown that some patients have their anxiety raised by repeated exposure to clinical information – this concerned a video made for patients prior to their endoscopic examination (insertion of fibre optic tube through the mouth to reach gastrointestinal parts, given without general anaesthetic). The latter patients are classified as 'repressors', those who prefer not to visualise unpleasant events. 'Sensitisers', who use the repeated information for desensitising themselves, did have better control during the examination. The criteria used to measure recovery rates from operations, and hence success for psychological pre-paration, have been shown to be misleading. Johnston (1984) argues that patient recovery is *not* necessarily a unitary process: researchers commonly assume that their multiple indices (length of stay, reported pain, medication and mood check-list scales, etc.) are measuring the same dimension, which may not be the case. Hospital policy can also influence the length of stay, and physical fitness can determine post-operative mobility. Psychological information has been shown to influence pain, but not the length of hospitalisation.

However, the psychological interventions have in common a lack of critical scrutiny of the hospital regime which, in the first place, produced patient alienation, especially the admission procedure. Psychologists have a professional worry that nurses may object to their intrusion into patient care, or perform themselves the pre-operative strategies, which indeed a number are now doing.

To modify hospital regimes, a patients' charter has been suggested, on the lines of consumer rights. A determined proposer is McNair Wilson, the only MP dependent on renal dialysis. He is angry about his own hospital experiences: such as being given antibiotics to which he was allergic and losing patches of skin; an unremoved stitch which turned septic, requiring a further operation; all part of his catalogue of misfortune. Patients, in the charter, would have rights to weekly progress reports (written if requested), and hospitals would have a complaints procedure. After patients have been told of their planned treatments, they should be able to consult their own GP about it. The mechanics of operating such a scheme would be the key to its effectiveness. Would family doctors find the time for 'impartial' discussion with patients on proposed hospital treatments?

Finally, the role of 'nurse advocate' is being floated to 'protect' patients' interests, presumably against doctors. The argument is that nurses have a greater understanding of their patients' needs, because of more frequent contact. This puts them in a strategic position to negotiate on their behalf, for example, with the doctors' proposed clinical regime. With patients who are severely mentally handicapped and with others incapable of communication, nurses should already be playing this role. There is however the danger in granting advocacy rights *carte blanche* that 'competent' patients could become fodder, with their dependency increased, via nurse assertions for further professional autonomy from doctors and others. Nurses are entrenched in the hospital system, and any intepretation of patient-needs they make will be set within the frame of what *they* define as acceptable working conditions.

THE GRIFFITHS' BEACON

From the *NHS Management Inquiry Report* (Griffiths Report), 1983–84, some relevancies for the hospital will be discussed. Griffiths decries the lack of the general management role embodied in an identifiable individual to give leadership and direction, to take responsibility for developing plans and securing their implementation, and to evaluate their results. Prosaically, Griffiths writes, 'If Florence Nightingale were carrying her lamp through the corridors of the NHS today, she would almost certainly be searching for the people in charge.' The general manager is needed to steer the hospital on a safe course in the uncertain future, whereas at present it is rudderless. With decreasing resources, decisions will have to be made quickly, and an effective management would be able to provide the same level of care more efficiently at lower cost. The 'appropriate' leadership will capitalise on the dedication and expertise of all disciplines and staff by motivating them into greater savings. These could be ploughed back and used for new health initiatives. Merit money and other incentives would be used. 'Non-efficient performers' would be redeployed (where?), and dismissed as a 'last resort'.

The general manager can be appointed from the existing hospital teams, or from outside (he is thinking of business and commerce), as decided by 'local requirements'. With typical Griffiths' solemnity, he asserts that the best of the consensus management approach (previously decried for its lowest common denominator decisions and slowness) will be harnessed and its worst aspects discarded. The strong general manager will release personal energy lower down the line and revitalise the organisation, with more staff training and appraisal. The central issue is that the NHS has enormous expenditure, but with no profit motive as a performance spur. As precise management objectives are set exceptionally, and as clinical evaluation is rare, there is currently no realistic accountability. No business firm would tolerate this state of affairs; it would soon collapse. As one solution, Griffiths suggests clinicians (the big spenders) should be involved more closely in the management process.

The Committee of Public Accounts (CPA) (1983–4) provides ammunition for Griffiths. The DHSS had set a target for health authorities to achieve by 1984–5, namely a 10 per cent reduction of revenue expenditure spent on management. This had been costed at £30 million, involving 3–4,000 staff. The CPA reported that only £10 million had been saved and commented that the evidence given it by health authorities on manpower control was 'quite inadequate'. There was no assessment that the new growth in management was justified. Paradoxically, the Commons Social Services Committee (1986) were informed by the DHSS that the NHS over the past two years had pruned unnecessarily 12,000 jobs i.e. above the government's target. Most were in nursing, ancillary and 'domestic' work. GPs, even in inner city areas, had not applied for government funds available for modernising their practices. Again, rectification of defects in 13 newly-built hospitals would cost at least £30 million, yet Health Authorities had not considered it necessary to vet the designs proposed by commissioned consultants. To date only one per cent of the figure had been recovered from contractors and consultants. Mr Maxton, a member of the CPA, commented that it was four years since the defects in the Royal Hospital for Sick Children were first noted by the committee and that Mr Rennie (from the Scottish Home and Health Department) had then promised to vigorously pursue those at fault ... 'Four years seems to imply not a very vigorous pursuit.' The original contractors had even received further fees for remedial work. Mr Rennie explained that to recover money by arbitration was a lengthy, legal process.

The Griffiths report is thin and vague; written more like a 'briefing memo' (to non-health specialists in the cabinet?) than as a detailed, operational programme. Pilot projects had been set up in six hospitals and four districts, involving clinicians in management budgets, but the findings were not available to Griffiths. The National Association of Health Service Personnel Officers complained that if the Sainsbury organisation received similar recommendations for restructuring its management from an external consultant, far more evidence and investigation would be demanded before embarking on the new proposals!

Griffiths, like its forerunners, transforms the patient into an accounting principle. No cognisance is given to findings on client needs. The Royal Commission on the NHS research paper, Patients' Attitude to the Hospital Service (1978), discovered, for example, that 40 per cent grumbled at being woken up 'too early'. The NALGO memorandum was critical that there was no mention of the Black Report on inequalities and health. Griffiths did not enter the debate on restructuring society.

After decrying Griffiths, NALGO, however, argued its own vested interests concerning the conditions of service for the proposed general managers. In particular it argued against limited contracts. Would specialist general managers be appointed, or would a member of each management team be expected to take on the role in addition to normal duties? If the latter, extra payments would be required.

It is symbolic that only at the end of the report does Griffiths focus on patients. In a brief section, 'patients and the community', he emphasises: 'underlying all that we recommend is the desire to secure the best possible services *for the patient* (his emphasis), the logic being that an 'active' management will automatically make patients 'central'. There is the hint that the NHS Management Board could instigate market research to obtain patients' perceptions. Griffiths offers no judgement on the effectiveness of Community Health Councils

(CHC) and lay members of Health Authorities in representing consumer interests.

The National Consumer Council surveyed in 1984, the information needs of CHCs; approximately half, i.e. 114, responded. Almost half of these were unhappy with their relationship with the DHA. The dissatisfactions involved their exclusion from crucial decisions affecting patients, especially hospital and ward closures. Although having the legal rights to consult, many CHCs were inadequately supplied with appropriate information: DHAs also delayed information. This was the experience of Hammersmith and Fulham CHCs, when they sought information on Well Women Clinics and Patient Activity Reports. The majority of CHCs had never even been approached by their DHA to enquire about their needs.

The gist of Griffiths is that present managers have security of appointment irrespective of performance. But will the 'new, dynamic leaders', on 3–5 years' contracts, galvanise the organisation? Griffiths offers no evidence on the key assumption between management style and productivity, defined in the broadest sense. The management literature offers no firm conclusion. There are fashions in management principles as elsewhere: in the 1950s the participatory leadership styles of the Human Relations school were in vogue. Management style is also a function of worker and union strength.

The Nuffield Centre for Health Services Studies' memorandum reversed the Griffiths' thesis, by arguing that the position of general manager could be very vulnerable. Many organisational members are well placed to 'sabotage' him/her, transforming the role into one of 'scapegoat' for all that goes wrong. Further, the proposals for using 'merit money' for non-clinicians are dubious, and even the awards to doctors have been seriously questioned. It is doubtful, too, if a review body similar to that for clinicians could be assembled to peer-review non-clinicians, for example, administrative staff or technicians.

The Social Services Committee, 1983–84, however, assented to Griffiths, though with reservations. It recommended that Regional and District Authorities should be compelled to specify, in future accountability scrutinies, how their version of general management is being operated. By a separate general manager, or by a nominated individual from within the present 'management team'? The general manager's role was also ambiguous concerning 'professional responsibilities' and the relationship to the chairmen of health authorities. If Unit functional managers, e.g. Directors of Nursing Services, reported to the Unit General Manager rather than to a District Nursing Officer, the latter would become 'surplus'. There would then be no need for a nursing management level above Unit level, save in an 'advisory capacity'. The committee was also totally opposed to part-time managers, since such appointments could not fulfil the daunting task set by Griffiths.

Summarising; we can refer to Sir Kenneth Stowe's (Permanent Secretary) evidence to the CPA. He stated: 'the Griffiths' report is really the last step in a sequence of steps which have a rationale to them.' Whether it is a 'last step' remains to be seen. The Guillebaud report 1956, posited that the NHS could be moulded along stricter commercial lines, following other nationalised industries, like the railways. The NHS commenced life with hospitals run by a chief executive, namely Medical Superintendents. But prior to Griffiths the chief executive or general manager models had been rejected. In Patients First 1979, a government consultative paper, the idea was again rejected, being thought incompatible with 'professional independence'. Now professional independence is too costly a burden to finance, especially when wider economic choices have to be made.

CONCLUSION

Disputes over the efficacy of hospitals are not new. The nineteenth-century debates on hygiene and care have their twentieth-century counterparts expressed in financial accountability. Hospital organisation has been comparatively under-researched. It is perhaps the last inheritor of the Weberian bequest, via Classical Management. Typically, client relationships were never seriously acknowledged in such models. Smith's (1964) description of hospitals as organisations at cross-purposes with themselves remains apt.

The difficulties of operationalising both academically and practically, those concepts developed 'elsewhere', are great. Leatt and Schneck (1982), for example, in analysing the relationship between technology, size, environment and structure in nursing units, delineated technology under the headings of 'uncertainty', 'instability' and 'variability'. Variability was the degree to which there existed variations between raw material and techniques. Translated into the hospital context, 'raw material' might be the number of patients offering a broad spectrum of health problems. In another context Griffiths is being translated according to political dogmas.

The reality of the organisation is now being mediated by the 'health surrogates' of performance indicators. These bring the danger that they may encourage new games of bureaucratic ritualism, played at the expense of consumers.

REFERENCES

Bennett J V 1979 Incidence and nature of endemic and epidemic nosocomial infections. In Bennett J V and Brachman P S (eds) *Hospital infections*. Little Brown, Boston

Blau P M 1963 Critical remarks on Weber's theory of authority. *American Political Science Review* 57: 305-16

Burns T, Stalker G M 1961 *The Management of Innovation*. Tavistock, London

Burrell G, Morgan G 1979 *Sociological Paradigms and Organisational Analysis*. Heinemann, London

Committee of Public Accounts 1983-4 *Manpower Control, Accountability and Other Matters Relating to the NHS*. HMSO, London

Coser R L 1963 *Life on the Ward*. Michigan State University Press

Davis A G 1982 *Children in Clinics*. Tavistock, London

Eiser C, Patterson D 1984 Children's perceptions of hospital: a preliminary study. *International Journal of Nursing Studies* 21: 45-50

Freidson E (ed) 1963 *The Hospital in Modern Society*. Free Press, New York

Gofman H, Buckman W, Schade G 1957 The child's emotional response to hospitalisation. *American Journal of Diseases of Children* 93: 157-65

Goss M E W 1963 Patterns of bureaucracy among hospital staff physicians. In Freidson E (ed) *The Hospital in Modern Society*. Free Press, New York

Gouldner A W 1952 *Patterns of Industrial Bureaucracy*. Free Press, Illinois

Great Britain DHSS and Scottish Home and Health Department 1968 *Report of the Committee on Hospital Scientific and Technical Services*. HMSO, London

(Grey Book) Great Britain, DHSS 1972 *Management Arrangements for the Reorganised NHS*. HMSO, London

Griffiths NHS Management Inquiry Report 1983-4 *Social Services Committee*. HMSO, London

Hall D J 1977 *Social Relations and Innovation. Changing State of Play in Hospitals*. Routledge and Kegan Paul, London

Haywood S C 1983 Politics of management in health care: a British perspective. *Journal of Health Politics, Policy and Law* 8: 424-43

Janis I L 1958 *Psychological Stress*. Wiley, New York

Jaques E (ed) 1978 *Health Services. Their Nature and Organisation and the Role of Patients, Doctors, and the Health Professions*. Heinemann, London

Johnston M 1984 Dimensions of recovery from surgery. *International Review of Applied Psychology* **33**: 505–20

Langer E, Rodin J 1976 The effects of choice and enhanced personal responsibility for the aged: a field experiment in an institutional setting. *Journal of Personality and Social Psychology* **34**: 191–8

Leatt P, Schneck R 1982 Technology, size, environment and structure in nursing subunits. *Organisational Studies* **7**: 221–42

Martin J P 1984 *Hospitals in Trouble*. Basil Blackwell, Oxford

Revans R W 1964 *Standards for Morale: Cause and Effect in Hospitals*. Oxford University Press

Rolston H 1982 The irreversibly comatose: respect for the subhuman in human life. *The Journal of Medicine and Philosophy* **7**: 337–54

Rosengren W R, Lefton M 1969 *Hospitals and Patients*. Atherton, New York

Schulz R, Harrison S 1983 *Teams and Top Managers in the NHS, a Survey and Strategy*. King's Fund Centre, London

Seeman M, Evans J 1962 Alienation and learning in a hospital setting. *American Sociological Review* **27**: 772–82

Shipley R H, Butt J H, Horwitz E A 1979 A preparation to re-experience a stressful medical examination: effect of repetitious videotape exposure and coping style. *Journal of Consulting and Clinical Psychology* **47**: 485–92

Smith H L 1964 The hospital's dual status system. In Simpson R L, Simpson I H (eds) *Social Organisation and Behaviour*. Wiley, New York

Wessen A F 1958 Hospital ideology and communication between ward personnel. In Jaco E G (ed) *Patients, Physicians and Illness*. Free Press, Illinois

Wilson N R 1954 Teamwork in the operating theatre. *Human Organisation* **12**: 9–14

Wilson-Barnett J 1984 Alleviating stress for hospitalised patients. *International Review of Applied Psychology* **33**: 493–503

Woodward J 1970 *Industrial Organisation: Behaviour and Control*. Oxford University Press

Woodward J 1974 *To Do The Sick No Harm. A Study of the British Voluntary Hospital System to 1875*. Routledge and Kegan Paul, London

Zerubavel E 1979 *Patterns of Time in Hospital Life*. University of Chicago Press

Chapter seven
MEDICAL ERRORS

If you pick up a textbook on nursing and medicine, it is extremely unlikely that there will be a prominent section dedicated to 'errors'. These texts will be resplendent with procedures to follow, supported by appropriate research findings. There will be warnings of possible reactions, e.g. in the giving of drugs; also listed will be the statistical chances of recovery from specific surgical interventions. The adverse effects suffered by the patient are assumed not to be caused, as a general rule, by the practitioner. The texts also assume that all practitioners are competent humanitarians, and that professionalism is pervasive, so that only those best fitted to practise (in a Darwinian way) have emerged. Although these manuals give no details of the administration of medicine in different settings, there is again the assumption that this would be effective and would match the differing skills of practitioners with the appropriate diagnostic and treatment cases. Finally, there is an almost total neglect of the warning of the Renaissance physician Paré (1500–1590), who became the influential leader of the College Saint Côme: Namely that there is a fundamental difficulty in asserting that the patient has been cured directly *by* a doctor, or *because of* the doctors' endeavours.

Other facts contradict the medical mask of being error free. Cosmopolitan medicine has always claimed scientific validation as its legitimating foundation, constantly emphasising that the climb to the summit of achievement has been through 'trial and error'. Given practices are tested then, if found wanting, discarded in favour of more appropriate alternatives. Cosmospolitan medicine has claimed an affinity with Kuhn's (1970) methodology: namely a step by step advance over a long period of 'normal science' within the reigning paradigm. The dominant frame gradually decays when it can no longer contain the accumulative readjustments. This leads to an inevitable, revolutionary change, when a new paradigm successfully emerges. To subscribe to this version of knowledge construction means, by definition, that errors must have been committed as part of 'normal' scientific development. Unfortunately it is patients who are the focus of the application of medical knowledge!

Other facts reveal the presence of errors. Medical and nursing staff are very aware of them. Their everyday conversations are punctuated with 'horror stories' explaining them. This form of story-telling acts as an unofficial training manual, instructing others about possible clinical dangers and providing various means of avoidance. The media, too, has its bouts of moral panic. A recent headline ran: *MOTHERS' AGONY IN CAESARIAN BIRTHS (Guardian,* 13 June 1985). It is claimed that more than 500 women a year are awake during caesarian operations, the problem being to anaesthetise the mother sufficiently without damaging the unborn baby. The calculation is a difficult one, with the error having been reduced from 4 per cent to 1 per cent of all caesarians since 1975. However, the number of caesarians has increased from 6 per cent to over 10 per cent of births during that period. In private medicine the rate is doubled, the same figure as in the USA.

Consumer litigation is increasing in the USA, providing a lucrative income for lawyers. The doctor–patient relationship is primarily an economic one. Health maintenance constitutes a large percentage of personal income, and clients want value for money. The medical profession is trapped behind the mask of its own success. If hearts can be successfully transplanted, then clients expect a successful outcome for their 'mundane' backache. Increased expectations from medicine are also leading to increased litigation in the UK. There are now more opportunities for medical errors to proliferate even though, paradoxically, the overall 'expertise' of nursing and medical staff is rising (as indicated by more training inputs). There are now more nurses than there are NHS beds. Although the staff ratio is a difficult one to assess, between 1978 and 1983 there was a real increase of nursing staff of 6 per cent (allowing for the reduced working week); however the number of hospital in-patients increased by 12 per cent and out-patients by 7 per cent. The administrative rules routinising staff and medical practices have multiplied enormously. New directives/guidelines are in continuous circulation – bound in folders requesting, 'read, initial and pass on'.

As more behaviour becomes rule-governed, the chances for deviation increase. Sponging and feeding patients are now clinical activities. It does not follow that former, complex medical practices, once routinised and 'simplified', have drastically reduced their risk factors. For example, epidural anaesthetic (spinal) is now routine for childbirth, but is still potentially dangerous if inserted wrongly by a fraction, or if not correctly topped up. Another aspect of error is exemplified here, i.e. that all mishaps with the technique are not known. The DHSS does not centrally record them, and the frequency of error that is offered by the medical profession, of 1 in 1,500–2,000, could well be an underestimate. Compensation for errors is often settled out of court, with the Medical Defence Union having made about 500 such settlements up to 1983.

How an error is defined depends largely on the clustering of a large number of factors – not least the validity of the baseline of normal practice and the moral intent of the practitioner. Here we discuss the various categories of error, since all are not of the same order. If, as suggested, errors are an integral part of the doctors' practices, then it necessitates exploring how doctors are taught to handle them as part of their professional activities. Finally, doctors frequently blame their patients for the failure of their treatment regimes. The non-compliant patient, who disobeys doctor's orders, has now a prominent place in medical ideology. The view from the 'other side' – the patient's modification of treatment – will also be discussed.

WHAT IS A MEDICAL ERROR?

A useful starting point is to examine the *Annual Report of the Health Service Commissioner* 1984–85, colloquially known as the Health Ombudsman. He investigates grievances against the NHS. The number of complaints received was 9 per cent fewer than the peak of 1983–84, but at 815 was an increase over all earlier years. Of the 443 investigated, 47 per cent were found to be justified. The grievances are categorised not only by function – Nursing, Medical and Administration – but also into two other permeable categories: 'failure in service' and 'handling of complaint' by the authority. Failure in service includes examples as diverse as community and laboratory house-keeping. Complaints against the medical staff are further subdivided: 'lack of or incorrect information', 'attitudes' and 'failure in non-clinical procedures'. The NHS Act 1977 (and NHS Scotland Act 1978) setting out the role of the HSC stipulates that matters of clinical judgement are to be excluded. This is where most grievances *would have* fallen. Grievances against nursing are subdivided into: 'failure in care', 'lack of or incorrect information', 'attitudes' and 'maltreatment'.

The language of the report is significant. It is obvious that alleged errors are being investigated and, even when substantiated, the report meticulously avoids the term. This is used only once, when a Health Authority apologised to the HSC for its 'admitted error' when it illegally destroyed the first-year medical records of a mentally retarded boy, whose father needed the information for the case for compensation he was pursuing under the Vaccine Damage Payment Act 1979 (W45/83–84).

Errors are usually translated into 'failure to follow the correct procedure'. For example, an accident form was not filled in when an old lady of 84 years sustained unexplained facial injuries on the ward (W336/82–83). The phrase 'strayed from their own standards' is used where hospital staff failed to heed a wife's warning about her husband's drug reaction; he subsequently died (WY9/84–85). 'Most serious failure' was used when a charge nurse disobeyed an instruction to arrange for the duty doctor to see a mentally handicapped 19 year-old patient. His mother found him wandering around the grounds barefoot, partially dressed and suffering from a chest infection. He died soon after (W385/83). A 'serious failure in the service' occurred when a duty doctor arrived much later than he could, after being summoned, for he was not occupied elsewhere (W309/83–84).

It is implicit that the errors investigated are of two types: omission and commission; a classification frequently used, as recently by Mizrahi (1984). Those health personnel who interface directly with clients are the ones most likely to be the focus of a complaint. The chef's bad cooking, or the electrician's failure to repair equipment, do not figure, although they too contribute to the maintenance of the treatment environment. The refusal to assign the term 'error' (or 'mistake'), when justified, may in part be because the HSC not only perceives his role as investigatory, but also as remedial: encouraging the criticised members to take the necessary steps to avoid a repetition. By avoiding the critical stricture, 'error', the HSC hopes to promote sufficient goodwill to facilitate reform. The HSC notes that 'failures in service' are repetitive and provide valuable lessons for all.

Medical error can stem from uncertainty. Behind the public mask of medicine, radiating professional power and confidence, all kinds of doubts persist. We have seen (Ch. 2) that there are disputes concerning the different models of diagnosis. For most illnesses there are a host of treatment philosophies. Medicine recognises polar extremes, the conservative and liberal stances. In orthopaedics the conservatives favour traction and braces; with breast cancer such surgeons prefer radical mastectomy, not lumpectomy. With cancer treatment, general surgeons, radiation therapists and chemotherapists seriously dispute one another's claims. Knafl and Burkett (1979) initially singled out orthopaedics for studying how trainees acquired medical judgement, on the assumption that it would be one of the least ambiguous specialisms. This premise was rudely shaken when they discovered that its students were taught that their own specialism was one of the *most* ambiguous. Their tutors impressed on them that they would be taught things that do not always follow the textbook!

Fox (1959) has distinguished three basic types of uncertainty that disturb physicians. First, when they have incomplete understanding or control over the available knowledge: no-one can possibly keep up to date with the escalating findings. A second uncertainty derives from the limitations in current medical knowledge. The expert doctor can pose questions for which there are no existing solutions. The third uncertainty is a compound of the first two; being unable to distinguish between personal ignorance and the inadequacy of current medical knowledge. One prime purpose of medical socialisation is to teach trainee doctors how to handle uncertainty, without precipitating unpredictable and troublesome outcomes.

Fox studied in the 1950s a metabolic research unit, which represented an extreme context of uncertainty, since there were no recognised treatments. Amongst others, they were testing the yet untried steroids on patients with Addison's disease. The question of medical error was therefore not a consideration. Uncertainty was openly faced and patients were fully informed. They were incorporated into the experiments as professional colleagues; supplying doctors with detailed self-monitoring data. Gallows humour was a favourite technique used by doctors for releasing the personal tensions of uncertainty in treatment and the deaths of patients regarded as friends.

The baseline of medical knowledge, established at one point in time, must be the obvious frame for normal practice; but this is continuously shifting. There can also be simultaneous and contradictory solutions to a doctor's problem. Many established truths have been found subsequently to be patently fallacious. In 1903 the French Academy awarded the physicist Blondot a prize for his discovery of N-rays; just after the discovery of X-rays. The N-rays turned out to be a figment of his hallucinations. Would the doctor be committing an error of omission if he delayed treatment until it had been 'completely' validated? Damaging side effects of a treatment may take many years to appear. In the early 1970s, children who would have suffered from dwarfism, were treated with a hormone extracted from the pituitary glands of corpses (approximately 40 were needed to treat one child).

The hormone is now banned in the United States, after the discovery a decade later, that there is a danger of some contracting the fatal Creutzfeldt-Jacob disease from a virus attacking brain cells and nervous system. A 'safe', but expensive genetically engineered hormone is now on the market. This example could be considered by most as a normal or justified error. Goldthorp and Richman (1976) show how medical baselines can switch overnight. The ancillaries' strike of 1973, blocked the planned intake to a maternity unit: primigravidae (mothers having their first baby), —Rh mothers and those over 31 years of age were now deemed suitable for domiciliary delivery, yet the day before they were risk categories for hospitalisation only! Clearly resources cannot be divorced from the issue.

Minogue (1982), while accepting the distinction between negligent and non-negligent errors, denies that we should consider a third category of 'fallibility' suggested by MacIntyre. 'Non-negligence' is caused by the general lack of existing knowledge; hormone treatment for dwarfism would be a candidate. The 'fallibility' category however is 'independent' of human intervention, and rests on the statistical frequency of outcomes. For example, it is explained that 1 in 1,200 recipients of smallpox vaccination will suffer a dangerous reaction. Also the attribution of negligent error cannot be applied to the adverse case, especially if the patient is forewarned of risk. The analogy is evoked that disease, like a hurricane, depends on specific historical conditions, some of which are unknowable. Minogue is opposed to this view of non-culpability, arguing that if it became the dominant thinking then all medical errors would be defined from a purely quantitive position; the definition of error in any specific case would then cease to be a moral or qualitative issue. By focusing on the idiographic, medicine would be detracted from its search for general and substantive laws.

The notion of error is further extended when medicine is subservient to a 'wider' frame of ethical reasoning. Rosner (1983) cites the position of the Jewish orthodox doctor, with whom divine guidance and the teachings of the Torah are supreme. The doctor in a fundamentalist Islamic state is also a parallel. Jewish law forbids driving or using instruments on the Sabbath, which affects the doctor who acts as the agent of God. The violation of corpses is forbidden - to undertake an autopsy could therefore be an error. Precedents created by Maimonides (1135-1204) the Spanish rabbi and philosopher (who became physician to Saladin), provide the basis for compromise. The physician *can* treat 'critically' ill patients on the Sabbath. Modern surgery has created new ethical demands. The removal of any organ from the body necessitates its burial by Jewish law. With transplant surgery the recipient's heart would be buried, but what would happen to the donor's heart (assuming it is Jewish) after the recipient dies? Does it revert back to the donor for burial? Rabbinical debate continues.

HANDLING ERRORS

As Hughes (1958) has reminded us, all occupations have devised techniques for handling atypical occurrences. The medical profession has had long experience of solving errors in its own way, the public lacking an effective voice. Arluke (1977) analyses how the ritualistic format of the 'death rounds' controls and systematises events which are threatening to medicine. In the large USA teaching hospitals ceremonies called the death rounds take place weekly. Not all deaths are errors, but death challenges the collective values of the medical group, exposing its failings. By neutralisation strategies death is routinised. A member of the medical staff takes the audience through the clinical sequences culminating in a death. Using a slide presentation, X-rays and other tests are logically arranged, the trajectory creating the impression that death/error would be inevitable. Death ceases to be the focus of the exercise; the clinical complexity of the case takes over. The reviewer's skill comes to the fore; these are occasions for doctor's talents to be publicly reinforced. Patients' deaths thus cease to be a medical consequence. Two other features sustain the programme. First, the reviewer never presents his own cases of death/errors, second, each case is kept separate, so that there are no accumulative comparisons with other cases, and the identification of dominant patterns of errors is prevented.

Mizrahi (1984) has depicted how everyday errors come to be located within the ideology of medical groups. She spent three years studying how 105 house officers (interns), just graduating from medical school, faced the challenge as they progressed through a large public hospital, a private hospital and a Veterans' Administration – all with different intakes. One half of the house officers admitted responsibility for one or more very serious errors. That was only the tip of the iceberg. Coping mechanisms for distancing errors were deployed – i.e. a hefty collection of rationalisations were used. The disease was frequently blamed; the patient would have died within a year 'irrespective' of the error, was the argument of one houseman who never understood what was happening to a patient's electrolytes, thus causing a young death. Their own tiredness and the system are other justifications. It is possible that 'tiredness' was indeed a real factor since house officers do work very long hours. Another rationalisation often used was the fact that anyone makes mistakes, and therefore that a house officer is 'entitled' to his. The personal nature of medicine is also projected as there are often no ground rules to cover many cases. You just have to go in and 'try'. They became their own internal adjudicators, except for serious errors which became litigious. Because of their cloistered work setting, the issue of revealing errors to the interested parties, patients and their relatives, was not of prime consideration, and therefore not a restraint. In time an aura of acceptance of others' mistakes takes over. Mizrahi never discusses whether this acceptance is more characteristic of the public than the private hospital, where patients are less influential. Not all house officers were successful in coping with errors. This could be a matter of personality, or outgroup status, but Mizrahi does not elaborate.

Other studies of medical socialisation concentrate on how errors committed by interns are mediated through their relationships with controlling superiors, and how these errors can be 'retrieved'. Bosk's (1979) study was based on 18 months' participant observation in the surgical (high status) training programme in an elite Californian teaching hospital. The research role adopted was an interesting one: he helped wheel the medication trolley and chart racks on rounds with doctors. His data fell within the comparative frames of two different surgical activities. One had a high research base and the other was more clinically orientated. These differences, however, turned out to be insignificant. The same rating of error was common to both.

Surgery is a precise activity: errors are immediately visible. Parts of the body are removed and rearranged, with the surgeon's scalpel the agent. In psychiatry, contrastingly, medical intervention is unobtrusive. Medical errors are more easily attributable to the patient. Light (1972) explains how a patient's suicide 'becomes' the latter's responsibility. In contrast, when a surgical patient dies the question asked by colleagues becomes: 'what did you do?'. Bosk describes how surgeons have their taxonomic ordering of errors: technical, judgemental, normative and quasi-normative.

Technical errors committed by interns will be forgiven by the supervising surgeon, even the most serious, if two rules are fulfilled. First, the intern must report the error immediately, so that its effects can be ameliorated. Second, the intern must not make a habit of committing the same error — this would then be incompetence. Technical errors are regarded as essential teaching material.

Judgemental errors are matters of deploying inappropriate strategies of treatment, such as making the wrong choice of operation, necessitating 'excessive' post-operative surveillance. It is inappropriate, too, for interns to perform 'heroic surgery' – the prerogative of specialists.

Normative errors are those breaking established social etiquettes. They threaten the hospital conventions, which in turn reflect hierarchical ranking and reciprocity. Interns must co-operate, for example, with nurses, for the latter manage the essential human relations on the ward, including the ebb and flow of relatives – who can be troublesome to the surgeon. Interns can resent experienced nurses offering 'helpful' suggestions, fearing that their competence will be undermined with patients. Normative errors are more serious than technical ones. They represent a permanent defect in moral character and cause unpredictable breaches in the supervising surgeon's relationships. Repairing these cleavages consumes unnecessary time.

Quasi-normative errors are specific. They break only the idiosyncratic conventions of the supervising surgeon. All have their own style, some keep a tight control over their interns, others do not. To use independent judgement with the former is 'mutiny'. Surgeons also develop variations in their surgical technique, and these must be followed by their interns. Quasi-normative errors may seriously affect an intern's career; the supervising surgeon may not support his promotion, since the intern is not his mirror image.

Bosk also has a catch-all category of errors – 'exogenous'. This is a catalogue of other sources of errors: by nurses, unco-operative patients (who get referred too late for successful surgery) and machine breakdowns, etc.

Errors provide important insights into the dynamics of professionalism, which has always stressed the virtues of its collectivity and self-policing to maintain standards above those of public morality. However, surgeons are extremely reluctant to challenge inferior, technical performances by peers; the very errors most life-threatening to the patient. They are happy to criticise colleagues' moral lapses, such as inappropriate behaviour on resource committees, etc. Technical errors can easily be accredited to the unknown factor 'X', a patient's distinctive disposition, genetically and socially determined lifestyle. It is unlikely that other colleagues were there to witness the faulty operation. A moral error is on public display for all: like a black hole in the social fabric it could drag them all into its ramifications. However, they sift out and check all errors by interns. The total application of professional control is thus on the 'pre-professional'. When an intern has been absolved from a technical error, and the damage is repaired, his indebtedness feeds back, helping to generate the collective attachment of professional solidarity.

ERRORS IN PSYCHIATRY

Psychiatry is the most disputatious branch of medicine. The history of its acceptance within the medical fold was stormy; its knowledge base considered lacking in 'scientific' credentials. Psychiatry's peripherality still remains. Light (1975), summarising surveys of USA medical students, shows that psychiatry is ranked as one of the most poorly taught specialities; psychiatrists are less competent and less clear-thinking (but more likeable) than surgeons. One trait characterising potential psychiatrists is 'high death-anxiety'.

As the thrust of psychiatry is to sanction some behaviour and to legitimate other forms then, some have argued, a primeval error is endemic in the whole enterprise. 'Appropriate' behaviour is relative and problematic, even within the same society. The behaviour defined as 'psychiatric disorder' by one group of psychiatrists can be interpreted by others as an 'alternative means of communication', or 'personal exploration of the limits of human experience' – i.e. rational responses to an alienating world. Even psychiatrists working with the same diagnostic categories can differ in how they apply them to the 'same behaviour'. Diagnosis proceeds from 'appearances' (ch.2), with the imputation of motives to clients' subjective accounts. Psychiatrists rarely diagnose patients in their own natural settings.

Colby and Spar (1983) refer to the unreliability of diagnosis as causing the fundamental crises in psychiatry. If the patient describes himself as depressed, is he clinically depressed? In its attempt at greater precision, psychiatry is continuously refining and multiplying its diagnostic categories. The new categories all conveniently fail to specify what is normal!

Colby describes how diagnosis fluctuates. In the 1950s catatonic schizophrenia was common and paranoid schizophrenia less common. Today their frequencies are reversed. The once prevalent hebephrenic schizophrenia has now disappeared. This tells us more about psychiatrists' *beliefs* than it does about patients' behaviour. Even Van Gogh's former diagnosis of schizophrenia paranoia has been over-turned. Khoshbin of the Harvard Medical School (*Observer* 4 August 1985) now declares him to have suffered Geschwind's syndrome. Symptoms include sudden changes in sexual interest, a 'viscosity' to changes in behaviour and hypergraphia – a compulsion to paint or draw!

In 1980 the American Psychiatric Association brought out its Diagnostic and Statistical Manual (DSM) mark 3, the summation of a committee of experts' review of the literature. To reduce the numbers whose disorder cannot be fully diagnosed and to enhance professional certainty (but not predict patient outcome), all the major diagnostic categories now have 'atypical' sub-categories, e.g. 'atypical anxiety disorder'. As Colby and Spar critically note — before it can be decided who does not fit all the (main?) requirements of 'anxiety disorder', it must be first stipulated what these are – but DSM 3 does *not* specify! In their exposé of diagnostic unreliability, conducted in the form of the Socratic dialogue between an inquirer and an array of psychiatrists/ mind experts, further doubts are cast. When the DSM 3 manual was completed, psychiatrists were invited to field test the categories. Almost half of the prime categories of adult disorders were found doubtful. In the practical world of psychiatry, anyway, few bother to diagnose strictly according to the 'book'. The statistics therefore compiled from practice, lacking the standardised base, are later compiled into data indicating national frequencies. Not only is the mental patient (especially those with non-organic disorders) socially constructed during diagnosis, but so are the future 'norms' of the illness, which loop back to influence future diagnostic regimes.

These criticisms are known to psychiatrists, who respond by arguing that even 'physical' medicine is an art. Some of their diagnostic categories do have high levels of agreement – e.g. paranoia. Further, they assert, psychiatrists take account of category un- reliability when diagnosing, being aware of the impact any mental illness label may have, for example on employment opportunities. This practice only intensifies the moral dilemma of the psychiatrist. Livingston and Zimet (1965) have argued that, as students, psychiatrists have non-authoritarian personalities. Again, later in career psychiatric error and doubts are often publicly paraded in court especially in murder trials, when psychiatrists for the defence and prosecution give counter-versions of the defendant's 'state of mind', and whether or not he really 'heard' voices telling him to kill.

Rosenhan's experiment (1973) still has lessons for those trying to distinguish the 'sane' (normal) from the 'insane' (abnormal). Sane people gained access to twelve different psychiatric hospitals. The pseudopatients included a psychology student, three psychologists, a paediatrician, a psychiatrist, a painter, and a housewife. After faking symptoms of hearing dull and hollow voices, of the same sex as themselves, they were admitted. Inside, they stopped their faked symptoms and behaved normally, although most had never visited a psychiatric ward. The pseudopatients were never detected by the staff, but were by the patients. The researchers openly wrote up their field notes in the wards. The official records on three of the pseudopatients attributed their writing to a pathological symptom. The patients knew exactly the purpose of the notes and asked the researchers if they were part of an inspection team, or if they were professors!

One teaching hospital, on reading the research report, argued that the experiment would not have been possible there. Rosenhan arranged for the staff to be informed that over the next three months at least one pseudopatient would attempt admission. Evaluations of 193 patients were made; 41 were assessed by at least one member of staff as 'phony'. One psychiatrist suspected 23! Rosenhan and others conclude that once a patient is psychiatrically committed, then any aspect of his behaviour is potentially part of the illness. Hanging around waiting for the canteen to open was considered, by one psychiatrist, as an aspect of oral-acquisitiveness syndrome. But mealtimes structure the day, there being little else to do.

ETHNICITY AND PSYCHIATRY

Ethnic diversification since the Second World War has brought into sharp focus diagnostic limitations. Although national health statistics are not ethnic-sensitive, as in the USA, there are sufficient findings for disquiet. The NHS was founded on the planning assumption that it would be dealing with a homogeneous population, conveniently ignoring class differences. The Royal Commission on the NHS (1981) noted in passing that the special needs of ethnic groups require sensitive handling. No specific suggestions were made for implementing a comprehensive policy. There have been responses from the DHSS and health authorities for targeting compaigns on given problems – sickle-cell anaemia, rickets and maternity care. Mental illness has never been particularised. The problem for psychiatrists has been one of distinguishing how far a patient's presenting symptoms are representative of a culture with shared experiences (which could be a sub or occupational culture), or represent 'genuine' individual differences, possibly filtered 'distortedly' from the enveloping culture. In traditional society this dilemma is not as pertinent.

Psychiatrists working within cosmopolitan medicine usually use the personal differences model, often with gender typing, following the established medical model. Ethnopsychiatrists have always used the concepts of normality/abnormality present within a given culture.

They explore these concepts in the patient by examining the way symptoms mediate the private and public symbols of that culture. They play down biological determinism as a root cause of mental illness. Others are seeking (e.g. with depression), the hormonal basis of the disturbed circadian rhythms: cortisol, prolactin and melatonin have been indicted – but only offer a partial explanation. The USA has greater experience of accepting the relevance of ethnicity as the frame within which to practise psychiatry. Illness is considered an explanatory and exploratory model and not an entity. Ethno-psychiatrists treating the Hopi Indians of south-east USA do not dismiss as delusion their cosmic version of a world ordering, based on spirits.

Misunderstandings can abound, leading to a greater degree of error, when diagnosing members from the new commonwealth. Blacks of Afro-Caribbean origin have their own theories on the causes of misfortune leading to 'madness'. Rack (1982) has summarised these. There is the belief that other people can plan your madness through Obeah: Obeah men and women have supernatural powers of witchcraft. They can be evoked for good (healing) or evil. Poisoning is a favourite way of attacking another. Another theory is that 'tainted blood' can be inherited, often unknowingly, which under certain circumstances will incapacitate. The after-effects of birth can also precipitate disorder. Women who do not get sufficient rest will find that their body does not correctly reconstitute itself. There is also the notion of 'studiation': too much studying can 'turn' your head and drain your life energy.

These lay theories do have a logical trail, but could appear preposterous to those lacking understanding of their cultural contours. For example, in a peasant society interlaced with active reciprocal networks, to study means not only to engage in a different activity but to isolate oneself. Studying is a solitary activity. Isolates in these societies are suspect people. New ideas from learning may also oppose the conventional truths. In nineteenth century England, working class people educated beyond 'their station' were considered as a moral threat by aristocracy. The after-effects of birth have their parallel in cosmopolitan medicine, with its stream of post-partum mental illnesses: post-partum psychosis; puerperal insanity; gestational psychosis; insanity of pregnancy, of puerperium and of lactation; toxic and infectious exhaustive psychosis, etc. Childbirth as a disrupter of hormones/identity is only another metaphor for expressing black lay theory of 'incompleteness'.

The patient–psychiatrist clash also arises from the different expectations from the consultation. Psychiatrists use the Sherlock Holmes method of gathering evidence, collecting inductively all the symptoms, then using substantive reasoning to locate the disease. The patient gets irritated by this rambling and 'time-wasting' approach. He starts with the assumption that the psychiatrist, being clever, should know what is wrong. The patient is primarily concerned with the 'why' question. Why misfortune has singled him out? He may see no connection between his treatment (pill-taking) and the cause of illness. If he is a Pentacostalist believing in divine intervention, he may speak constantly of God in his everyday conversations – God is by his side; will help him; talk to him; plan his future, and so on. Such reiterations could be easily mistaken for one of the syptoms of schizophrenia, that is the body losing its boundary. Rastafarian beliefs and language can also confuse the untutored psychiatrist. As part of the back-to-Africa movement, Rastafarianism has all the characteristics of a retreatist, millennium sect of the oppressed.

The non-judgemental style of therapy can be confusing. Its requirements of introspection and intellectual exploration of personal motives are misunderstood. The free-floating exercise is seen as purposeless. The style can also be inappropriate to some white working-class people with 'low verbalisation'. They are more accustomed to receiving orders. If the psychiatrist plays the 'father figure', as part of the transference dynamics of therapy, this again can be misunderstood. Many West Indian households are matrifocal: fathers can be rather shadowy figures.

Concern has been drawn to differential diagnosis rates, patterns of referral and treatment. Those of West Indian origin have an above-average admission rate for mental illness. They are four times more likely than whites to be referred via the police and mental welfare officer. The Runnymede Trust (1983), summarising the existing literature, goes on to explain how black psychotics are twice as likely to be detained under section 136, of the 1959 Mental Health Act. The police are allowed to move to a place of safety anyone found in a public place judged to be dangerous to others, or to him or herself. These powers are used where constables have no right of arrest. Males of West Indian origin are also three times more likely to be admitted for schizophrenia than are UK-born males, but have a lower rate of affective psychosis (e.g. depression psychosis). They have a higher rate for paranoia, and are twice as likely as whites to be misdiagnosed and have the original diagnosis changed more frequently. Rastafarians are more prone to misdiagnosis of schizophrenia. Blacks are more likely to receive Electro-Convulsive Therapy (ECT), yet fewer are classified as suffering from depression. They are more likely, too, to receive major tranquillisers compared with whites with the same diagnosis.

Asians show a different pattern; a below-average rate of admission to mental hospitals, and a below-average suicide rate. Males present symptoms of 'physical' complaints and females complain of sleeplessness, sweating and a spinning head. To reveal mental illness in a family would taint it, spoiling marriage opportunities. Asians have a denser, supporting family network than do Afro-Caribbeans. By delaying referral they tend to offer more serious conditions, and alternative treatment by hakims is frequently used.

Unless psychiatry takes serious note of racism as an influence on mental illness and on its own practices, then ethnic patients are more likely to be forced into unsatisfactory diagnostic categories. Littlewood and Cross's (1980) study of an East London General Hospital showed how the staff considered that blacks were more in need of ECT and intra-muscular medication. They were more likely to be seen by junior members of staff, often black. The authors conclude that the medical staff have either recognised medical conditions in blacks that others have not or, more likely, that their medical behaviour followed racist stereotypes.

Racism has many prongs. Discrimination can compel lower rates of social mobility in a consumer society which stresses success; create feelings of persecution; induce low self-esteem; use the excuses of social isolation and personality barriers as defence mechanisms. The racism equation (like the stress model) is not always a simple equation. As Rack points out, Pakistanis are more discriminated against than Poles, but they have a lower rate of paranoia. Burke's (1984) study of psychological disturbance among West Indians living in North Birmingham shows that the age group 45–64 of married persons has the highest rate of depression. His explanation is that these have suffered the emotional tragedy of their children being forced by racism into downward mobility and into inferior jobs or unemployment. Much depends on the strategies adopted to cushion the effects of racism. Strong participation in community politics, or sect membership, can provide confirmation of meaningful black identities and a release of social tension.

Mercer (1984) argues forcibly that racism, both overt and institutionalised, has constructed a pathological model of 'black culture'. It has been criminalised by the projection of the 'mugging syndrome'. Family life (and child rearing) is portrayed as 'defective' by the welfare agencies because it is not patriarchially ordered, and has a high rate of illegitimacy. 'One-parent families' are however a broad based trend, and are not the prerogative of blacks. The black family is very much an historical adaptation to a high male unemployment. It is not a 'fixed' entity, and variegates during its cycle. Black culture is forged within a culture of poverty, and academic studies often emphasise limitations of social skills, little initiative and high welfare dependence. This pathological picture cannot help but infiltrate white psychiatry, distorting its perceptions. Some psychiatrists now use the category 'West Indian Psychosis' (for a sudden onset of violent behaviour and hallucinations). It is questionable whether this is an endogenous psychosis, as much as the product of black stereotyping. When black clients present persecution symptoms, some are realistically grounded, a product of a hostile society. There is much in the argument which locates blacks, especially, as still filling a colonial status within a white metropolitan culture.

THE NON-COMPLIANT PATIENT

Failure of treatment is increasingly blamed on the non-compliant patient; medical literature on this subject has been doubling every five years since 1965. Not all 'bad' patients distort their treatment. Rosenthal *et al.* (1980) reinforces the nursing literature by distinguishing eight types of 'problem patient': the demanding; manipulative; the violent and irrational; the complainers of pain; the careerists (do not belong in hospital, not really sick); the non-compliant; those who try to control treatment; and the unpleasant ones – described variously as 'nuts', 'weird', 'bitchy', 'schizo', etc. Non-compliance causes problems for nurses with doctors. If medication regimes are manipulated, then nurses have to spend unscheduled time with them. Non-compliance decreases with both older patients and those with chronic illnesses. Those who try to control treatment threaten the professional hegemony. Bad and angry patients can be referred to the psychiatrist, who can classify them as 'projective paranoiacs'.

The super-compliant patient, such as the uncomplainers of severe pain in the post-operative phase, also cause medical problems. As Lorber (1975) points out, doctors and nurses frequently disagree on the moral rating of the same patient. Doctors have their own rich crop of typifications: 'crocks', 'termers', 'turkeys', 'gomers'. Mizrahi (1984) reveals a particularly obnoxious one: SHPOS (super-human piece of shit), who was blamed by one intern (who arrived late) for dying on him. Two features are common. First, medical and nursing staff take little, or no responsibility for causing their patients' 'deviance' through their support of alienating hospital structures. Second, they develop tactics for 'distancing' themselves from these patients – by avoidance, neglect, rapid discharge, and punishment – all of which can hinder their medical progress.

The greatest rate of non-compliance is with self-medication – the most extensive form of treatment. Patients who fail to comply fully with their prescribed medication range between 30 per cent and 60 per cent, and even as high as 90 per cent has been recorded. Non-compliance is not a new problem for doctors, who tend to overestimate the rate of their patients' conformity. To admit high rates, would be tantamount to declaring oneself a bad doctor. Non-compliance has no determining variable: there is no significant association with social class, IQ ability, education or marital status. Any disease is likely to have its non-compliants. Those who take drugs over a long period, having been prescribed a cocktail of drugs with frequent application, those taking drugs for mainly asymptomatic disease (44 per cent of those in the United States with high blood pressure are not aware of it), and those taking drugs with bad side effects – all have tendencies towards non-compliance. There is a higher level of compliance with medication for short-term, symptomatic, and acute disease, such as sexually transmitted ones, with their stigma of being unclean.

Anyone is a potential non-complier. Diabetic children (Belmonte 1981) have cheated when self-administering urine tests to monitor blood sugar levels. The children were taken to summer camps for diabetics, as doctors believed that group learning was the most effective. The children however believed that if their sugar level was normal, they were cured. An important point emerges. Patients operate with their *own* existentialist relationship with their medication. Non-compliance, the doctor's definition, takes on different meanings when reviewed through patients' eyes. Under the heading of non-compliance whole sets of different activities can take place. Diabetics develop their own 'favourite spot' on the body for injections. Doctors warn against this on infection grounds. The old, who have seen treatments come and go, can be 'critical users'. They, too, are very body conscious, with changes through ageing. Their 'scatter gun' approach to self-medication cannot wholly be attributed to forget-fulness. Doctors themselves are notoriously non-compliant when sick, whether in the West or in the USSR.

There are no accurate means for assessing non-compliance. Counting pills left in their container tells us nothing about the frequency of use. Some patients will double their dosage if symptoms intensify of if they have 'missed' a day. Others will crush their pills if hard to swallow, even though coated with a substance to make them pass intact through the stomach. Doctors' and pharmacists' directives give only the meagrest of detail – number to be taken and frequency. The measurement of metabolite level (produced by the drug's absorption in the body) often does not give a 'true' reading. Lithium, used extensively for bipolar affective disorder, has a very rapid absorption rate. A patient dosing himself before seeing the doctor could indicate the proper therapeutic level.

The compliant patient is an appendage of the doctor's version of the ideal healing relationship. This paternalistic model is a consensus one. It is based on the assumption that the doctor knows best. Patients can be so overwhelmed by their condition that full explanations will only add to their burden. Most patients are incapable of comprehending sophisticated medical facts. According to the doctor's rational calculations, slices of the truth will be passed to the patient. As in the Parsonian sick role (Ch. 3), patient passivity is taken for granted. Non-compliance is therefore 'sabotage', negating the doctor's good work. This model does not question the efficacy of treatment. Some studies show that there is actually no connection between compliance and treatment results. Heszen-Klemens's (1984) data on Polish doctors, treating TB, coronary heart disease and catarrhal inflammation of the gums, exemplifies this. The paternalistic model is hard to sustain when many modern ailments are not susceptible to 'full' cure. The rise of the knowledgeable patient presents another 'threat', since these patients are the most critical of doctors. Blaming the victim, as Ryan calls it (1976), is now a major feature of all service professions, and not just medicine. Social workers are addicted to this explanation. Despite their rise in professional status, the results of their labours are becoming more problematic, with public criticism mounting. Blaming the victim is one of the major symptoms of staff 'burnout', together with increased alcohol use and routinised work performances.

Another medically-centred explanation for patient non-compliance is imperfection in communication between doctor and patient. The assumption is again that patients are unreliable; they selectively remember parts of the doctor's instruction. Ley and others (1976), for example, has shown that patients forget between 37 and 54 per cent of the information on leaving clinics and surgeries. Goldthorp and others (1976), in their study of 250 gynaecological patients, showed that 45 per cent could either offer no biological linkage, or gave incorrect information, about the part of their body which had been diagnosed in need of treatment. The communication model does not question the doctor's right to define the requisite information for the patient. The doctor's role is to use the appropriate strategy for conveying it, within the time limits set by him. The consultation is not an open-ended question and answer session. Yet few doctors encourage patients to take notes, let alone tape the instructions! Doctors could then be pinioned to their advice, if it should prove faulty.

Another medical model deployed is the manipulative patient. Simply, these patients are intent on scheming their way through the consultation for their own ends. Although the doctor may adopt a 'mutually negotiated' style of consultation, these patients will not keep to the 'rules'. Patients will deliberately lie, thus leading the doctor into error, if he accepts blindly their information. Hecht's (1974) study of TB patients showed that over 60 per cent made errors in recounting the drugs they took. Even mothers lie to doctors about the drugs they administer to children. Bergman (1963) notes that about half lied about the administered penicillin dose. Alcoholics, drug addicts and overdosers are regarded as natural liars. The manic patient has an established reputation as a potential 'trickster': often sharply perceptive, they 'enjoy' reeking havoc with relationships inside and outside the psychiatric setting. This medical model is again angled to a one-sided morality. Doctors' lies and deceit (withholding information) are not equally bracketed. Placebos are considered a legitimate part of the doctor's armoury against disease.

Once doctors diagnosed that medical errors were patient-induced, then the next step was to seek out factors inhibiting compliance and then devise comprehensive medical regimes – later called Health Belief Models (HBM) – to remove these limitations. These usually relied on altering the situation factors to reduce the 'environmental barriers' (rearranging daily timetables, etc), and giving a heavy input of information on the cause of the disease and the effects of treatment. The premise of the 'rational man', whose life had been restructured by medical enlightenment, led doctors to assume that compliance would logically follow. The HBM had the fallacious assumption that the public operated with the medical definitions of health. HBMs were medical tools for controlling the patient 'at a distance' – the weakness before being that doctors were powerless once the patient left the consultation. HBMs, relying heavily on the work of psychologists, were first used in the USA in the 1950s to predict patients' responses to preventive health campaigns. The problem of non-compliance was an additional interest. Not all HBMs deserve the title of model, many are but crude listings of relevant variables. Calnan's (1984) recent testing of the HBM to predict attendance at screening clinics and breast self-examination classes for the detection of cancer, shows it to be of little value.

As we have seen (Ch. 2), patients were often selected for medical treatment in specialisms of scarce resources on the assumption that their personality and social position would mesh smoothly within the adopted HBM. The predictive expectations were often dashed. The non-compliant patient had re-emerged victorious. Research then focused on the limitations of the model, forcing a realistic exploration of patients' own interpretation of the meanings of their illness. Cummings's (1982) study of non-compliance among dialysis patients illustrates this trend. He found that the patient's level of knowledge was not associated with compliance, except for one aspect of the treatment – the taking of phosphate binding medicine to stop heart attacks. There was little association between family support and compliance. (This was a major criterion for selecting dialysis patients.) The patient only complied with the treatment regime to the degree that his illness was considered disruptive of family life. Younger patients regarded their illness as more troublesome than did older patients. Young patients were often under parental care and more hopeful of being offered a transplant.

There is some recognition of the impossibility of constructing HBMs to accommodate the full range of clients' perceptions and practical reasoning, yet models geared towards a single principle invariably fail. Medicine has encouraged other trends for reducing non-compliance. In lifelong conditions, like diabetes, there has been an amount of 'demedicalisation'. The diabetic is encouraged to take more responsibility, experimenting with diet and insulin level in accordance with his lifestyle. The doctor's role is now more one of evaluator. Errors are now directly attributable to the diabetic's misjudgement, and he must 'try harder' in future. Another trend is building more controls, direct and indirect, into treatment. Taylor (1984) showed that there was a very high (92 per cent) chemotherapy compliance among breast cancer patients, a treatment with severe side effects, like constant nausea. Chemotherapy is potentially life-saving and administered intravenously is seen as a direct medical intervention – all the background factors therefore being conducive for compliance. Taylor argues, however, that the doctor's active monitoring and chasing programme if appointments are broken, and the patient's use of psychological coping techniques – imaging, self-hypnosis, relaxation and faith healing – were still significant. These not only help ameliorate the unpleasant side effects but also allow the patient to buttress the doctor role in jointly managing cancer. The responsibility for failure and error is now *shared*, with an illness of uncertain prognosis. In the USA the strategy of written contracts, formulating the joint responsibilities of doctor and patient in, for example, the treatment of hypertension, is now appearing.

The patient-centred approach to compliance starts with the importance of client biography as a potential multi-strategy response to the doctor and treatment regime. The patient is destigmatised from being deviant, it being recognised that patients have preferences. Ben-Sira (1976) and others have shown that doctors' affective behaviour and genuine interest is strongly related to patients' satisfaction with their skills and treatment. Disabled war veterans judged the advice given on sex handicap from fellow veterans as superior to that given by expert doctors, who have never suffered in the same way.

Conrad's (1985) study of USA epileptics' self-regulation of medication is a detailed exploration of patient rationales. His sample was collected by the snowball, sampling technique, i.e. getting names from advertisements, invitations and others' recommendations: the sample of 80 mainly lower-middle class with an age range from 14 to 54 years, and with 44 women. Epileptics commented that doctors had great difficulty in matching the medication with their particular sequence of 'fits'. Their self-regulation was an attempt to 'round off' doctors' incomplete knowledge. With the use of modern drugs, such as Dilantin, epileptics were no longer confined to colonies. Some states once curtailed their rights of marriage. Restrictions on employment have also been reduced. Epileptics are now widely dispersed within society, so that few knew fellow-epileptics. The decision on self-regulation was therefore an individual one, but patterns did emerge. Self-regulation was performed for 'normalisation', with about 40 per cent using this technique, that is altering the daily dose for at least several weeks and stopping the drug for three consecutive days. Self-regulation operated to remove the drug's side effects, such as rashes, yellow skin, partial impotence and sluggish speech – all social impediments. Others wanted release from drug dependence, to disaffiliate themselves from the unpleasant, pharmaceutical image associated with mental illness and hard drug users. Epileptics would 'top up', as a precaution, on high risk occasions, such as before examinations and tiring journeys. Self-regulation was also used to explore the limits of the disorder, to demystify their disease and to make more complete the body and self. Self regulation mimics the doctor's prescribing habits of 'try it and see', but is more finely tuned to individual needs.

CONCLUSION

Errors in medicine are a general occurrence. The Durkheimian position would regard a certain percentage (if that could be quantified) as 'normal', for without errors we could not be certain what doctors meant by 'good practice'. Errors are deviations from any aspect of the medical process – whether knowledge, techniques or process. Not all deviations can be classified as errors. Their negligent and fallacious properties depend upon competing interpretations of 'reasonable' risk and 'due care' in the face of uncertainties. Professional hegemony has attempted to make itself the final arbiter, very much reducing the patients' and the public's rights in what are essentially questions of universal morality, of defining the self.

The consumer approach of the 'best buy' in the USA provides more possibilities for legal redress. The average doctor pays over £24,000 per annum in insurance premiums: in the UK the figure averages £576. The 1986 premium rose by 70 per cent; the Medical Defence Union anticipates an accelerating rate of litigation. The greater chance of litigation creates the paradox that the doctor is compelled to keep up to date, but also resorts more to defensive, over-medicalised practices – often not in the patients' 'best interest'. British law, heavily distilled from the case of Bolam against Friern Hospital Management Committee (1957), has laid down that medical negligence is very much a question of whether a doctor's performance was in accordance with that accepted by a responsible group of doctors practising in the same speciality. Who constitutes the responsible group (and by definition irresponsible?) was left open. Although the professions acclaim their code of practice, their operating rules are *not* inscribed on tablets of stone. By its response to errors, the dynamics of the profession – its rules in action – are explicated. The earliest models of medical socialisation suggested that its values were formally transmitted from a well-defined medical culture, being socially injected into students. Professional rules are not neatly parcelled to permit that kind of transmission. It is through the involvement in errors and their rectification that combinations of the profession's often contradictory rules become accessible, examinable and learned.

The non-compliant patient is readily blamed for distorting the path of medicine, a major cause of errors. This tack helps to preserve the integrity of medicine's knowledge base. But it is wrong to consider the non-compliant patient as necessarily malicious, or self-destructive. A complex variety of behaviour is contained under that term. Illness, especially long-term and chronic (or ageing) creates a disengagement of the body from the control of the self. The body 'containing' the sickness can appear actively hostile, rebellious and uncontrollable, thereby undermining the self. To impose a sense of order over the illness the patient uses self-regulation of treatment. The doctor directs his treatment towards the generalised, or statistical patient. Patients individualise that baseline.

REFERENCES

Arluke A 1977 Social control rituals in death. In Dingwall (ed) *Health care and health knowledge.* Croom Helm, London

Belmonte M 1981 Problem of cheating in the diabetic child and adolescents. *Diabetes Care* 4: 116–20

Ben-Sira Z 1976 The function of the professional's affective behaviour in client satisfaction: a revised approach to social interaction. *Journal of Health and Social Behaviour* 17: 3–11

Bergman A B, Werner R J 1963 Failure of children to receive penicillin by mouth. *New England Journal of Medicine* 268: 1334–8

Bosk C L 1979 *Managing Medical Failure.* University of Chicago Press

Burke A W 1984 Racism and psychological disturbance among West Indians in Britain. *The International Journal of Social Psychiatry* 30: 50–68

Calnan M 1984 The health belief model and participation in programmes for the early detection of breast cancer: a comparative analysis. *Social Science and Medicine* 19: 823–30

Colby K M, Spar J E 1983 *The Fundamental Crisis in Psychiatry: Unreliability of Diagnosis.* C C Thomas, Illinois

Conrad P 1985 The meaning of medications: another look at compliance. *Social Science and Medicine* 20: 29–37

Cummings K M 1982 Psychological factors affecting adherence to medical regimens in a group of hemodialysis patients. *Medical Care* 20: 567–93

Fox R 1959 *Experiment Perilous: Physicians and Patients Facing the Unknown.* Free Press, Glencoe Illinois

Goldthorp W, Richman J 1976 Maternal attitudes to unanticipated home confinement: a case study of the effects of the hospital strike upon domiciliary confinement. *Practitioner* 171: 843–53

Goldthorp W O, Richman J, Hallam W 1976 The gynaecological patient's knowledge of her illness and treatment. *British Journal of Sexual Medicine* 2: 6–9

Health Service Commissioner 1984-5 Annual Report. Third Report for the Session HMSO, London

Hecht A B 1974 Improving medication compliance by teaching out-patients. *Nursing Forum* 13: 112–29

Heszen-Klemens I, Lapinska E 1984 Doctor–patient interactions, patients' health behaviour and effects of treatment. *Social Science and Medicine* 19: 9–18

Hughes E C 1958 *Men and their Work*. Free Press, Glencoe Illinois

Knafl K, Burkett G 1979 Professional socialisation in a surgical speciality: acquiring medical judgement. *Social Science and Medicine* 9: 391–7

Kuhn T S 1970 *The Structure of Scientific Revolutions*. University of Chicago Press

Ley P, Bradshaw P W, Kincey J A, Atherton T S 1976 Increasing patient satisfaction with communication. *British Journal of Social and Clinical Psychology* 15: 403–13

Light D 1972 Psychiatry and suicide: the management of a mistake. *American Journal of Sociology* 80: 1145–64

Light D 1975 The impact of medical school on future psychiatrists. *American Journal of Psychiatry* 132: 607–10

Littlewood R, Cross S 1980 Ethnic minorities and psychiatric services. *Sociology of Health and Illness* 2: 102–16

Livingston P, Zimet C N 1965 Death anxiety, authoritarian and choice of speciality in medical students. *Journal of Nervous and Mental Disorders* 140: 222–30

Lorber J 1975 Good patients and problem patients: conformity and deviance in a general hospital. *Journal of Health and Social Behaviour* 16: 213–25

Mercer K 1984 Black communities' experience of psychiatric services. *The International Journal of Social Psychiatry* 30: 22–7

Minogue B 1982 Malpractice; problem of universals. *Journal of Medicine and Psychiatry* 7: 239–50

Mizrahi T 1984 Managing medical mistakes: ideology, insularity and accountability among internists-in-training. *Social Science and Medicine* 19: 135–46

Rack P 1982 *Race Culture and Mental Disorder*. Tavistock, London

Rosenhan D L 1973 On being sane in insane places. *Science* 179: 250–8

Rosenthal C J, Marshall V W, Macpherson A S, French S E 1980 *Nurses Patients and Families*. Croom Helm, London

Rosner 1983 The traditionalist Jewish physician and modern biomedical ethical problems. *Journal of Medicine and Philosophy* 8: 225–41

Royal Commission on the NHS 1981 *Report*, HMSO, London

Runnymede Trust Bulletin (1983) *Race and Immigration, Mental Health, Racism.*

Ryan W 1976 *Blaming the Victim*. Vintage, New York

The term 'community' is one of infinite elasticity. For those promoting reform or peddling panaceas for our social, economic and political dilemmas, community has an instant appeal. Its chameleon-like form has been blended with a multitude of competing ideologies. Although most of its recent purveyors take care not to offer detailed descriptions of what a community actually is, their policies are predicated on the understanding that it *does* exist (or can be stimulated into existence) and that it *is* endowed with beneficial qualities involving 'group support'. The term 'group' also presents tortuous, semantic problems; covering all forms of relationships between family and state – many of which have also been designated as communities.

To illustrate from the plethora of uses of community, one increasing trend since the 1950s has been the use of community education; in part promoted by the *Plowden Report* (1967) encouraging parents' participation in the activities of primary schools. This was seen as a means of boosting children's attainments, especially in deprived areas, with early parental support raising ability within institutional schooling. This initiative promoted the Education Priority Areas programme, with compensatory spending concentrated on deprived areas, in the hope of breaking the 'cycle of deprivation' found in such areas.

The Community Development Programmes, very much followed the earlier American experience of injecting aid and 'leadership' into inner-city areas. It was assumed that a stable 'culture of poverty' was congealing, creating fatalistic dependence on the bureaucratic councils. The programmes aimed to activate local self-help activities. It was erroneous though, to transpose the logic of the American culture of poverty thesis. Lewis's thesis (1961) never fitted even the

Mexican and Puerto Rican poor, the source of his studies. The poor do not possess an undifferentiated culture, cocooned from the influences of the wider society – a self-contained 'community'. Neither the local authorities nor the people they hoped to marshall, supported these 'external' spokespeople and the programmes therefore faded. Most urban aid programmes are now channelled via city hall and government.

Community policing is intended to increase the visibility and familiarity of the beat policeman, thereby expecting to reduce crime. The notion of local partnership between police and community is ambiguous. The police interpret it as a strategy for improving their criminal intelligence; but black minorities and others want themselves to control policing policies. Community radio was set up to reflect news of special interest to those within its reception area. However, most of its output, especially music, is national or international. Community newspapers are more successful in giving the majority of space to local news.

Groups with distinctive activities have been accredited with having community attributes, including business, deviant subcultures and gangs. The latter often claim territorial rights (turfs) to parts of the city, as found for example in Chicago, San Francisco, or as described by Patrick (1973) for Glasgow. The scientific community espouses similar fraternal ties with its claim to validate its members achievements.

Health and welfare agencies (like the Church before them) have dominantly rallied round the community emblem. Community Health Councils, formed in 1973 to represent the needs of immediate consumers, have nominated membership, a democratic version not appealing to all. The community label has been tagged to nurses, pyschiatric nurses, doctors, dentists and psychologists, all with differing ties to health institutional frameworks, often determined by political considerations. Community psychiatric nurses largely apply the hospital model merely in a different context, since psychiatrists are reluctant to relinquish professional control. Some practitioners, such as health visitors and district nurses, operated without the community tag, long before its popularity.

We next locate the notion of community within social thought, seeking to disentangle its main strands, which will be matched with the intent of some recent welfare and psychiatric reforms. The promise of Primary Health Care (PHC) in the less developed world will be referenced. Western planners assume that 'natural' communities, such as villages, are the ideal base for health initiatives.

LOSS AND RESURRECTION OF COMMUNITY

All societies have a concept of community, to offer a sense of belonging and personal identity. These versions are usually portrayed by familial characteristics, like mutual support and reciprocity. The Ancient Greeks deliberately limited the size of cities to maintain the 'feeling' of cohesiveness and participatory democracy for their free citizens. Those who threatened its harmony were expelled. Tribal societies, like the Dogon of Sudan, laid out their villages modelled on anatomical principles, symbolising wholeness, sense of order and continuity. All activities – waking, greeting and farming, etc. – were prescribed, to fit their moral order. Medieval towns in Europe were also designed to represent the cultural hegemony of the Church, the font of law. Communion and community had a common ring.

As Nisbet (1967) shows, a major preoccupation in the nineteenth century was for the 'loss' of community. The pessimism was engendered by the impact of the two revolutions – the French and Industrial. The fabric of the old order was shredded by the rise of new classes, by secular philosophies of legitimacy, by mass movement from the land, and by the new capitalist mode of production stressing individual competitiveness and success. As community was embedded in a traditionalism now 'swept away', concern for how the new (and yet unknown) social order could be sustained was a priority of philosophers and sociologists. Comte, who feared the excesses of the French guillotine, argued that the restoration of community was a moral imperative. He was not hankering for a restoration of feudalism and established religion, which he abhorred; as an evolutionist he regarded the most advanced society as being one which is founded on the principles of natural science. Sociology, too, was to be built on those principles and its positivist laws would provide the direction and shape to the emerging pattern of social relations. According to Comte, the new form of community could be engineered, based on a science of morality, to act as a social stabiliser.

Tonnies gave the clearest formulation of the problem in his book *Gemeinschaft and Gesellschaft*, published in 1887 when he was only 32 years old. Following the thesis of his predecessors – that nascent industrial society was floating on different organising principles – he spelt out the characteristics of Gemeinschaft (community) of pre-industrial society and Gesellschaft (association) of the new order. Earlier, Maine, the English lawyer, in his *Ancient Law* (1861), had also elaborated the shift as a movement from kinship and status to an industrial society based on universal values and contract regulated by the state. Gemeinschaft was based on blood (kinship), place (neighbourhood) and mind (friendship). These fostered an intimate cosiness, which encouraged mutual support, stability and agreement, enduring over time. Gesellschaft meant impersonality, change and decisions made on rational calculation of the best bargain struck by individuals. Tonnies was careful not to say that Gemeinschaft features could not be found in industrial society, but believed that they were the exception. He also noted that women expressed more Gemeinschaft values than men. It is interesting to note that today women do carry the load of 'community care', but not because of their Gemeinschaft natures. They have been socially conditioned from birth for household and caring roles.

Others followed the Tonnies' line. Simmel in his *Metropolis and Mental Life* (1903) argued that urban man was different. He was bombarded with so many sensory stimuli that he was forced to fragment his life into separate social spheres for survival. The sense of wholeness epitomised in Gemeinschaft had gone. Relationships were now treated as arithmetical exercises. Many individuals had no sense of belonging and were marginal and outsiders. Durkheim (1893) argued further that the guiding principle for integrating industrial society – a new division of labour – could produce abnormal forms, leading to a lack of integration and anomic suicide – by the sudden dislocation of normative values. In fact all the examples he uses of division of labour in his book of the same title were abnormal. The USA urban sociology tradition extended these arguments: to Wirth (1938), urban society was rootless with high geographical and social mobility. Primary relationships (face to face) had been replaced by secondary (impersonal) ones. The high density of the city precipitated social problems and rising crime rates.

Tonnies accepted that industrial society could recapture the lost spirit of Gemeinschaft; his analysis permitted a form called pseudo-Gemeinschaft. This could be done through state welfare benefits as was occurring at this time in Germany, with Bismarck's Insurance Reforms. Another way was to 'inject' social skills and 'appropriate' moral values into society. It is from these sources that the modern community initiatives have gained momentum. Durkheim posited that work could be the nucleus of new 'occupational communities'. Each would provide a harmonious structure, balancing the demands of state and family. Further, via moral education, a new value consensus would be cemented. The helping and caring professions of today, whose knowledge base is founded in the social sciences, are inheritors of the Durkheimian thrust. With their expert knowledge of human behaviour, they intended to create and sanction new, worthy identities for their clients. Psychiatrists *et al.* resemble a new spiritual vanguard: consultation and counselling is analogous with confession. At one time social workers hoped that their application of Freudianism would be the spur to a new self-awareness in clients and society.

The notion of loss of community was more widely taken up. The Human Relations school of management, owing its inspiration to Mayo (1949), believed that all conflicts, especially industrial, were caused by its disappearance. Democracy by itself could not save society from further disasters, such as the First World War. Our technical skills have outpaced our social skills. In established societies (pre-industial) the guilds had harmonised the two, or so the argument ran. Mayo's solution was to create modern replicas: he believed that man's greatest desire (instinct?) was to be in association with others. Although trade unions could create group solidarity, Mayo disregarded them as being an inferior form of social organisation. Managers were to be entrusted with the creation of work groups, led by 'natural' leaders (supervisors) trained in social skills, who would guide the group towards the 'common goals' (managerial ones). Some firms, with their own housing and other amenities, tied workers more closely into model communities: Owenism was an early nineteenth century precursor.

Political and religious movements have tried to socially engineer entirely new communities, by largely disengaging from society. The kibbutz movement starting in Palestine at Degania in 1909, was based on a reversal of the values of the Jewish ghetto. The latter, Tonnies would have recognised as a perfect Gemeinschaft! Working on the land, not commerce and Talmudic scholarship, had now the highest prestige. Democratic rights for its members, emphasising equality for women, were to be achieved by the abolition of private property and by radically changing the family, separating the responsibility of child-rearing from it. The term 'husband' and 'wife' became 'pair' (in Hebrew 'zug'). It is difficult to maintain the ideological purity of alternative communities, geared to the creation of a new vision of humanity. Sharp conflicts emerge. The young, educated in the original values of kibbutz life, clashed with the older generation wanting an easier life with some private consumer goods. Women never achieved equality, for the prestigious manual work was allocated to men. They found themselves in the communal laundry, washing for all the men in the kibbutz. A managerial elite appeared, when the kibbutz profitably entered into the competitive product market.

Therapeutic communities, of which there are many forms (some residential, some hospital-based, etc.), are similarly attached to ideological cornerstones of communal life. They are also strained by juggling democratic decision making with the maintenance of their founding principles. By restricting their intakes to certain categories – usually age, type of mental illness and social origins – they have attempted to maintain the 'faith'. It is difficult to insulate alternative communities from external change.

In the 1950s sociologists researching the urban jungle discovered that the traditional working class still had 'pristine' communities. Willmott and Young's discovery in Bethnal Green, for example, recharged the community myth. Extended kinship, mutual support, open door dropping-in, sons following fathers into the same jobs, were exalted. The other side of Gemeinschaft was not emphasised: family feuds, violence and the dominance of mum's advice, delaying daughters seeking antenatal care. American studies of ethnic groups, especially blacks, also sustained the image held by professionals that the disadvantaged were ideal targets for community initiatives. The current view from the other side of inner cities, where the old and infirm are barricaded behind doors with multiple locks, has done little to dint the enthusiasm of community decanters.

Summarising, community is capable of multiple interpretations. This ambiguity sustains its application by powerful interests. Hillery (1955) has collected 94 definitions; all they had in common was some agreement that it involved people! Stacey (1969) argued that it was no longer a useful abstraction and suggested that 'societal subsystem' may be a more profitable substitute. Some recent subscribers to community treatment avoid all definition. Community is something 'out there'. Shepherd (1979) considered community psychiatry as the best possible clinical care given in communities and their institutions 'outside' total institutions such as asylums. Again, Hunt (1985), senior medical officer at the DHSS, sees community care as the 'alternative' to long term institutional care for the chronically sick, etc. Contrastingly, one official faction within social work, represented in the *Barclay Report* (1982), still subscribes to the romantic, conservative version of community functioning in holistic harmony. The social worker's role then, is to tap and focus the existing human resources, layered as informal, caring networks of friendship and common interest, operating within geographical proximity. A picture replicating the one found in the earlier *Seebohm Report* (1968).

The obverse of community is infrequently held up for inspection. Community carried to extreme can incite a narrow parochialism; detracting from an understanding of the wider, societal power structures, which actually sets the agenda for so much carried on in the name of community. The success for one community's endeavours in lobbying resources, or in thwarting the design of planners (e.g. for new motorways), is at the expense of others. By underplaying the existence of intra-community conflicts, a crude analysis of community dynamics is offered. It is often through conflict that residents come to recognise common interests. Disagreement and support gathering, generate a vitality and interpretation of the community's values. The spirit of Gemeinschaft involves the full disclosure of feelings, although not all would be comfortable living continuously with total exposure and continuous intimacy. Having the capacity to move offstage, and into privacy, provides practical alternatives for living.

Altruism can exist without community. Psychologists claim evidence for an 'altruistic personality', with a high level of moral commitment. Pensioners, who themselves are in need, give very generously to charity. Over 5 per cent of consumer expenditure is on gifts for others. The success of Live Aid illustrates the hidden reservoir of altruism.

COMMUNITY ORIENTATION

Many factors have clustered around the community direction. There is the crisis of capitalism, built around the suggestion that high economic growth is no longer possible. Former health and welfare commitments, based on large-scale institutional care, are becoming too costly as we move towards a zero growth economy. The former arguments in favour of size, efficiency and economy of scale are now largely discarded. The last fling was the 1974 NHS reorganisation, when the large hospital (following the industrial model) with 'clear' lines of authority, was thought to be the way of improving staff communication, morale and patient care. The new managerialism, with administrative career opportunities for nurses, was also a design principle. Treatment outside (within the community) is now considered 'cheaper'. Future health cuts directed at community services will have less public impact than those which close or partially close a 'visible' hospital, with vociferous pickets at the gate.

The Schumacher message of 'small is beautiful' of the 1960s has gradually influenced political thinking of both right and left. The humanitarian and organisational benefits of 'small' could be translated into small 'institutional size' and 'community'. The impersonality of large organisations came to be recognised in poor industrial relations and high labour turnover, not only in factories but also in the NHS.

Anti-state centralism and anti-authoritarianism became embodied in the community shift. Community also came to represent a more meaningful participatory democracy – clients influencing the flow of services.

Psychiatric hospitals felt the first impact of the new community shift. The effects of long-stay incarceration were shown to have transformed these hospitals into expensive, human warehouses. Barton (1958) published his *Institutional Neurosis*, describing how patients became pathologically adapted to the hospital routines, which unfitted them for normal life. Goffman's (1961) rich ethnographic account of life in a closed institution showed, again, how the notion of effective treatment was a misnomer. Patients had to develop their own inmate culture (secondary elaboration of organisation structure) for survival. Before release, they were forced to follow the career of the typical psychiatric patient constructed by the staff: to deny this imposed diagnosis was proof of their mental illness. Closed institutions came to be known as processing plants (even 'snake pits', as portrayed in the film of that title) for stripping identities. Some USA state hospitals held over 12,000 patients. The anti-institutional mood, especially in the United States, was fuelled by the civil rights movements for minorities. The mentally ill fitted the scene as a 'depressed' minority with few rights. Inquiries into hospital scandals of mistreatment intensified the community fire. The Ely Hospital Enquiry of 1969 examined allegations of staff mistreatment and the pilfering of property from patients, 75 per cent of whom were subnormal or severely subnormal. Senior nursing staff were more concerned with upholding the *status quo*, than with letting junior staff ameliorate conditions on the ward. It is now government policy to build small or medium-sized units of no more than 100–200 beds for the mentally handicapped. Existing hospitals of over 500 beds are not to be expanded.

Demographic-medical trends also provided compelling rationales for community care. The increase in the aged has been accelerating. Between 1901 and 1981 the number aged over 65 years rose from 1.7 million to over 8 million. Crucially, for the purposes of care, the numbers aged 85 and over are estimated to rise from 620,000 in 1983 to one million in 1995. One in ten pensioners are likely to be incapacitated by Alzheimer's disease. Extrapolations also indicate that 20 per cent of the UK population suffer from undiagnosed 'psychiatric disorders' needing treatment. In their report to the Joint Commission on Mental Illness and Health, Plunkett and Gordon (1960) made an earlier claim for the USA, after reviewing 11 community studies probing this instance. The Midtown Manhattan (New York) study found that 80 per cent of its sample contained some instance of psychiatric symptoms. Institutional stay for these two groups alone, the infirmed elderly and psychiatric patients, would have emptied present health budgets, and more.

One of the preconditions for community emphasis came with the 'pharmacological revolution'. Chemical control, at a distance, of psychiatric patients was made possible when largactil was first synthesised in France in 1950 by Rhone Poulenc. However some countries, Germany and Spain, with engrained hospital regimes, actually increased their psychiatric intakes until 1975. Some professionals dramatically changed their treatment philosophies. Rehabilitation and integration became the new goals. The Education (Handicapped Children) Act, 1970, decreed that all mentally handicapped children had the right to education within LEA schools in England and Wales. The Jay Report (1979) stressed that those professions caring for the mentally handicapped should adopt a social work perspective, a shift from the nursing care model. Sweden had set the example with realistic attempts at reshaping the community to their needs. Rehabilitation for the elderly was also measured by their sustenation in the community; this often meant home confinement.

COMMUNITY AND HELPERS

There are no government, national reviews to test the success of 'community support'. We are left with an assortment of case studies, all indicating common themes, for example, that care is primarily a close family matter, and a major burden falls on women. The supported members resemble 'social detritus', or, following Spitzer (1975) 'social junk', usually being politically powerless to influence improvement-decisions. Being unproductive, they are an economic burden on society. They (and often their helpers) become members of a heterogenous welfare-benefit culture, kept isolated from related dependent groups, with different disabilities, by the specialisation of the caring professions, whose fragmentation emphasises one set of needs and not another. The physical retreat to the house (often a room), immobility, and the hostility of public places (lack of ramps, bans on wheelchairs on 'safety' grounds, stigmatisation of those with spoiled identities and residents' campaigns opposing the location of proposed community residences) – all contribute to isolation and invisibility. The final theme becomes one in which the helpers themselves are badly in need of support.

Pressure groups do act on their behalf, and some do have success. The United Neighbours Group in Action, in California, the home of minority rights, has had major successes on behalf of the aged. Using militant, consumer tactics formulated by Ralph Nader. Their target, in this instance was the rapacious nursing homes. Mencap, in the UK, has used sophisticated publicity to advance the cause of the mentally handicapped.

To detail the above points. Jones and Vetter's (1984) study of those who care for the elderly (they interviewed the informal carers of 256 dependent elderly) showed that two-thirds were spouses and daughters, and 10 per cent of the carers were not related. Over three-quarters of the carers were women, and two-thirds of the carers lived with their elderly. The household chores and personal assistance to the elderly became the major responsibility of the carers. Shopping was the only significant activity that the carers shared with others, and was apparent that there was no large network of community helpers rushing to volunteer assistance to the aged. When a carer makes an elderly person her responsibility (especially by sharing the same household), potential help from other kin diminishes, further isolating the carer and the dependant. Other studies have shown that over one-third of the carers have reduced their external socialising. However, here, only 11 per cent admitted that caring for their elderly dependants affected the frequency of contact with friends. We are not told the range of friends each carer had. It is possible that those with few friends tend to take on a caring responsibility. Nearly one-fifth of the carers admitted to being under 'considerable' stress. Women use, especially, friends of the same sex as confidants for sharing secrets and for releasing emotional burdens. Reducing this outlet is the carer's main regret.

Charlesworth and others (1984) set out to compare the coping strategies of male and female carers. Not claiming representativeness for their sample of 255 elderly (all of whom had been referred to specialist services), they interviewed 157 informal carers. Again, the bulk of the care was provided by the immediate family. There was a tendency for sons to care for fathers, while daughters were more likely to share the household of the dependant. Charlesworth's study reemphasised that carers of the elderly are themselves in mid-years: over 40 per cent were over 60 years of age, and many had their own personal health problems. The categories of carer and dependant are therefore not always discrete. Male carers tended to have more agency support, receiving, for example, assistance from home helps and meals on wheels. Male carers also had longer breaks from their dependants, who were received into long-stay units. Women carers tended to have day care or short-stay care for their dependants. Women carers also received assistance at a later stage than their male counterparts, often at a point when they could no longer cope.

The researchers were careful to admit that the differential support given to carers was not part of a deliberate, discriminatory policy. But sex stereotyping was an important factor. Women are conceptualised as 'instinctive' carers, their apprenticeship in housework readily equipping them for the future household management of the elderly. The common imagery of the dependent elderly is one of regression to infantilism. (The mentally handicapped are often considered too as inhabiting a permanent childhood.) Caring daughters are therefore treated as though they were renewing their motherly functions of child rearing. As a parallel point, the *Finer Report* on one-parent families (1975) adopted a similar posture and regarding fathering as a flawed role, the assumed qualities of male instrumentalism being inadequate for recognising and caring for the needs of small children. It advocated a concentration of service support on the lone father, to enable him to continue his employment.

Mental handicap was the subject of the most clearly formulated policy for any disadvantaged group. *In Better Services for the Mentally Handicapped* (1971), the government set precise objectives over a 20-year period. The Labour government set up the National Development Group, with outside experts to monitor progress and recommend changes for improvement. The Group was disbanded in 1980. The exact number of mentally handicapped is not known. There are different classifications: 'intelligent quotient' is the usual discriminator. Below a score of 50 is 'severe'; 50–70 is 'mild'. The long-stay hospital clients were to be reduced. Those remaining were to be accommodated in settings resembling 'homely conditions'. There was to be a move from large hospitals to smaller units, emphasising treatment rather than permanent residential care. The dominant impetus was to change the responsibility for care from the NHS to local authorities. The health authorities also transferred money along with those clients now placed under the local authorities, to be used not just for support services but also for the cost of housing and education.

How successful is this 'systematic' community initiative? If the crude criteria of reduced, hospital residential-stay are used, there has been some 'success'. However Wistow (1985) shows, this is a paper victory. Patient death rates were mainly responsible for reduced hospital residential stay rather than an actively managed policy of rehabilitation and discharge. Too many hospital-based careers were at stake, inhibiting full implementation. In 1981, 75 per cent of the budget designated for the mentally handicapped went to hospitals, yet they looked after only 30 per cent of clients.

The Development Team overviewing progress for the mentally handicapped has produced numerous reports criticising the bad co-operation between health authorities and the social services. One report (1982) singled out Kent. Ayer (1984) is pessimistic about the community response from social workers. He researched North Humberside, interviewing 132 mothers whose children, between 3 and 17 years old, were attending special schools. All acknowledged that home was the best place for their children, but the support needed from social workers was deficient. Ayer comments that being mentally handicapped was allocated low prestige in the post Seebohm reorganisation, not being easily located within the social work ideology. There was confusion whether it was generic, family therapy, or specialist, etc. With the children in schools, it was considered that the major needs of the family had been satisfied. Seventy-five per cent of the mothers found both social workers and health visitors unhelpful. Almost half had a poor opinion of their family doctor – another lynchpin of community care. There was complete recognition that schoolteachers were the most supportive.

Wilkin (1979) pointed to the undemocratic pattern of domestic labour. (Ayer admitted that he only talked to mothers, because they are the major prop of everyday care.) Fathers limited themselves to few tasks, mainly lifting the child or 'babysitting'. They were not primarily responsible for toileting, dressing and, in particular, changing nappies. (Some mentally handicapped can be permanently incontinent.) Men tended to avoid this 'polluting' activity involving human excreta, thereby doubly stigmatising the women's caring roles. It is not clear how this separation originated. Societies have historically imposed taboos on women for being polluting at birth and menstruation. Their 'transitional' status at these times threatened the well-defined, patriarchially dominated social structure. How their renewed candidature for polluting work permeated the modern household is by no means clear.

PSICHIATRIA DEMOCRATICA

In 1978 Italy enacted the most extreme reform of mental health. It dismantled the bulk of its psychiatric institutions, rather than initiate a policy of gradual phasing out – the style of the USA and the UK. In

1961 Italy had 113,000 in-patients; by 1983 this had fallen to 30,000. The 1963 Kennedy Act setting up Community Mental Health Centres (CMHC) and the UK 1959 Mental Health Act (later strengthened by Keith Joseph's December, 1971 Memorandum specifying that all mental hospitals were to close down in 15 years), urging community care, had produced lamentable results. The effects were hidden by the lack of a comprehensive social accounting of dischargees. The discharge policy became known as the 'revolving door' policy – discharge followed by re-admission. One study in the early 1970s showed that 30 per cent of discharged schizophrenics did nothing in the daytime. In a follow-up study of New Haven, Mollica and Redlich (1980) examined the treatment in 1975 of those patients who would have been either prime candidates for the state hospital, or would have been 'missed' by the system. There was clear class bias in 'community treatment'. These low-status patients received treatment from semi- and non-professional clinicians, as hospital in-patients or as out-patients at community units. Psychiatrists more frequently encountered middle-class patients.

The movement for Italian reform was called psichiatria democratica (PD). It included psychiatrists, sociologists, nurses and socialist politicians. Their enemy was 'establishment psychiatry'. Famous anti-psychiatry figures formed the vanguard: Foucault, Laing, Goffman and Szasz had all published sharp, if not vitriolic attacks. Szasz in his *Myth of Mental Illness* (1974) argued that 'mental illness' was a legal and moral question, and not a medical prerogative. Psychiatrists were clearly violating their oath to do the patient no harm. The Italian contingent of PD – Basaglia, Thomasini and Jervis – had previously tested some of their radical ideas in small-scale experiments. PD was determined not to replicate the errors of capitalist reforms.

PD was most influential in Northern Italy, with its communist and socialist regional governments. The group made lengthy preparations prior to the 1978 Mental Health Act. Mass media publicity, public meetings and conversion 'teach-ins' were held with those likely to be affected. The existing staff were guaranteed a policy of no redundancy or change of salary, when the institutions closed. The wards were thrown open to the general public; inmates were taken to local events, as part of a programme of mutual familiarity. Attempts were made to find guaranteed employment for the future ex-residents. One plan was the forming of work co-operatives, engaging in sub-contracting. The co-operatives would also be a model for learning and practising life skills. There were plans for sub-dividing the hospital property into flats for the aged and the most handicapped. For those unable to work,

PD was promised that they would receive small, personal allowances to encourage their independence.

PD did not adopt the naive view that a change of cultural environment would solve all problems. While decrying institutional care, it accepted the need for drug therapy, and to a lesser degree, counselling. Electro-convulsive treatment and psychosurgery were forbidden, as medieval vestiges. The community centres catering for ex-patients were de-professionalised. They had no staff rooms, not even for the director. Psychiatrists did keep, however, the right to write prescriptions. The new clients could drop in at will; they were not obliged to present themselves to the staff. At the centres decisions were made collectively. A few centres kept a small number of residential beds: staff and clients there had daily meetings.

How the success of the scheme is assessed is very much a matter of ideology. PD resembled a political movement. One major critic, Jones (1985), has shattered the optimistic image, largely reflected from the Trieste area, where real endeavour went into the reforms. Elsewhere many ex-patients are sleeping rough and fed on charity, lacking assistance and treatment. As there had been no psychiatric training for nurses since 1975, their competence is suspect. The deskilling of doctors has lowered morale. Increased dosages of drugs are regularly used. The pattern of care rarely fits the model laid down in the Act. Many CMHC are grubby and chaotically organised. Elsewhere patients queue up for treatment at the out-patients of general hospitals. The south of Italy has largely escaped the Act. The Church there is powerfully entrenched, running most mental institutions under the guise of hospices. Locked wards and patient restraint are still used. To avoid the Act, patients, by change of nomenclature, have now become 'guests'! Admission of new patients to mental institutions was forbidden. One unintended consequence of the PD reform has been the growth of psychoanalysis. The latter was not defined as a treatment regime: Marxists regard it as 'intellectual mysticism'. As with other community reforms, women members of households have shouldered the burden.

Defenders of the reforms, like Ramon (1983), argue that these are still in a transitional phase. PD was weakened by the untimely deaths of Goffman, Foucault and Basaglia; Basaglia was very much its charismatic leader. To routinise the 'succession crisis' a more unwieldy bureaucratic, national committee was devised. There was a loss of reforming momentum. The common problem, lack of resources, was present too in Italy. The ideologically charged coping-network of community rarely materialised. Although the family tradition is strong in Italy, most did not welcome the return of their relatives, having severed their ties with them. By and large there has been no national evaluation of the scheme. Those arguing for its success claim that the suicide rate has not increased.

Without following the Italian path, there is the tendency in England and the USA for CMHCs to become more politically infused. Political activism is the practical means for extracting resources: needs and social justice are then a matter for negotiation. When CMHCs in the United States are zoned, it is inevitable that they will reflect the prevailing ethnic and class interests. As emotional crises increasingly involve questions of ethnic identity, it follows that the mental health issues cannot be treated in a social vacuum.

Black CMHCs are diverging in treatment philosophies from white, with their emphasis on racism as the prime cause of mental illness and with their demands for black cultural and economic development. Jones (1985) has advised against following the American experience. She claims that the goals of the CMHCs have been too diffuse, by attempting to solve the manifestations of inequality. The growing movement of transcultural psychiatry would argue differently. Mental illness and social context cannot be artificially separated.

SOCIAL NETWORKS

The study of social networks has been used to make less opaque the concept of community. Networks are the mapping out of the linkages between people and institutions. Networks can be classified in different ways. They can be described by their shape: being 'open', and expansive to admit others; being dense, clustering tightly around a few members, etc. Networks are also transmitters of services, goods and ideas, and can therefore be classified by the processes of interaction. Some are 'totalistic', as found in closed religious orders; others are for a specific purpose. The housebound aged may use a child only for running errands.

Boissevain (1974) has classified networks in terms of zones and degrees of personal intimacy. The first is the personal zone of the immediate family, with regular contacts; the second is the intimate zone of friends. The third is the effective zone of friends and relatives, seen infrequently, but which can be activated by, for example, health crises, or by moving to be in closer proximity, as when elderly parents buy a house near one of their children. The fourth zone is also effective, which includes non-related but strategically important people, like doctors. The fifth zone is the nominal zone, including those known by hearsay, or only fleetingly. The local MP and representatives of agencies would be candidates. If specialised help was needed, these sources would be tapped, sometimes via an intermediary whose social network presently includes these. Those in need often hook on to representatives of the social services by following the informal instructions of existing clients, known reciprocally from, for example, their intimate zone.

Networks have many practical and academic uses. It is through social networks that individuals have their identity sustained, or changed. Networks also have predictive value. Bott (1957) one of the early users, deploying the anthropological method of tracing kinship links, showed that couples who had separate networks were also likely to have segregated conjugal roles within the household, as exemplified by the traditional working class. By focusing on the kaleidoscopic potential of social networks, it was expected that a more meaningful construct of community would emerge. Reviewing social networks and their dynamics immediately played down locality and cultural homogeneity as the fundamental bases of community. The latter track had driven the concept of community into an idealistic bolt-hole. Urbanisation and industrialisation did not destroy communities; they exist in multiple forms, depending largely on how people made *use* of their locality. Within sociology itself network analysis was originally hailed as the methodological tool which would bridge the opposition between macro sociology, which concentrates on social structures, and micro-sociology, which elaborates participants' subjective interpretations of their own reality. Network analysis also encouraged the application of mathematical sociology, applying numeration to the frequency and direction of interaction, and treating the exercise as graph theory.

There are many studies illustrating the relationship between networks and illness behaviour. Suchman (1974) discovered that over 70 per cent of people discussed their symptoms with others before seeking professional, medical assistance. Those social networks, with friends predominating, accelerate the seeking of medical care. Networks therefore modify the perception of the seriousness, or not, of symptoms. Those abruptly removed from close kin networks succumb more easily to stress-related disease. The Japanese who migrated to California have a higher rate of coronary heart disease than those who migrated to Hawaii. The key variable is that those in the USA have a less connected network to insulate them from the faster pace of life. The more rapid rates of rehabilitation from alcoholism, severe burns, and dismemberment have all been correlated with close networks – for the assurance and approval of the patient's new identity.

Pattison and Hurd (1984) have shown how different psychiatric disorders are matched with variations in networks. These were classified according to the Pattison Psychosocial Inventory, using measures of emotional intensity, contact, reciprocity and instrumental base. The latter refers to others being positively valued for themselves, but who also supply assistance when needed. There is little value in treating an individual in ignorance of his network characteristics. The network of a 'normal person' has a total of 25-30 persons, with subgroups of family, friends, relatives, neighbours and work associates: each accounting for five or six members. Reciprocity and instrumental help are symmetrical, with positive emotional support, being stress-reducing. The 'neurotic-type' network is smaller, with about fifteen, with fewer relatives and friends. This network frequently supplies negative emotional responses, conducive of isolation and asymmetry in relationships. The neurotic is given little corrective feedback, so that stress tends to spiral. The 'psychotic-type' network is smaller still, 10 to 12 people all locked in an emotionally charged closed system, generating perpetual anxiety, with the transmission of conflicting communications.

There are, of course, well known criticisms of network analysis. The first is apparent from Pattison's classification: do psychotics become psychotic *then* gravitate to psychotic networks? Or do they become psychotic because they are in a psychotic network? If the former, the 'pre-psychotic' network is then the most significant. Although networks claim to explain process, most of the studies are 'static' and of a functionalist type. There is also the question of the impingment of the 'invisible network': that is, the one not physically mapped out by the researcher. Respondents do locate their activities to 'significant others', which may not be apparent. The term 'friend' is a troublesome one to operationalise, with a long listing of different characteristics. Nevertheless social networks have allowed some useful entrées into the community labyrinth.

PRIMARY HEALTH CARE AND COMMUNITY IN THE LESS DEVELOPED WORLD

Primary health care has been signposted as the major way forward for immediately improving the health of those in the less developed world. These countries still have a large rural base although it is reducing under the impact of urbanisation, and are deemed ideal candidates for community-based health schemes. It is assumed, especially by western planners, that villages will be the 'natural' springboards for rapid self-health initiatives. The Alma Ata declaration of WHO at Geneva 1978, set a target of providing a basic health service for all by the year 2000. Primary health care (PHC) also expressed the democratic way with community partnership. The enterprise was assumed to be more effective when communities largely decided their own goals and provided collective labour for hygiene measures, such as latrine digging and securing a safe water supply, which would symbolise villagers' unity and pride, encouraging further progress.

PHC contained two ambiguous meanings. It was intended to be the first health care people came across when sick; and also to identify a comprehensive health delivery process. The planners ignored at first the fact that these societies often had flourishing traditional healers, whose remedies had already been consumer tested. They could in any case only be totalistic if the government allocated the necessary resources to furbish the health centres with equipment and staff for handling medical emergencies. The fate of community care has been mixed, being more successful in socialist states, like China, where there is effective political planning. PHC is the first stage of the medical referral system, the whole mirroring the political echelons of local and regional government. Peasants have high status, the Chinese revolution (unlike the USSR) being peasant inspired. Thus heavy health investment has been placed in the rural PHC communes, but towns still remain advantaged.

PHC had generally fared badly in Africa. Villages are not always meaningful entities, often being the creation of colonialism. Pastoralists and some agriculturalists lived in dispersed, shifting hamlets. The Kikuyu and Thonga, for example, originally did not live in villages. Africans were often forced into villages for administrative convenience. The British could then enforce a poll tax on the head of each household. Those who could not pay were forced to enter the market economy, initially road-building, later plantations and mines. In many villages, sub-lineages are the important structures of self-help. Villages are often fragmented units, riven with land and marriage payment disputes; Indian villages are sharply divided on caste lines, with the Harijan (untouchables) often denied access to wells, despite the Indian constitution forbidding caste discrimination. Tanzania has continued the policy of forcing peasants into large, rural units for PHC. Peasants often object, because they have longer distances to their fields.

Geest's (1982) explanation for the secondary importance of PHC in

Cameroon has general application. Former colonial countries are left with urban elites (often western educated), who dedicate less resources to rural areas. They inherited large urban hospitals, practising cosmopolitan medicine, which consume a large part of the health budget. In Cameroon in 1980 only 18 per cent of the budget for drugs went to the rural areas, even though, the towns contain only a quarter of the population. Even this figure is probably an overestimation, as the census is often rigged in favour of the urban areas. Again, only 7 per cent of the cost of administration was spent in the countryside. The government will not give full support to PHC, as democratic participation at the village level may prompt wider demands for regional autonomy.

Health workers sent to initiate PHC can be badly trained, with little commitment, sometimes being reluctant conscripts who would prefer careers in urban centres. As strangers, with no village affinity, they are often unable to rally traditional support. Lacking adequate funds and with a shortage of medicine, health workers would be unable to use health care as a 'reward' for village labour, which is a major disadvantage since villagers will participate if they can see some immediate, tangible effects of PHC. When PHC schemes are directly sponsored by foreign aid they are especially vulnerable, since this maybe switched as a matter of political expedience.

In the mid-1970s Nigeria planned a fully integrated health service. The country was to be divided into health units, each of 150,000 people. These were to be interlaced with 20 health clinics (village-based), 4 primary health centres and 1 comprehensive health centre (CHC). The CHC was not only to receive referrals, but was also to provide back-up for PHC. The administrative bureaucracy proliferated. In 1976 the Implementation Agency was set up, with six different sub-committees; each rapidly spawned its own sub-committees. For example, the strategic committee, which was to specify the steps for initiating the health plan, set up six sub-committees: for records, logistics (planning), training materials, health manpower (for costing effectiveness of service and manpower projections), community health organisation and management training. All the planning was done at the Ministry of Health at Lagos. The Implementation Agency, responsible for translating the national scheme into action, was given no financial control over the programme's expenditure. The rudimentary essentials of PHC were ignored: community support was not widely canvassed. Improving the infrastructure of rural transport and the cleaning up of polluted water supplies was neglected. The politicians rode on the back of the health proposals, making extravagant promises that the federal government would pay compensation for the land used for health buildings. Some were paid, others not! Each of the Nigerian states demanded modifications to the plan, to suit their own 'real' needs. The Hausa and Fulani of the Islamic north did not favour a family planning emphasis, fearing its effects on the patriarchal structure.

The Nigerian experience was an example of a heavily administered drawing-board exercise, a case of the urban planners knowing best. If the national scheme had taken off, further errors would have been compounded, such as the installation of health managers in posts, while still undergoing the necessary training to do the job! Nigerian optimism was based on the continuous high price of its oil exports within the newly formed OPEC agreement. The health budgets of all less-developed countries are vulnerable to dramatic changes in the price of their primary export (raw materials) on the world market, where the developed world usually has the price advantage. These fluctuations have had an adverse effect on the success of PHC.

Geest has even argued that corruption can be a more effective means of health distribution to rural communities, avoiding the excesses of centralist planners who fail to deliver PHC. Rural communities often run out of state allocated drugs, or receive those which have now become obsolete. In contrast, urban health workers can receive 'benefits' from western-based pharmaceutical drug companies for favoured purchases. Few less-developed countries have accepted WHO advice to selectively purchase 200 essential drugs. Kenya once purchased a ten-year supply of a drug, which had a two-year expiry! Urban health workers often return to their villages with gifts of medicine, stolen from their clinics. Geest argues that these personnel should be allowed to purchase drugs at the wholesale price, thereby encouraging private medical entrepreneurship in rural communities.

Another way forward for PHC is to harmonise the mechanistic structure of state bureaucracy with traditionalism. The latter is flexible and adaptable, and can be a vehicle for health improvement. But medical elites often regard tribal healers as 'primitives'. MacCormack (1981) has argued that traditional practitioners should play a legitimate part in PHC. The WHO has suggested that they form their own association to supervise standards, modelling themselves on the professions. This is possible in India, where Ayurvedic medicine is long established, with its own medical schools and certification. Elsewhere, others, like spirit mediums, owe their competence to the fact that they once cured themselves from a serious illness. It is rare for them to sanction fellow healers, and they are too widely dispersed to monitor each other, even if they so wished. Their legitimacy stems from consumer validation. Traditional healers do not wish to be incorporated into government schemes as low-ranking health workers. They earn more money from their own practices, regarding many of their health methods as superior, especially in the psychiatric field. There have been examples of a good working relationships between the two health belief systems, e.g. at the Fann Psychiatric Hospital in Dakar. Although African traditional medicine reaches 80 per cent of the population, it is mainly disapproved of by the state schemes, whose health workers do not wish to see their professionalism undermined. Traditional healers, however, are continuously enhancing their skills by extracting from cosmopolitan medicine that which they regard as beneficial.

CONCLUSION

After the nineteenth century fears that community had been lost, it is now evoked as the major solution for our ills. The multiple imagery of community is more powerful than its substance. Although confusion reigns as to what its characteristics are, the ambiguity allows others to read what they will into it. One confusion is whether 'community care' means care in the community, care by the community or care for the community. The spectre of community raises a strange paradox. Those who decry the diminishing influence of the family go on to endow community with exaggerated familial characteristics – of automatic support and ever-charged coping networks.

Community is now the convenient antidote against remote state control, professional dominance and the alienating large institutions, etc. Local participation and 'freedom' are expected to shift mountains. But 'community' is not ideologically free, whether in the developed or the third world. Its parameters for action are set elsewhere. In the health field professionalism may have discarded its hospital white coat, but not its gatekeeping and resource allocation functions. Control is more disguised. In the less developed world PHC at the community level can vary between being coercive, with enforced programmes, or supportive, with genuine attempts at long-term health co-operation originating from the local level.

REFERENCES

Ayer S 1984 Community care: failure of professionals to meet family needs. *Child: Care Health and Development* 10: 127–40

Barclay Report 1982 *Social Workers: Their Roles and Tasks*. National Institute for Social Work

Boissevain J 1974 *Friends of Friends, Networks, Manipulators and Coalitions*. Blackwell, Oxford

Bott E 1957 *Family and Social Network*. Tavistock, London

Barton R 1958 *Institutional Neurosis*. Williams and Williams, Baltimore

Charlesworth A, Wilkin D, Durie A 1984 *Carers and Services: A Comparison of Men and Women Caring for Dependent Elderly People*. Equal Opportunities Commission

Durkheim E 1956 *Division of Labour in Society*. Free Press, Glencoe, Illinois

Finer Report 1975 *Report of the Committee on One-parent Families* (2 vols) HMSO, London

Geest S V D 1982 Secondary importance of primary health care in S Cameroon. *Culture Medicine and Psychiatry* **6**: 366–83

Goffman E 1961 *Asylums*. Doubleday, New York

Hillery G A 1955 Definitions of Community: areas of agreement. *Rural Sociology* **20**: 111–23

Hunt C B 1985 Implementation of policies for community care – the DHSS contribution. *Health Trends* **19**: 4–6

Jones D A, Vetter N J 1984 A survey of those who care for the elderly at home: their problems and their needs. *Social Science and Medicine* **19**: 511–14

Jones K 1985 Lessons from Italy, the USA and York in McAusland (ed) *Planning and monitoring community mental health centres*. Kings Fund, London

Lewis O 1961 *Children of Sanchez*. Random, New York

MacCormack C P 1981 Health care and the concept of legitimacy. *Social Science and Medicine* **15**: 423–8

Maine H S 1861 *Ancient Law*. Murray, London

Mayo E 1949 *Social Problems of an Industrial Civilisation*. Routledge & Kegan Paul, London

Mollica R F, Redlich F 1980 Equity and changing patient characteristics. *Archives of General Psychiatry* **37**: 1257–63

Nisbet R 1967 *The Sociological Tradition*. Heinemann, London

Patrick J 1973 *Glasgow Gang Observed*. Eyre Methuen, London

Pattison E M, Hurd G S 1984 The Social network paradigm as a basis for social intervention. In O'Connor W A, Lubin B (eds), *Ecological approaches to community and clinical psychology*. Wiley, New York

Plowden Report 1967 *Children and their Primary Schools, A Report of the Central Advisory Council for Education, England* (2 vols) HMSO, London

Plunkett R, Gordon J E 1960 *Epidemiology and Mental Illness*. Basic Books, New York

Ramon S 1983 Reforming psychiatry, lessons from Italy. *Medicine in Society* **10**: 39–44

Seebohm G F 1968 *Report of the Committee on Local Authority and Allied Personal Social Services*. HMSO, London

Shepherd M 1979 in foreword Goldberg D, Huxley P *Mental Illness in the Community. The Pathway to Psychiatric Care*. Tavistock, London

Simmel G 1950 in K Wolf (ed) *The sociology of G Simmel*. Free Press, Glencoe Illinois

Spitzer S 1975 Towards a Marxian theory of deviance. *Social Problems* **2**: 638-51

Stacey M 1969 The myth of community studies. *British Journal of Sociology* **20**: 134-47

Suchman E A 1974 Sociomedical variations among ethnic groups. *American Journal of Sociology* **70**: 319-31

Szasz T 1974 *The Myth of Mental Illness*. Harper and Row, New York

Tonnies F 1957 *Community and Society*. Harper Row, New York

Wilkin D 1979 *Caring for the Mentally Handicapped Child*. Croom Helm, London

Wirth L 1938 Urbanism as a way of life. *American Journal of Sociology* **44**: 1–24

Wistow G 1985 Community Care for the mentally handicapped: disappointing progress. In *Health Care UK, an economic, social and policy audit*. CIPFA

Chapter nine

ALTERNATIVE MEDICINE

The title is a misnomer. Other names used to express this pot-pourri of medical activities are equally inadequate: 'marginal', 'quasi-marginal', 'fringe', 'quack', 'holistic' and 'traditional'. A recent addition, 'complementary medicine', is in vogue, indicating that it is not in opposition to established medicine, but only seeking 'partnership'. We shall keep the label 'alternative medicine', as a convenience. Accepting the World Health Organisation's crude description, this refers to those forms of health care usually outside the 'official' health service. The latter is inevitably cosmopolitan medicine, which has the power to define and designate what it considers beyond its professional pale. The labels, 'quack' and 'fringe', already bias the proceedings with the imputation that they are either fraudulent, or of little consequence.

Two trends are clear. Cosmopolitan medicine is taking more interest in some aspects of alternative medicine, not necessarily to proscribe and ridicule it as in the past. The public is also making more use of its services, thereby publicising and legitimating its treatments. Advertisements for alternative medicine are common in the quality papers; some invite their readers to train as practitioners in their specialities. Treatments offered can be: hypnotherapy, aromatherapy, primal analysis (for alleviating birth trauma), astrological counselling, shiatsu (a Japanese remedial massage, similar to acupuncture, but with finger pressure applied to the body's meridian points for energy stimulation), reflexology (an Indian and Chinese diagnostic and therapy system, which uses zones on the feet as the source for influencing the body's organs), and biofeedback (means of monitoring and controlling the body's forces, especially blood pressure), and so on. The sales list is endless for health foods, herbs, devices for rheumatism (e.g. copper bracelets), spots, migraine, sleeplessness (e.g. magnetic pillows), tension (e.g. relaxation tapes) and obesity (e.g. micro diets). The USA has over 5,000 astrologers, who have been consulted by 35 millions (estimate) for health and business purposes. Travel agents arrange trips to 'psychic healers' in the Philippines, for those desperate in the terminal stage of cancer. They are supposed to operate without puncturing the skin! Personal columns frequently record thanks to St Jude for recovery.

Attempts to portray alternative medicine and cosmopolitan medicine as polar opposites will prove futile. The use of the unorthodox and the orthodox are themselves value judgements. This distinction is often made within both alternative and cosmopolitan medicines. For example, chiropractic in the 1930s went through political and philosophical schisms. A chiropractor uses manipulative therapy on the spine; the entwined nerves being the source of many body disorders. It is a revival of techniques used by ancient Egyptians, Sumerians and Chinese. The orthodox, who were nicknamed the 'hole in one' or 'straights', wanted to keep faith with the principles of B. J. Palmer, the son of the founder who took on his father's charismatic mantle. Others wanted a mixed treatment, away from the spine, combining homoeopathy, naturopathy, cranial adjustment, dietetics and iridiagnosis. (Iridiagnosis, then a passing craze, was a method of diagnosing disease by examination of the eye: it was alleged that the eye was divided into 40 concentric zones radiating from the pupil; changes of colour of zone and shape would reveal the disease and its body location.) Iridiagnosis is now making a comeback. Some of the 'unorthodox', to escape the conflict, left to join a nature cure association. According to Baer (1984a), the 'mixers' are today winning in the United States.

To consider alternative medicine as unscientific, or pre-scientific and untested, creates similar problems. It is true that there have been many frauds. The vrilium stick invented in Chicago in the 1920s was sold as a necklace to ward off germs. The Federal Government banned it in 1950, it was rat poison! Its promoters claimed it was an unrecognised form of radioactivity. There is dispute about other treatments tested and shown 'useless'. The Nobel prize winner for chemistry, Linus Pauling, was stopped from promoting vitamin C as an alternative treatment against cancer. His research ran counter to the dominant research investments (which have not made much progress over the decade).

Practitioners of alternative medicine rarely run clinical trials, or use a methodology recognised as satisfactory by cosmopolitan medicine. They are generally opposed to animal experiments as a first testing stage. Their main validation is consumer satisfaction. Homoeopathic practitioners will argue that the proof they offer is that they will cure patients whom cosmopolitan medicines have failed, such as those with allergies. Their treatment is now available under the NHS, and many pharmacists stock their medicines. To counter the frequent accusation that alternative medicine relies on suggestion for its effects, it is noticed that homoeopathic medicine will also cure 'non-suggestible' animals. To do clinical trials using the 'double-blind' technique, (i.e. randomly allocating dummy drugs unknown to both doctor and patient) is not feasible. Homoeopathic medicine, like many of its counterparts, particularises its treatment to meet each patient's needs. The medicines used also do not create unpleasant side effects. Very detailed history taking and attention focusing is very much part of the treatment, creating patient confidence. Mixed treatments can be used, compounding the difficulties of 'controlled' trials e.g. acupuncture is often combined with special diets for obesity and other conditions. As shown in Chapter two, there is much in cosmopolitan medicine which is persisted with, despite poor results. The working of the ubiquitous aspirin still remains a mystery.

Other features of possible disjunction include the organising principles of knowledge; the degrees of complexity; the metaphoric imagery, e.g. mechanistic, naturalistic or unitary; and the advancement of knowledge beyond existing frames of ideas. However, it must be stressed that both alternative medicine and cosmopolitan medicine accept illness as undesirable and as an imbalance.

Homoeopathic medicine, for example, may appear to be founded on the reverse principles to those of cosmopolitan medicine. Its originator, Dr Hahnemann, a German doctor, last century based treatment on the key principle of the 'law of similia', i.e. 'like cures like', a principle known to Hippocratic medicine (incidentally the reasoning behind imitative magic). Giving identical substances that actually *cause* the disease or symptoms, will tend to stimulate the body's combative resources. Modern drugs, in contrast block, or directly attack, the disease. Hahnemann collected about 3,000 substances, which he published in his text *Materia Medica*. His discovery first began with his taking cinchona bark (from which quinine is extracted); it gave him malarial symptoms. The other operative principle is the law of 'minute dosages'; some prescriptions are in their millionth part. However, the law of similia was recognised sixty years later when vaccination was adopted by cosmopolitan medicine. Today homoeopathic medicine also uses chemically made compounds ('non-natural') for its treatment. Some of Hahnemann's original substances, like crushed bed bugs and lachryma filia (young girls' tears), have been discarded.

Natural treatments are not the preserve of alternative medicine, although this is a common fallacy. Naturopathy, the ancient precursor, operates on the simple principle that the body has its own inbuilt healing forces. The Ancient Greeks and tribal society would perform their major healing ceremonies in the open air, often near water – being exposed to the universal elements on sacred ground, the homeland of spirits and deities. When healing shifted from treatment centres like temples, healers would still sanctify the home of the sick as part of the remedy. Naturopathy insists that the body must maintain harmony by correct posture and diet (mainly vegetarian), and by regular fasting for elimination of waste products. This health recipe is not alien to cosmopolitan medicine – albeit 'submerged' under the heavy investment in mechanistic treatment. What naturopathy offers as a way of life, cosmopolitan medicine crudely designates as preventive medicine. Water therapy is also being acknowledged as a serious treatment.

'Natural' treatments also underpin new forms of alternative medicine – those emphasising the more spiritual (divine) forces shaping human life. Nineteenth-century examples are Mrs Baker Eddy's Christian Science Church, explaining that illness is caused and cured by the mind; and Spiritualists who rely on external astral energy for health support. Their roots have direct lineage with Christ's healing ministry. Christian Science followers were even forbidden to study anatomy and hygiene, for these were irrelevant distractions from good health.

Cosmopolitan medicine has been criticised for its mechanistic approach, but this appears also in some alternative medicines: chiropractic relies heavily on physical manipulation, although most practitioners are forbidden to perform surgery and to administer drugs. Switzerland is the only European country to recognise legally chiropractic; USA, Canada, Australia and New Zealand have also accepted it. Holistic medicine is fast becoming the 'in-word' in cosmopolitan medicine. In 1983 the British Holistic Medical Association was formed to expand its range of techniques, including counselling, meditation, acupuncture and osteopathy, etc. Most doctors would regard the holistic approach as the ideal. They also argue that the pressure of time inhibits its adoption. GPs' complaints that far too many patients waste their time on 'trivialities' may be a confused response! Trivialities are often the key for mutual exploration of totalistic concern.

To propose that cosmopolitan medicine is far more complex (because of its scientific base) builds another sandcastle. The multiplication of diagnostic testing leaves an incomplete jigsaw and an increasingly ragged view of humanity. Many alternative medicines are complicated syntheses within cosmologies, offering solutions to the human predicament. Ayurvedic medicine, one of the oldest, is circumscribed by classical Indian philosophies (e.g. Nyaya and Sandkhya), with man embodying all the universal substances: the five elements (panchbhuta) of fire, earth, air, water and ether; each having their anatomical connections; and the humours (tridosas), which are the major diagnostic clues. Dianetics (founded in 1950 by the science fiction writer, Hubbard), uses, a technical vocabulary – with mental health therapy becoming 'auditing' and painful memory residues, 'engrams' – and also offers a universal view. Engrams produce disease, the most powerful engrams are intra-uterine developed; Dianetic therapy, through its many levels, will produce a 'clear' state (salvation) and thus release repressed human potential.

Many alternative medicines claim to have developed beyond existing medical knowledge. The interpretation and treatment of mental illness by Dianetics (later transformed into Scientology), brought it into hostility with conventional psychiatry. Reich, too, extended Freud's ideas, needless to say in a way unacceptable to Freudians. Freud once refused to psychoanalyse him. Reich asserted that he had reduced the mental energy of the libido to scientific laws. Freud had always regarded psychoanalysis as a transitional method, until natural science had become sophisticated enough to reveal the mysteries of the mind. The new substance discovered by Reich was called orgone (or primordial) energy. Incomplete orgone balance generated sickness, especially cancer. Reich died in prison, on 3 November 1957. He had refused to accept the injunction of the USA Food and Drug Administration on his distribution of orgone boxes (which stored the energy). The FDA ruled that the boxes were fraudulent and that orgone did not exist. It was claimed that orgone boxes, alternately layered with metal and wood, trapped the energy which was piped to patients. Reich's ideas in his book, *Function of the Orgasm*, (1970) further alienated him from psychiatry. Lack of orgasmic potency cause neuroticism and bellicose societies. 'Make love not war', the anti-Vietnam war slogan, was derived from Reich.

Summarising, alternative medicine consists of a diverse crop of health restorative activities. That is one of its appeals; personal preference and temperament can find their niche. Many of their fundamental principles are not alien to cosmopolitan medicine: indeed, some were discarded along the scientific way, such as astrological and humoric causation. Others are 'illegitimate' extensions of existing medical knowledge. Some techniques are even being 'smuggled back' into cosmopolitan medicine.

We now shift the debate along three broad fronts and examine the social impetus behind the recent ascendancy of alternative medicine; this necessitates some details about its consumers. We then further discuss the relationship between alternative medicine and cosmopolitan medicine. Some, like osteopathy, are demanding full professional status, while others remain mortally opposed. Finally, the impact of cosmopolitan medicine's recent colonisation, as *the* official health service, of some third world countries will be reviewed, and new relationships with traditional medicine will be disentangled.

ALTERNATIVE MEDICINE, SOCIAL CHANGE AND USERS

Alternative medicine has always contained an 'anti' element. One dominant element from the nineteenth century onwards has been a reaction against secularisation (but not all forms of rationality). Religious sects were one form of anti-establishment protest, each plugged into distinctive social strata, with their own dilemmas. Sects offered a unitary world view; healing was often central, being one way of experiencing the divine will and of confirming one's status in the grand order of things. For example, the Elim Church, developed in Ireland during the First World War reflects the social tensions of the time. Its original membership were the despairing poor, promised hope and redemption in the world to come and fellowship in this. Their teachings stress that healing should be first sought from God, but this does not rule out later help from medicine. The most faithful are those cured directly by God. All religions have stressed the power of prayer for healing, but some make this central. In their evangelical campaigns, spontaneous healing was to the fore, being one of the nine spiritual gifts. When treated by doctors the cure is always attributed to the holy spirit working through the medical profession.

In contrast, Christian Science had a different appeal. Under the charismatic leadership of Mrs Eddy, the sect was centralised, and made fully dependent on her revelations. Christian Science was not a religion of the oppressed and was more orientated towards this world, having an intellectual appeal. Each member was given the capacity for self-healing. Eddy's manual, *Science and Health*, contained the recipes for healing, denying the existence of the body. Sickness and sin were mirages, distorting thoughts which had to be denied. They were the product of the malevolence of 'animal magnetism'. The lower middle class, and especially women, became its main adherents.

Nudelman (1976) addresses a fundamental issue: how do healing sects maintain their integrity, especially after losing momentum with the passing of their charismatic leader, and when counter evidence from the outside world pounds them? Nudelman shows that Christian Science has made little impact in the developing world, where there are major health hazards which can be alleviated by better diets and vaccination. Christian Science does best with healthy populations. The health status of Christian Scientist is above average, and smoking and drinking prohibitions are usually maintained. The reduction in tobacco related diseases (heart and lung disease) provides proof of the effectiveness of Mrs Baker Eddy's teachings. One survival tactic is not to publish membership statistics, thereby curtailing debates on growth rates. Support tends to be upheld from converts from the older age groups, who may experience lingering health problems unmoved by cosmopolitan medicine. In Nudelman's sample of Christian Science students, with males over-represented in the form of engineering and physical science subjects, most had made contact with cosmospolitan medicine. This appeared in contradiction to their beliefs. A number of Christian Scientists, however, came from families where only one parent was of the faith, so that cross-pressures existed for seeking medical assistance. Other students recognised their own inability to cure themselves, but added that it worked well with others. Christian Science teaching has a major 'exemption clause' which allows visits to doctors for alleviating pain derived from a 'mechanical symptom' as distinct from a spiritual symptom. Self-definition in this self-help religion becomes all important.

Many alternative remedies originated in the United States, particularly the cultural influence of the frontier – Mid West, with California later becoming important. The roving medicine man with his universal cure; the itinerant preachers with one foot on the ladder to heaven; and self-help and individualism (e.g. bone setters), all flourished in areas lacking doctors. Husbands delivered their own children. California now spawns more cults and health movements than any other state. Dianetics started there. Leary's LSD movement of the 1950s found a home in South California, after he was sacked from his lectureship in psychology at Harvard for unofficial drug experiments. LSD is an hallucinogen, similar to mescalin (extracted from a cactus) used by Indians in South-east USA in religious festivals. Leary thought LSD would be useful for treating schizophrenia, as well as for general use in 'opening' the door of perception. 'Drop out and turn on' was another hippy slogan of the 1960s. Leary escaped from jail and is now in exile in Algiers.

There has always been the tendency for health movements to crystallise into political and religious cults. Dianetics has sought status as the Church of Scientology, partly for tax relief and partly as a result of political hostility towards it.

Herberg (1960) has argued that the USA is historically rootless, with descendants of the original migrants constantly seeking status security: and one way has been through contact with alternative medicine. The West's increasing interest in eastern religions and philosophy has been another spur. Nuclear physicists have also turned to Taoism and Hinduism, etc., in an attempt to find new meta-imageries to embrace their data on the hidden world of sub-atoms. Eastern meditative techniques can easily accommodate western individualism.

Further encouragement for alternative medicine arises from a disenchantment with cosmopolitan medicine. Some are repelled by its disaster syndrome; others by its mass consumerism approach; and some desire to get back to 'nature' – thereby hoping for purity and truth. Part of the women's movement hopes to rediscover the lost wisdom of the muses.

The roll call of disasters is mounting: thalidomide and child deformity have left a lingering memory. The once 'safe' and liberating contraceptive pill now has hidden dangers – those over 35 years of age are recommended to abandon it, to lessen chances of thrombosis and heart attack. The miracle tranquillisers like Largactil, have been shown to have taken their toll. Tardive dyskinesia (TD) sometimes results, with patients losing control of leg, face and tongue movements. In most cases TD is irreversible, even getting worse if tranquillisers are stopped! TD can only be dampened by increased doses of tranquillisers. Roche, the largest supplier of the drug, calculated that 150 million people now take it, perhaps leaving as many as 30 million people as TD sufferers. The mid-brain disturbance is not reversible. Medical supporters argue that TD also occurs in those not tranquillised, mainly the old; and that without tranquillisers schizophrenics would experience even more personal suffering. But doubt exists about whether informed consent was obtained before administering the drug, with patients aware of the risks of TD.

Different client groups have different grievances with cosmopolitan medicine. Many multiple sclerosis sufferers are dissatisfied with the lack of progress in orthodox research. Self-help groups circulate details of alternative treatments: decompression chambers (used by divers) and snake venom therapy in USA clinics are being tried. Women's health clinics are gaining momentum, after the model of the Boston Women's Health Movement.

To keep their clientele, changes have occurred within cosmopolitan medicine; ranging from Odent's and Leboyer's use of natural elements for childbirth (babies born into darkness, quietness and water) to hospitals offering more domesticated surroundings and alternative birth positions to delivery on the back. Some are now using replica sixteenth-century birth chairs. Moving around, squatting or maintaining an upright position distributes pressure from the baby's head evenly around the vaginal opening, reducing the possibility for tears and the need for episiotomies. The supine position of hospital birth was introduced for the convenience of nineteenth-century male obstetricians.

Hazell (1975) has made one of the few studies of the home delivery movement in the USA. Midwifery at home is illegal in California. Only doctors are allowed to attend domiciliary deliveries, but they are usually unwilling. Lay midwives operate outside the law. Hazell's data was based on 300 couples she observed in the San Francisco Bay area, and she had open access because of her midwifery expertise. She was trained at the Maternity Centre Association which, under medical pressure, ceased to engage in domiciliary deliveries in 1965. The users were white, 'average' Americans, with the father gainfully employed. Only about 10 per cent could be called hippy. Hospital expenses were not a consideration. Home birthers were not bound together by organisational ties, or by relationships of kin and friendship, their interest in natural childbirth being part of a wider ecological concern. Home delivery was not simply a protest against the impersonality of hospital obstetrics, but was a celebration of each couple's 'togetherness'. Some births had traits of sexual ecstacy, emotions which could not easily be displayed in hospital. Fathers had a purposeful role, actively helping in delivery. The placenta would be buried in the garden, the spot often planted with a new rose bush. Some couples would eat the placenta, raw or cooked. Home birthers accepted fatalistically the potential birth dangers. They were not inhibited from seeking medical assistance for serious illness, although half had a previous 'bad' experience of medicine and distrusted doctors.

Ethnicity as a focus of new political identity has forced cosmopolitan medicine to consider cultural variations and treatment regimes. In the USA the offerings of traditional medicine are taken seriously. Marsella and White (1982) have traced these linkages in the field of mental illness, a specialism where it is easiest to have a rapprochement of ideas (as opposed to surgery). American psychiatry has always had a strong existentialist representation. For reasons of diagnostic errors, interview bias, etc., research is showing that about half of all ethnic minority clients (mainly blacks, Hispanics and Asian-Americans) refuse, after one visit to return to CMHCs for further treatment. Three contradictory solutions are offered. Anthropologists suggest that folk medicine is given official credence and its practitioners become state employees. The mental health agencies argue that more effective delivery is needed, with CMHCs located closer to the different ethnic groups. Leaders of the Hispanic community, for example, argue for more multicultural interpreters (which will increase job opportunities for the educated unemployed), fearing that indigenous healing would lead to 'cheap' medicine for the 'unsophisticated' and to restrictions on health choices.

Lefley's (1984) discussion of the emerging combinations between cosmopolitan medicine and alternative medicine shows how the surface distinction between the two becomes blurred. Nigeria has evolved two models. First, the 'non culture-bound' treatment, with the therapist recognising the importance of local ritual, and using it when appropriate. The other model – the 'culture-bound' approach – does more than acknowledge local ritual. It stresses the convergence of folk and psychiatric healing themes, often using the two healers. The latter model of joint responsibility is mainly absent in the United States, for reasons of professional politics. Instead, folk healers (Hispanics, usually Puerto Rican) have various connecting ties: they arrange for referrals; participate in the training of psychiatrists, or act as cultural experts; more rarely, they act as cotherapists in the same mental health centre as the psychiatrist. Folk healing – involving prayer, lifting of spells, exorcism and 'drugs' – is not performed in health centres. The complete traditional regime remains separate and therefore can be classified as 'alternative'. However, in Puerto Rico, the Therapist-Spiritist Training Project is fast moving towards the synthesised approach. There are regular meetings on neutral ground between spiritists and professional therapists for mutual training sessions, and reciprocal referrals are occuring.

There is no co-operation between Pakistani traditional healers, hakims, and the NHS. There are two types of healers. Those already settled in England and the 'renowned' ones, who tour Europe from Pakistan. These visits are well publicised in advance, and consultations take place at hotels and Islamic centres. Rack (1982), relying on Aslam's data, notes that most cases are psychosomatic, sexual disorders and mental illness; all of which receive little sympathy from cosmopolitan medicine. A hakim's treatment is often supplemented with prayer. In Aslam's sample only 4 per cent said that they were more satisfied with British doctors. Hakims are clearly breaking the law in prescribing medicines covered by the Medicine Acts, but are not prosecuted. There are other points of conflict with cosmopolitan medicine. Unani medicine classifies many of their medicines as 'hot' and deleterious for some illnesses. Some hakims' medicines are considered dangerous and useless. The spoons used for preparing baby remedies contain high proportions of lead. Magsol, used as a remedy for gonorrhoea, is mainly sugar and sand!

The numbers who consult alternative practitioners are not fully known. The Threshold Survey 1981, indicates that 10 million people visited them; however details of mode of referral, length of treatment and cost are more hazy. Stanway (1982) is more specific: in 1977 over 80,000 visited the out-patients departments of the six homoeopathic hospitals run by the NHS. More people treat themselves (offered advice from pharmacists) than visit GPs. The sale of do-it-yourself health monitoring equipment is becoming big business: blood pressure and blood glucose monitors and various testing kits (e.g. pregnancy) are leading the way. Doctors are used now for second opinions.

Most people gravitate to alternative medicine after contact with cosmopolitan medicine. Moore (1984) illustrates this point with the case study of a Centre for Alternative Therapies: offering acupuncture, Alexander technique (posture re-education), homoeopathy, bio-feedback, hypnosis and others. Over half the patients came with pains and allergies, with the presenting symptoms having persisted for a mean of nine years. The chief referral route had been friends. Although most studies show that the popularity of alternative medicine has been rising in proportion to the discontent with doctors, most of these patients had good relationships with GPs; 22 per cent had actually been referred by them. It is interesting to note that approximately the same proportion (about a quarter) said they were 'rushed' by both their GP and by the doctor at the centre. The study is silent about the organisational context of the centre. Fee payers expect to buy time, as well as treatment. Perhaps it was run on the system of hospital appointments? After eight weeks' attendance over half said that they were much improved.

Conservative government policy is advantageous to alternative medicine, via the restraint of public expenditure. The NHS is the largest employer in Europe, and in 1981–2 it spent £145 million on office equipment alone. As well as direct staff cuts and savings on a reduced list of prescribed drugs, etc., the Conservative policy also involves reducing direct demand. Self-reliance and private health insurance have been encouraged. The largest private sector is the 'disorganised' one of alternative medicine. Private health insurance provides more of the 'high-tech' used in the NHS, but in pleasant hotel-like conditions. Private health insurance often does not cater for mental illness, the aged and for chronic 'lingering' cases (back pains, arthritis and 'non specifics', etc.). Alternative medicine is an instant medical hypermarket and the supplier of a vast range of cures. If payment for 'item' extends in the NHS, there will be an additional incentive to gravitate towards alternative medicine. Many practitioners match their fees according to the capacity to pay, like pre-war 'family doctors'.

Socialism, as a conglomerate political philosophy, has always contained a streak of 'health faddism'; social purification, the creation of a new and better society has traded on notions of going back to nature for one of its inspirations. In practical terms the Labour party recognises itself, however, as the legitimate guardian of the NHS, defending the status quo, together with its medical hegemony. The radical feminists are opposed to the NHS's lack of sensitivity in catering for women's needs. They prefer more deinstitutionalised medicine, in the form of women's clinics, as part of their wider aim of raising consciousness and the reclaiming of their bodies. Some self-help groups have incorporated 'medical techniques' e.g. menstrual aspiration (very early abortion) and brought them into conflict with cosmopolitan medicine. On the whole however their health approach is preventive.

ALTERNATIVE MEDICINE AND PROFESSIONAL ORIENTATIONS

As explained, there is no clear division of principles between alternative medicine and cosmopolitan medicine. Also, significantly, there is no agreed classification which will locate the multitude of alternative medicines. Crude axes suggest themselves: fraudulent/scientific; sacred world view/secular; totalistic body focus/specialist part. These axes have value as an iron maiden or rack, but much depends on who is defining what and to whom, e.g. chiropractic (orthodox) concentrates on the spine, but also stresses general well-being.

All practitioners express common concerns for standards and the validation of their practices. Alternative medicines can be shuffled into broad bands according to how they wish to realise these aims. At one extreme are 'closed groups': only initiated members can participate in their healing practices. Validation is by caucus (church elders, lay assemblies or other knowledge experts) who keep the articles of 'faith'. Closed groups are not concerned with outside approval. A much broader band covers the open associations of alternative medicine which receive clients. Some of these may know little about the knowledge base of their treatment, but play a keen role in validation. They can vote with their feet. Closed groups proselytise. Open groups are market orientated, using professionalism as their reference point, acknowledging that it has come to signify quality control and trust. Open groups do however, make different appeals to professionalism, and we now discuss how they achieve this.

There are four major professional orientations. *Closed groups*, which are largely anti-professional, professionalism having become synonymous with those power structures challenging their existence. Among the *open groups* are those which: (a) utilise the institutional rhetoric of professionalism as management props; (b) want to achieve independent professional status; and (c) want professional status under the umbrella of cosmopolitan medicine.

Professional symbols have universal recognition. Witch doctors in African towns were quick to adopt them, as they were seen as blending with the modern urban image and in keeping with the expectations of their aspirant clients. The office is used by them for consultation; the white coat is the standard garb; and herbs and charms are dispensed in hygienic bags. The source of misfortune is now divined as unfair competition for promotion at work and not the village clan. Witchcraft has in these ways absorbed the new tensions of industrialisation. Davis and others (1984) provide an interesting example of how USA occult practitioners, and fortune tellers, articulate their professional authority in manipulating clients. Interest in the occult has increased rapidly over the last twenty years; the manufacture of tarot cards, witches' regalia and paraphernalia are big business. Boles, one of the researchers with Davis, was a trained practitioner in psychic readings. Twenty-one practising fortune tellers (non-gypsies and white) were interviewed; one allowed the researchers the access to clients' records.

Fortune tellers prefer the titles of 'psychic advisers' and 'readers'. Contrary to expectations it was not the poor and elderly (marginalised groups) who were clients, but those in their thirties and forties; half were high school educated, and half were women. Males attended primarily for venereal disease and sexual dysfunction (usually impotence). Psychic advisers are licensed, and their consultation and waiting rooms display their credentials – often mail-order degrees.

Special links with the spirit world are also emphasised. Religious artefacts and statues of saints are prominently placed. The strategy is to convince clients that the session is no different from a doctor–patient, or priest–supplicant, consultation. Some occultists reinforce the analogy by referring to themselves as 'doctor', 'professor', and even 'bishop': female practitioners frequently call themselves 'sister'.

Occultists take extensive medical histories, covering the major anatomical parts and concentrating on the genitalia if VD is indicated. Products are sold under the guise of prescriptions. Davis lists: headache pillows; Uncrossing Bath Salts (frequent bathing is recommended for all conditions); and Go-Go Tablets, a sexual restorative for couples. Clients are not given sick roles. Occultists operate with a dual model of disease. They deal with unnatural causation – misfortune caused by others, and natural causation. Occultists always recommend that clients see a doctor, for dealing with the biological component – i.e. the natural aspect. Doctors allocate sick roles, whereas occultists offer spiritual ones. Doctors welcome the financial benefits from referred patients, tolerating the pseudo-medical activities of occultists.

Treatment for sexual dysfunction parallels medically formulated sex therapy. Tension releasing activities are used, including the recommendation of initial abstinence, which removes feelings of failure. The prescribed medicines – oil rubbed into the genitals, candle burning and accompanying prayers – have ritualistic import. If the client lacks a sexual partner, the occultist will hire a surrogate, who is tutored in the significance of the 'therapy'. Occultists caution against miracle cures. Long-term patients allow deeper therapeutic exploration. Conforming to the Protestant work ethic, clients have to work through their complaint.

Osteopathy presents a contrasting picture. In the United States osteopaths were granted legal rights as separate medical practitioners. They ran skilful political lobbies to advertise their claims from a tight, centralised body. Four states have a system of two-fold licences – the second permits osteopaths to use major surgery. The picture is more complicated, because in 1962 the medical and osteopathic associations in California merged into the University of California College of Medicine, Irvine. This move was opposed by the American Osteopathic Association, which blocked a similar merger in the state of Washington. It sponsored a new anti-medical group of osteopaths in California and got a ruling from the New York Supreme Court that osteopathic qualifications from Irvine should not be recognised. As Wardwell (1972) shows, USA osteopaths filled a major gap in primary health care, substituting for the shortage of general practitioners. The mechanistic principles of osteopathy were not incompatible with the biological disease model of cosmopolitan medicine. By compromising some of the principles of their founder, Still, who was opposed to drugs and surgery, they have moved their practices towards cosmopolitan medicine. Still had claimed divine revelation for his methods, curing almost everything – dandruff, yellow fever, diabetes, obesity, and impotence, etc.

English osteopaths are trying to achieve comparable status. Conditions are against them. Their numbers are much fewer (USA has 17,000), and primary health care is much better developed. Politically distant from their parent association, osteopaths have flitted around a number of associations, thereby weakening their political representation. Baer (1984b) has charted this tortuous history. The British Osteopathic Association was founded in Manchester around 1910. By 1921 a rival organisation, the Manchester College of Bloodless Surgery, started by Looker, was teaching both osteopathy and chiropractic. The Incorporated Association of Osteopaths Ltd was founded in 1925 by the Looker graduates, who were disbarred from membership of the British Osteopathic Association. In 1936 the Incorporated Association of Osteopaths, after new mergers, became the Osteopathic Association of Great Britain. In 1978 the reformulated London College of Osteopathic Medicine only permitted doctors as students, thus sharpening the division between medically qualified osteopaths and others. Baer points to more ramifications: some naturopaths joined forces with osteopathy, setting up joint societies, such as the British Naturopathic and Osteopathic Association. Naturopathy waned in the 1950s when cosmopolitan medicine promised instant cures with 'miracle' drugs. The Society of Osteopaths appeared in 1973, after splits among the College of Naturopathy and Osteopathy, but there is still a large sprinkling of other societies, some with European connections.

To achieve professional status, which is tantamount to a monopoly position for its members' skills, osteopathy needs the patronage of powerful clients. In the USA judges, senators and businessmen, 'worthy community voices', vouch for it. A strong governing body for assuring training and certification is needed. Osteopathy's British history is one of factionalism, which does not instil public confidence. Three Parliamentary bills, attempting to promote a register for osteopaths, were defeated in the 1930s, being opposed not only by the weight of cosmopolitan medicine, the universities and medical schools, but also by other representatives of alternative medicine –

namely the British Chiropractors Association and the Chartered Society of Massage and Medical Gymnasts. Ideological rivalry between American chiropractors and osteopaths spilled over, with osteopaths claiming that some of their concepts had been filched. The favoured position of American osteopathy had also been seen as detrimental to the recognition of chiropractic.

Since the 1970s osteopathy has mounted a more concerted effort at professional recognition. It has established academic links with higher education. The Council for National Academic Awards would be prepared to consider the proposed degree in osteopathy sponsored by the Polytechnic of Central London and the School of Osteopathy, if the Department of Education and Science would recognise the degree for grant purposes. Sir Norman Lindop, a former director of Hatfield Polytechnic, was appointed principal of the School of Osteopathy. He had influential connections, being a lay member of the General Medical Council and chairman of the Lindop Report, reviewing the processes of validation in the Public Sector of Higher Education. Osteopathy was represented on the 1976 Ministry of Health working party investigating remedies for back pain, a costly scourge of industry. To date the trend is for some medical practitioners to absorb osteopathic skills either directly by being trained in them, or by using 'trusted' osteopaths for referrals under their control.

Summarising, except for closed sects/political groups, alternative medicine has displayed a dominant interest in professionalism, for consolidating the power and prestige of its practitioners and for market regulation. How it succeeds, for example in achieving full independent professional status, will depend largely on how it projects the validity of its case – political acknowledgement from powerful elites, both medical and non-medical being essential. Even occultists survive, by not attempting to undermine the medical hegemony. They are therefore permitted to drape themselves with professional trappings.

TRADITIONAL MEDICINE AS ALTERNATIVE MEDICINE

We go on to elaborate further the changing role of traditional medicine, and extend the debate (Ch. 8) on PHC. The popularity of traditional medicine in large parts of Africa was partly due to its greater accessibility, with cosmopolitan medicine predominant in the urban areas. Heggenhougen's (1980) analysis of Malaysia's medical pluralism does however add new dimensions. Malaysia's economy is more than buoyant. It has one of the fastest rates of industrial growth; even Japan manufactures electronics there because of its labour efficiency. Its modernity is reflected in stringent traffic laws to control the proliferation of cars, in the increased proportion of students gaining higher education and, not least, in its heavy investment in cosmopolitan medicine, especially in rural areas. Lack of accessibility to cosmopolitan medicine *cannot* be put forward here as the reason for the sustenance of traditional medicine. Prior to cosmopolitan medicine, traditional medicine was the dominant system. It only became, technically, alternative medicine *after* being replaced by the western official version.

People of Indian origin, mainly Tamils, have long used Ayurvedic medicine; the Chinese Malays utilise sinsehs, their traditional practitioners, and the indigenous Malays, mainly rural, have their traditional healers, bomohs. Heggenhougen quotes figures to suggest that there are as many full-time bomohs as there are doctors in the state health scheme, with ten times more as part-time bomohs. As with alternative medicine in the West, there is a gravitation from cosmopolitan medicine by those whose symptoms do not clear. Although there is a tendency for initial choice to be based on the type of complaint – 'physical' ones to cosmopolitan medicine and 'psychological' to bomohs – the picture is complicated. Bomohs are not only consulted for asthma, which has a psychological dimension, but also for boils and severe fractures. Cosmopolitan medicine is known to do well with worms and diarrhoea.

All the major traditions of alternative medicine have organised to form their own federations. They have been able to trade on their ethnic links and their vast client networks. Ayurvedic and Chinese medicine are advantaged too by having their own long established training schools. Half the sinsehs belonging to the Chinese Physicians Association are graduates from recognised training centres. Federations have also been possible because there is not the same proliferation of healing cults/groups as is found in the West. Bomohs may be divided into herbalists, spiritualists and bonesetters, but many are mixed practitioners. Although the Malaysian Medical Association is opposed to the official recognition of bomohs, the government is not that antagonistic. Bomohs represent a significant symbolic thread of Malay identity. The government is keen to emphasise that in nation building.

Heggenhougen notes other reasons for bomohs' popularity. Cosmopolitan medicine has its notable failures, and drug addicts in particular fare very badly. Malaysia has set a high priority in eradicating addiction. The death penalty is mandatory for drug trafficking. Addiction is considered an impediment to economic development. The more unstructured therapeutic context of bomoh practice is the more apposite for treating addicts. Waiting lists, often unpredictable as in the West, repel many Malaysians who prefer to drop in at the local bomoh's for immediate and understandable treatment. As elsewhere, traditional medicine has become innovative, widening the range of treatments by incorporating suitable techniques and drugs from cosmopolitan medicine.

Indonesia is also a modernising country which has made a determined effort to extend its official medical system, especially the psychiatric services, throughout its 27 provinces. Again, traditional healers are frequently utilised. Salan and Maretzki (1983) followed up the caseload of none traditional healers, all urban based, and had them interviewed by a psychiatrist and health official on home visits to discover reasons for their preference. The Indonesian official health system was seeking ways of blending its psychiatric delivery with clients' needs. The Mental Health Act of 1966 had moved care away from the custodial regime instituted by Dutch colonialism to an open style of hospitals. The contrasting cities chosen for the study were i) Palembang in S. Sumatra, which has a population of three-quarters of a million and is industrial with a mixed population, ii) Semarang in central Java, with a population over one million, containing the highest percentage of ethnic Chinese of any city; and iii) Denpasar in Bali, with a population of half a million, with a strong Hindu tradition, but expanding rapidly as a tourist spot. Three healers were chosen in each city. Some healers were excluded to make 'straight' comparisons easier with cosmopolitan medicine: e.g. a midwife cum herbalist and a healer who illegally used injections to treat cancer. As part of the client interview, the Cornell Medical Index was used. The researchers were most surprised to find that 70 per cent had received some treatment for mental illness from doctors prior to their visiting healers (other studies had indicated the reverse); 76 per cent transferred to healers because of a lack of improvement, and 16 per cent mentioned the expense.

Evaluating success is difficult, but 60 per cent of clients felt they had improved. This rate was not evenly spread across all healers. One trance healer achieved a hundred per cent improvement rate, according to clients' perceptions. Some clients did not want treatment, for instance 25 per cent just wanted advice on personal problems. Cosmopolitan medicine, based on the disease model, is not geared to that kind of demand. With chronic illnesses, 58 per cent felt improved with traditional medicine. It must also be noted that half the sample, according to the investigators, experienced illness of a 'self-limiting type', such as transient fever, mild gastritis, and muscle swelling because of trauma. However, their categories can be queried. They refer to mastitis caused by temporary physiological hormonal balance. This could be a *post facto* diagnosis. This condition can also have an important psychological dimension and be long lasting.

Although financial consideration was the second reason for shifting to alternative medicine, some healers can be more expensive. Elaborate exorcising ceremonies, with a large supporting cast, can cost £1,000. The diversity in styles of healing sessions allows for greater symbolic compatibility between client and healer. Healers using trances demand strict obedience of formal etiquettes, to control the potential danger from spirits. Other healers lay sacred objects on diseased parts, or use copper rings placed between the fingertips; others demand recitations from the Koran; others ask clients to stay at home for up to a week. Some healers visit clients' houses, some stay overnight and leave protective potions against disturbing spirits. Some healers live frugal lives, relying on client donations, others display opulence. Some charge according to health results. All healers allow clients to explain their misfortune without being hurried, and admit relatives to the session, as active participants, or not. These cultural minutiae convey powerful sentiments into healing, and contrast sharply with the impersonality of cosmopolitan medicine.

One major study has thrown doubt on the high esteem and treatment success accredited to healers. The idyllic scenario of 'illiterate' healers knowing better than the weighty battalions of scientific medicine may be partly a carry-through of the wishful sentimentality of liberal researchers. All anthropologists who study traditional societies have a tendency to 'fall in love' with their tribe or group. If client evaluation data is broken down, it is clear that some healers are rated much higher than others, and that dissatisfaction must therefore exist with some. Kleinman and Gale (1982) matched up, as far as possible, 118 patients treated by healers and 112 patients treated by doctors in Taiwan, and did a follow-up evaluation after about one month in their homes. The researchers called those treated by healers shrine cases; they were treated in temples. The samples in both groups were mainly lower and lower-middle class, and all were indigenous Taiwanese. The shrine group, as expected, had more socio-psychiatric conditions, but both caseloads were typical of the different treatment regimes.

The findings caused initial surprise. Client's ratings of improvement were almost similar: 86 per cent treated by doctors claimed improvement and 82 per cent treated at shrines claimed improvement. When health status was 'empirically' checked by the health team, more doctor-treated patients were found to have improved; 85 per cent as opposed to 76 per cent of shrine cases. On other criteria cosmopolitan medicine also had the edge: 93 per cent were satisfied with the doctor's style, but only 65 per cent with their healer's performance. More patients were satisfied with the time doctors allocated to them than were satisfied with the time healers allocated.

As Kleinman and Gale admit, their study did have a major flaw; the possible bias of the health care team who made the evaluations. Their leanings were towards cosmopolitan medicine: the senior member was a public health nurse trained in the scientific approach, and her influence may not have been counterbalanced by that of the other member, an anthropologist with a good rapport with the healers. The nurse's health interviews were very much longer and wider in scope than those given by doctors. Client's favourable assessments of their doctors may have been influenced by this 'unintended' interest. Both doctors and healers failed, however, to provide satisfactory support for some treatable psychiatric disorders. One factor the study omitted was details of the social networks of each group; it is through these that the cultural meanings of disease and remedies are often mediated.

CONCLUSION

It has been stressed that what is considered alternative medicine is the product of the powerful definers, who support establishment medicine. Cosmopolitan medicine has never progressed along a well-signposted path. Internally it is composed of many branches, with different emphases; while surgery stresses more specialisation, general practice and psychiatry will nod towards the virtues of holism, but add the rider they have not the time and resources for full commitment. Universal demarcations between cosmopolitan medicine and alternative medicine are not possible. Alternative medicine is multiplying its already luxuriant species. Some, which go by the name of alternative medicine, were formally within the fold of cosmopolitan medicine; others stretch its principles in directions not favoured by the doyens of cosmopolitan medicine. Megavitamin therapy, the ingesting of massive doses of vitamins, appropriate for each disease, is one example. Vitamin B3 for schizophrenia and E for skin complaints, have been condemned as useless and dangerous by the American Medical Association and the American Psychiatric Association. Now cosmopolitan medicine is quietly smuggling those aspects of alternative medicine it finds valuable, thereby consolidating certain of its shaky foundations: osteopathy, biofeedback and acupuncture are being practised by doctors, but on their own terms. Yet the external posture, as represented by the BMA's (1986) 'investigation' into alternative treatments, was that they were largely ineffective, lacking a scientific or rational base and could be dangerous.

Medicine originated entwined with religion, sacredness and supernatural power. Hippocratic medicine at Cos divorced itself from priestly healing, leaving the temples to handle intractable complaints. Cosmopolitan medicine became the inheritor of the secular and scientific world view. Alternative medicine has always had a place for the torch of religious healing, lacking a central organisation and thriving on diversity. Some alternative medicines overtly lacking religious frames, can still impart a sacred potency by the 'faith' they conjure up in the minds of their adherents. To visit the chiropractor, or naturopath one 'swears by', can resemble a private and miniature pilgrimage to Lourdes for salvation and the revealing of fundamental truths via illness.

Alternative medicines represent a lexicon of philosophies, whose appeal often matched unfulfilled aspirations. Wallis and Morley (1976) showed how Dianetics attracted mainly males in their thirties with white-collar jobs. With an above average education, many were experiencing 'status panic', due to restricted opportunities for social mobility. For some, Dianetics offered an alternative career as practitioners.

The nineteenth-century English believers in spiritualism were mainly working class, as they are today. Estimates indicate that in the 1850s over one million Americans were followers, out of a total population of 25 millions. The movement grew extemely fast; it was only in 1848 that the Fox sisters of New York 'explained' how the dead communicated through sharp raps. Shortt (1984) elaborates how spiritualism touched many social nerves. It rounded off the promise of evolutionary development by explaining that death was not a meaningless finality. Many prominent scientists initially subscribed to it, notably Wallace, the co-discoverer of evolution by natural selection. The ethereal dimension balanced the material one. Owenite socialism and women's rights got caught up in its appeal. From the 1870s spiritualism came under a vicious medical onslaught from the newly established discipline of neuroscience, which was staking out its professional claims. Neurologists wished to demolish any notion that the brain had supernatural properties, making its workings incompatible with scientific laws. Belief in spiritualism then became a mental illness. The 'spiritualist disease' had related symptoms of sexual disorders in women, e.g. hysteria of uterine origin, and of general paralysis in males; both sexes experienced hallucination. The cure included electricity and sedation. Spiritualism provides an example of the power of cosmopolitan medicine to define its opponents as insane, when their beliefs offer a powerful challenge.

The future of many alternative medicines will depend on whether the state will deinstitutionalise cosmopolitan medicine from its privileged position within the power structure. If Griffiths succeeds it will have made the most serious inroads yet into the protected garden of clinical autonomy. Parts of the medical profession have been turning against the Conservative government with their corpse rattling and shroud-raising publicity, which have been used to attack health cuts. The government may respond by promoting some alternative medicines in the name of greater personal choice. In the less developed world more serious attempts are made to investigate the claims of traditional medicine. In Zimbabwe, 4,000 healers have been officially registered as 'semi-professionals', to complement the country's 820 doctors. Tanzania has a similar scheme. The medical school of Dar es Salaam selects for training those amenable to cosmopolitan medicine, who are willing to teach hygiene, nutrition and will administer some western drugs. As government employees they are more in the way of medical auxiliaries than traditional healers. Such is the world-wide influence of cosmopolitan medicine to dictate the mode of health practices.

REFERENCES

Baer H A 1984a A historical overview of British and European chiropractic. *Chiropractic History* 4: 11–15
Baer H A 1984b The drive for professionalism in British osteopathy. *Social Science and Medicine* 19: 717–25
Davis P W, Boles J, Tatro C 1984 Dramaturgy of occult practitioners in the treatment of disease and dysfunction entities. *Social Science and Medicine* 19: 691–8
Hazell L D 1975 *Birth Goes Home*. Catalyst Publishing Co, Seattle
Heggenhougen H K 1980 Bomohs doctors and sinsehs — medical pluralism in Malaysia. *Social Science and Medicine* 14: 235–44
Herberg W 1960 *Protestant–Catholic–Jew*. Doubleday, New York
Kleinman A, Gale J L 1982 Patients treated by physicians and folk healers: a comparative outcome study in Taiwan. *Culture, Medicine and Psychiatry* 6: 405–23
Lefley H P 1984 Delivering mental health service across cultures. In Pedersen *et al*. *Mental Health Services*.

Marsella A J, White G M 1982 *Cultural Concentrations of Mental Health and Therapy*. Reidel, Boston

Moore J, Phipps K, Marcer D 1984 Why do people seek treatment by alternative medicine? *British Medical Journal* 290: 24–5

Nudelman A E 1976 The maintenance of Christian Science in scientific society. In Wallis R, Morley P (eds) *Marginal Medicine*. Free Press, Illinois

Pedersen P B, Sartorius N, Marsella A J 1984 *Mental Health Services. The Cross-Cultural Context*. Sage Publications, Beverly Hills

Rack P 1982 *Race, Culture and Mental Disorder*. Tavistock, London

Reich W 1970 *The Function of the Orgasm*. Panther Books

Salan R, Maretzki T 1983 Mental health services and traditional healing in Indonesia: are the roles compatible? *Culture, Medicine and Psychiatry* 7: 377–412

Shortt S E D 1984 Physicians and psychics: the Anglo-American medical responses to spiritualism, 1870–1890. *The Journal of the History of Medicine and Allied Sciences* 39: 339–55

Stanway A 1982 *Alternative Medicine*. Penguin, Harmondsworth

Wallis R, Morley P (ed) 1976 *Marginal Medicine*. Free Press, Illinois

Wardwell W I 1972 Limited, marginal and quasi-practitioners. In Freeman H E, Levine S, Reader L G (eds) *Handbook of Medical Sociology*. Prentice-Hall Inc, New Jersey

Chapter ten
UNEMPLOYMENT AND HEALTH

A high level of unemployment is likely to persist among the western industrial nations. Few would predict the return of the Beveridge (1960) norm of 'full employment' – unemployment of less than three per cent of the workforce. The Labour Party has trimmed its exuberant promise of the 1983 election, and now pledges to reduce initially unemployment by one million, if re-elected. The Conservative government makes no promises. Having ceased to talk of the 'cyclical upturn' in the demand for labour, its emphasis is on preventing further 'deterioration' of the unemployment statistics. The Beveridge figure largely held until the end of the 1960s. By mid-1979 unemployment had reached 1.4 millions, and in early 1986 it was around 3.3 millions, about 13.6 per cent of the working population.

How many are unemployed, and who they are, are matters of fierce ideological controversy. The government's opponents claim a figure of at least four million. In November 1982, there was a major change in the production of the offical statistics. Only those entitled to unemployment benefit were now included. Previously, all those registered as seeking and being available for work were totalled. Unemployed women, who never paid the 'full' insurance rate and could not claim benefit, were now excluded from the count. Community programmes, engaging about half a million (October 1985), have also minimised the official, unemployment statistics. Sinfield and Bartley (1984) illustrate another fast-growing group which are omitted, namely older workers 'taking' early retirement. In the last five years employed men aged 60–64 years have fallen from 85 per cent to 70 per cent.

Those subscribing to the 'loafer', or 'scrounger' thesis, point to the 'black economy', estimated by Lloyds Bank at 7 per cent of the GNP. However, many of the participants are not the registered unemployed, but those who are employed who fiddle the books, and non-registered unemployed. The annual Labour Force Survey of 57,000 households gives ammunition to both sides. The spring, 1984, count (excluding Northern Ireland) extrapolated that there were 940,000 recipients of unemployment benefit not 'actively' seeking work. On the other hand there were 870,000 seeking work, but excluded from the unemployment statistics.

To the unemployed themselves, quibbles over the 'real' figures will smack of sophistry. There are other considerations. As it costs £5,000 annually (1982) to maintain one unemployed person, that money is unavailable for health and welfare resources. Researchers who maintain that unemployment 'kills', base their thesis on its distribution. Brenner (1979) is one of the leading gurus. His macro-economic model of time-lagged relationships, is used internationally for comparing the effects of unemployment on ischaemic heart disease, etc. For the thesis to be plausible, it is essential that the unemployment calculus be accurate. Although the USA level of unemployment has fallen to about half the UK rate, its derivation is equally problematic: underestimating the black and Hispanic quotients. Most of the USA employment growth has been in the service sector, these jobs having doubled in the past 20 years. Kerr (1984) reports that the Australian 'hidden unemployed' probably equal those registered as unemployed; a household survey of unemployed women in New South Wales discovered that less than 30 per cent were registered.

The unemployed, like the poor, are not a homogeneous group. Fagin's and Little's (1984) detailed case-studies of 22 unemployed families reveals the complexity. A host of allied variables intervene: class, age, gender, stage of family development, prior employment/ unemployment biographies, and coping resources, etc. The economist's categories of frictional, structural and cyclical un-employment are too clumsy to capture the range of behavioural responses. The waiting period of frictional unemployment, before starting a new job, can be tension ridden for many in the present climate of economic uncertainty. Some who experience structural unemployment, with no local prospects of employment because their dependent industries have 'gone', can be 'adjusted' to their predicament. The long-term unemployed, for over one year, have increased to 40 per cent.

How one becomes unemployed is influential. To be individually singled out for redundancy, not in accord with the union principle of 'last in', is different from the mass closure of a community-based firm. With the Shotton or Consett steel closures, self-blame is out of the question. Unfair, international competition, the recession and lack of investment are factors beyond workers' control. There is no shame; all are in the same boat. There are open community campaigns and support, much of which is cathartic. While older workers may lament the loss of their jobs, Roberts and others (1982), commenting on their study of youth unemployment (attracting the greatest sympathy and most government schemes) in six high-unemployment inner-city areas – including Brixton, Liverpool and Manchester – argue that many specialist youth advisers will not find the anticipated picture one of despair. There is much self-imposed unemployment; e.g. 'refusals' to accept inferior jobs with little prospects. There is a great deal of 'making out'; 38 per cent admitted to undeclared, casual unemployment. The youths followed the leisure patterns of the 1960s, drifting in and out of unemployment.

We now go on to offer the following themes. First, a review of the changing meanings of work and the methodological difficulties of ascribing the influence of 'work' to 'non-work' activities. Theorising on the health effects of unemployment relies heavily on assumptions made about the significance of work. Second, an assessment of the Brenner genre of arguments – that increased stress on the unemployed is at the root of their 'new' illnesses. Finally, a discussion of the health implications of unemployment for selected groups – women, children and youth.

CHANGING SIGNIFICANCE OF WORK

The hangover of the Protestant work ethic is still strong, colouring attitudes towards the unemployed, especially the 'workshy' young. In 1965, 23 per cent of the unemployed were under 25 years; in 1985 they constituted over 50 per cent. In Europe, only Italy has a higher percentage. The levels of benefits are set so as not to discourage the take-up of employment, irrespective of whether jobs exist. The unemployed under-25s have swelled by the rapid erosion of unskilled/semi-skilled industrial jobs and by the demographic effects of the early-60s 'baby boom'.

In its 'purest' form, the Protestant ethic embodies 'ideal' qualities; a sense of purpose, dedication, worthiness, fulfilment of spiritual and community needs, and time regulated behaviour (as opposed to 'frivolous dissipation'), etc. High achievement on earth was an indication of being amongst the elect – the doctrine of salvation by work. The reality is different. Before the mass unemployment of the late 1970s, for many manual workers work was ceasing to be the central life focus (if it ever was). Bureaucratic rationalisation granted them less trust and autonomy, enlarging their alienation.

To survive at work they transformed work into 'play' and made a virtue of 'conspicuous loafing'. Roy's (1960) account of 'banana time' remains a classic description of how degraded workers attempted to capture, momentarily, glimpses of meaningfulness. Work can also be dangerous and take its human toll. Workers have gone mad on car assembly lines: in tyre plants new chemical products, like pliofilm, have increased the risks from leukaemias. Instrumental orientations to work can be strong, often involving a regrouping of one's existence outside the factory, impinging on family life. The strange paradox emerges: when unemployed, many yearn for those very same unpleasant conditions to fill an 'emptiness'. Work does however produce its 'surprises'. Occupations held in low esteem by others, like traffic wardens, are conceptualised differently by their members. Traffic wardens often reply that they enjoy the daily variety and the opportunity to meet people.

There are other philosophies of work besides the Protestant ethic. To the Greeks work was a curse; a condemnation of the gods. It brutalised the mind and soul. The Hebrews regarded it as a painful necessity, an expiation for the sins of their ancestors. Later traditions elevated it. The Pharisees ranked labour higher than 'idle' contemplation and scholarship, as necessary for good health. The Christian view, espoused by St Aquinas, was that work was only necessary for maintaing existence. If a man could live without it, so be it. He had a low opinion of commerce, and an even lower one of money-lending. However, the laws of usury gradually eroded, encouraging the consolidation of the Italian commercial states, and paving the way for capitalism.

Tribal societies never distinguished between work and leisure. Firth's (1939) description of Tikopian boat-building is pertinent. When the announcement was made that a new boat was needed, those interested would turn up. The event would be celebrated ritually with a feast. There was no payment to 'workers' according to labour inputs or 'unit costs'. The participants could claim reciprocal gifts from the 'owner' at a later date, involving shares of its catch of fish.

Theorising about the connections between ill-health and unemployment was inadequately developed between 1945 and the late 1960s. The unemployed, relatively few and unskilled, were subsumed under 'poverty research' which also included the elderly, the 'unemployable' handicapped and the employed low wage-earners with large families. Readjustments of welfare benefits and the targeting of special care by the helping professions, seemed the logical solutions. The socio-psychological dimensions of the effects of unemployment were not to the fore. Epidemiological studies of the effects of inequality were prevalent.

Before unemployment burst on the scene, sociologists had been worried by the expectation that a new society of leisure was on the horizon, and that people were perspectively unprepared for the consequences. They were wrestling with the problems of what was 'leisure', and what its relationship would be with work. Appeals could not be made to the theories of the nineteenth-century founding fathers: they had largely ignored the question of leisure. Engels had predicted, though, that an increase in leisure would increase the political awareness of the working class. Studies in the 1960s of the effects of the reduction in the working week on German and USA car workers had shown the reverse. Workers became more home-centred and all forms of community activities reduced.

The political left were apprehensive about the revolutionary potential of the working class in a society of increased leisure. The Annecy experiment in France, to encourage workers to use their free time more constructively, in intellectual discussion and art, failed. Dumazedier (1967) was forced to rethink the Marxist version of evolutionary change through the new stages of the 'leisure cycle': the lowest form being recuperation from work-fatigue; the highest, 'development', when self-improvement (politically) occurs.

Other researchers sought empirical connections between different types of work and leisure patterns. The 'contrast' and 'balance' theories owed more to ideological prescriptions: that work and leisure should be adjusted to provide the modern man with a greater sense of 'fulfilment' and 'harmonisation'. Specific accounts which showed that arduous occupations, like mining, produced an opposition pattern (contrasting) of leisure, while residential social workers produced an extension pattern (similar), did little to unravel the key variables. Practically, it would be near impossible for coal miners to dig coal in their leisure time! Leisure was also affected by many other factors, such as the type of community and the influence of the media. Some of the incomplete debates on leisure spilled over into unemployment studies. Women were mainly 'invisible' in leisure studies and had initially much the same fate in unemployment research. It was assumed that unemployment had minimal effects, the home being women's 'natural' habitat.

Work remains the dominant influence. Its contribution to social control is undisputed. There is no other activity which predictably locates so many people. The correlation between life chances (e.g. in education and morbidity) and work is high. The women's movement has revitalised the work ethic. Work provides a universal measure for gauging whether they have achieved equal status. Retirement patterns are also influenced by former work experiences. What has been called the fringe of work, i.e. marginal activities, is increasing, with the lengthening of professional training and with new educational demands. Unemployment has created new jobs, mainly semi-professional, in social work, in social services, and in retraining, etc. The time cult of work also pervades the rest of society. The sporting activities sponsored for the unemployed youth replicate the mathematical precision of the work ethic. Other unemployed develop strategies to fill the gaps left in their time schedules; some shorten the day by sleeping longer.

Straight comparisons with unemployment before the Second World War are misleading. Unemployment had lingered since the early 1900s, worsening after 1920. The mortality rates were very much higher then, especially for infants and mothers in childbirth. The means-tested benefits were not only much lower but varied according to locality. Forman's (1979) reconstruction of working-class life in St Helens illustrates the tried and tested survival tactics. Most had no money for buying their homes. Their major savings were in insurance and death benefits. Not being able to afford medical services, many utilised unofficial sources. Teeth would be pulled by showmen on the Saturday market. Hide-and-seek with debt collectors became a sophisticated art. In the mid-1930s half the population of the UK were still inadequately fed.

Bakke (1933), a research fellow from Yale University, who came to study unemployment, has left us meticulous observations on the London borough of Greenwich in 1931. Streets were more actively used by the unemployed. They ranked second in importance to the massive cinema-going – the dream palaces where personal worries temporarily melted away. The streets were used by all ages for parading and gossiping, providing relief from the overcrowded residences. The current 'loafing thesis' was strong in Bakke's day. He made his own street census to test it. Most 'loafers' were not permanent fixtures on the street. Today's loafers may have found some work the next day. The major point of congregation was outside the labour exchange on 'signing days', visits being impossible to schedule at a fixed time.

Today the unemployed are pressurised into private isolation, often being unable to dissipate their 'feelings' of despair in public sociability. Only youths attempt to colonise public territories, and even then their activities are often interpreted by the law enforcers as a threat to 'established order'. The bulk of the unemployed have experienced the abrupt impingement of job loss, having been conditioned to expect rising standards of living and annual wage increases. The 'impossible' has happened to them. They still remain confronted by a mass consumer society, enticing ever increasing expenditure. Their plight can be heightened by the close proximity of new, expanding electronic industries, often multi-national, represented for example by the silicon valley of central Scotland. The long-term unemployed, especially the under-25s, are more geographically widespread than their counterparts between the wars.

The unemployment rates for women over 25 years tend to be lower than for the corresponding male groups. The bulk of the newly created jobs are in the light and service industries, 'prefering' women, often on a part-time basis. The reason why the unemployment figures do not diminish proportionately with the creation of new jobs is that unregistered women slot into them. For women to bring an income into a male unemployed family is *not* in sharp contrast to the pre-war depression. Women at that time enlarged their domestic 'servicing' of middle-class homes. There are also far more one-parent families headed by working women. The black matrifocal family has long been an adaptation, both in the West Indies and the USA, to high male unemployment. White males, socialised into the role of dominant breadwinner, are severely de-statused by the role reversal of unemployment.

The 1920/30s research into the psychological dimensions of unemployment was at the stage of preparing its foundations. Most concerns focused on malnutrition, child mortality, fear of the spread of contagious diseases like TB, and the possible lowering of the moral and sexual standards - women turning to prostitution and child neglect. Infant mortality is a very emotive, demographic statistic. High rates can soon be blamed on a 'callous' society, namely the government of the day. Macfarlane and Cole (1985) draw the parallel between the speeches of the Prime Minister, Neville Chamberlain (12 November 1937) and Norman Fowler (October 1984), Secretary of State for Social Services. Both are taking credit for the lowering of the infant mortality rate and using it as a confident indicator of the overall health improvements. However, in 1937 it was 72.6 per 1,000 in unemployment-devastated Durham and 41.7 in prosperous Surrey.

Since 1945, society has become medicalised and and socio-psychological problem-orientated, with the growth of the new caring professionals. Their 'evaluation training' emphasises the recognising and seeking out of 'pathologies' and stress-related illnesses. The pharmaceutical revolution, with its mass production of tranquillisers, has created a climate of 'instant salvation' by pill. The threshold for bearing, unaided, personal miseries has arguably been reduced by professional intervention.

UNEMPLOYMENT, STRESS AND ILL HEALTH

Debates on the relationship between health and the economy are long standing. Malthus predicted that famine, disease and death would stalk the land if the population increased geometrically and food supplies only arithmetically. The relationship is not all one way. Increases in the standard of living can also bring their crop of health dilemmas. After 1950 there was an increase in male mortality from heart attacks in the prosperous USA; this trend was reversed with changes in lifestyle, independent of the economy. Durkheim explained in the last century how anomic suicide could occur during both a depression and during sudden economic improvements. Much depends, too, on the mode of health delivery, and its anticipatory responses to 'new' health demands.

Brenner, from the Johns Hopkins School of Hygiene and Public Health, is the influential doyen of the position that increases in unemployment directly cause health deterioration. The main explanatory mechanism singled out for this deterioration is 'stress'. The health effects are not immediately responsive to movements in unemployment statistics, but are time-lagged, that is they take time to work through. Brenner (1979) has longitudinally tested his model over the period 1936–76 on the mortality rates of England and Wales. Brenner's (1973) most meticulous research was to put the State of New York under his microscope for the period 1852–1967, when he traced the annual changes of psychiatric first admissions to both state and private hospitals. The admissions were classified by age, diagnosis, marital status and educational qualifications. He found that improvements in the economy predicted a decrease in first admissions and an increase in women's admissions.

Brenner has listed a number of pathological indicators sensitive to economic shifts: suicide and homicide rates, prison population, cirrhosis of liver mortality, cardiovascular mortality and general mortality rates (designated by sex, age and ethnicity). Based on the USA experience, Brenner (1971, 1979) has produced projections of 'additional' increases of mortality and morbidities generated by unemployment. If a 1.4 per cent increase in unemployment persists over six years, then there will be an 'extra' 920 suicides, 495 fatalities from cirrhosis and 20,240 from heart and kidney diseases, 4,227 new admissions to mental hospitals and 648 murders. Some indicators rise sooner than others: cardiovascular mortality has a three year 'delayed' effect after the crucial rise in unemployment. The cardiovascular effect, from this take-off position, will then persist for the next 15 years, even if unemployment decreases. The above calculations were for the period 1970–75.

Brenner's model now has *ex cathedra* standing with many and has been faithfully duplicated in other contexts. After the closure of the Dunlop plant at Speke, which increased Liverpool's unemployment by 0.8 per cent, it was projected that another 176 deaths would occur. Watkins (*Manchester Evening News*, 4 May 1983), Salford's senior registrar for community medicine, predicted that if the town's 15.9 per cent unemployment rate persisted for another five years, then there would be an additional 800 deaths, a 4.3 per cent rise in male and a 2.3 per cent rise in female admissions to psychiatric hospitals, a 4.1 per cent rise in suicides and a 5.7 per cent rise in murders.

The Brenner approach has its critics. Few would deny that unemployment does have deleterious health consequences, but further refinement is required of what is essentially a two-way relationship. Some of the objections to Brenner are as follows.

First, a very general point – that demographic projections from a 'normal baseline' (if such a condition existed) are dubious exercises. At best one can construct a number of possible scenarios, depending on the value judgements of the analysts. Demography is perhaps the most multi-disciplinary of all subject areas. Each contributory strand has its own level of analysis. There is no valid bridging subject which can successfully capture the core of all the others, which include psychological decision making in families, sociological stages of family cycles, macro economic changes, changes in health ideologies, and major political and local interventions. With the dogmatism of Brenner's model (offering precise figures), there is no way of knowing what the health status of the nation would have been without the onset of mass unemployment of the late 1970s. Thus we cannot confirm the figure for those 'extra casualties', caused by the intrusion of unemployment.

Second, the cultural context of unemployment changes. To build the experiences of the 1930s into current projections would be very misleading. We know, for example, that there are fads and fashions in medical diagnosis, especially psychiatry. With unemployment now culturally engrained, it has a ready-made explanatory value built into it. Anybody would be 'depressed' if they lost their job. It is possible that time-harasssed GPs are becoming even less discriminatory in sifting the 'causes' of patients' troubles. The sick role has an appeal to the unemployed with identity crises, offering a measure of intelligibility and sympathy for the plight caused by unfair and invisible market forces. Fagin (1984) explains how, when he commenced his pilot study for the DHSS, families being interviewed soon raised the health topics. These often subsumed the reactions to unemployment. The loss of esteem felt by the unemployed father can also affect other family members.

Third, a major weakness of Brenner is that he does not specify clearly the distribution of the new health casualties. They are not only restricted to the unemployed who, it has been emphasised, are not a homogeneous group. The methodological problem is similar to the one posed by Durkheim's aggregate use of suicide rates. The majority of those who are 'structurally susceptible' to suicide do not commit the act. Other factors must therefore be critical. Komarovsky's (1940) study of the effects of the USA depression of the 1930s on family dynamics succinctly illustrated this. Those families conforming to the Parsonian ideal, with the husband playing external instrumental roles, produced more distress for him when unemployed. Families with joint conjugal roles were more mutually supportive. Marriages with segregated roles between partners are less likely to discuss openly the ramifications of unemployment: many of today's unskilled and semi-skilled families would be candidates. The tendency would be to keep their feelings 'bottled up', released by outbursts of violence. But domestic violence is also dependent on the amount of household space. Employed parents living in caravans display an 'above average' rate of physical violence towards their children.

Brenner does take account of the re-employed; arguing that some will also experience ill health, with reduced status from having gone down-market, by taking new jobs not commensurate with their skills. Downward mobility is itself associated with illness, and with schizophrenia and suicide. Repeated ill health very often precedes the occupational slide. It must also be noted that those employed, with no experience of unemployment, also can have raised sickness rates. More people *consider* that their jobs are threatened. A Gallup poll reported (September 1980) that 38 per cent took this view. There is now more unreported illness at work, with the fear that health may be a major criterion used by management in drawing up future redundancy lists.

The depression has reduced the bargaining power of many unions. When firms are experiencing intensified competition and cash flow problems, there is even less incentive for unions to exert their rights under the Health and Safety Acts, so that working conditions further deteriorate.

When the self-employed become unemployed, they cannot claim unemployment benefit and are not part of the statistics. The country now has its highest number of self employed. This is one avenue the unemployed have taken, with the help of their redundancy payments. In 1984, there were 2.6. million self-employed, of whom 637,000 were women (almost double the 1979 figure). Lacking entrepreneurial skills and under-financed, many go into liquidation. Small builders are a high risk occupation. There is little health research focused on the self-employed segment of the labour market.

There are examples of health improving with unemployment. Work conditions can be so unpleasant that workers are glad to be away. Jahoda and others (1972) studied Marienthal, an Austrian factory village, which experienced a hundred per cent unemployment in 1929. For some, their health improved away from the noise and contaminated air of the weaving sheds. (Respiratory tract TB was common.) To spend more time outdoors was regarded as a blessing. The study is also interesting for producing one of the first analyses of how unemployment affects the 'sense of time'. The women complained about the unpunctuality of the men for meals. Losing the ability to conceptualise time is closely associated with some mental illnesses, being a disengagement from reality. The powerlessness and isolation felt by many resulted in less use being made of the public library, although the charges had been reduced. Wedderburn's (1965) study of redundant railwaymen also produces examples of older workers, who had experienced lingering illness, agreeing that their health had improved.

Brenner's use of stress, as a precipitant for deteriorating health, is difficult to operationalise. It has become a catch-all category, the bourgeois equivalent of Marx's alienation. Employment is not the only source of stress. There is the stress of going through separation and divorce (the latter averages 140,000 per year) and one in three marriages will terminate. There is no agreement how 'arousal stimuli' (stress) become translated into psychological and physiological consequences. Some personalities thrive on these challenges. Others can substitute coping mechanisms for filtering 'unpleasant' experiences. Stress will cause some to experience raised blood pressure, sexual impotence and disturbed sleep. While stress has been closely linked with ischaemic heart disease and mortality, doubt remains as to whether their variations accord with Brenner's premise. Doing cross-cultural comparisons compounds the difficulties; ischaemic heart disease, for example, has undergone nine successive re-classifications.

There have been recent calls from psychobiologists to restrict the use of 'stress'. Weiner (1984), who has revisited the modern source of the concept, Selye's primary studies on rats, informs us that in the last 50 years about 150,000 publications have addressed themselves to stress themes — often with little agreement. Weiner concludes that the concept should be either abandoned or modified. He would like to see 'stress' confined to 'damaging' activities (stimuli), which are unavoidable, and directly produce physiological damage. The effects of natural and manmade catastrophes could be therefore incorporated.

Other researchers have manipulated the time-lagging of health consequences and come to conclusions contrary to those of Brenner. Eyer (1977) examined the USA and found that the most consistent decline in national mortality corresponded with rises in unemployment; during the Civil War, 1929–33 and 1968–75. Some European countries, e.g. Germany, Denmark and Holland also do not follow Brenner's law. The USSR and Eastern Block countries all having full employment, officially, are replicating Western disease patterns, especially rising alcoholism and heart disease.

However, there are some empirical case studies confirming partially the Brenner ambit of unemployment, stress and ill health. Kasl and Cobb (1970) managed to find two USA firms, one urban located and the other rural, which were proposing to close. With a research team, including nurses, they compiled detailed medical histories from 79 per cent of the male labour force, all of whom had clocked up long service. There was a peak rise in blood pressure and serum uric acid during the period anticipating redundancy while at work. These indicators remained high during the immediate period out of work compared with a control group of employed. One worker committed suicide. The redundant did have more heart disease and hypertension, but their onsets were more likely to have occurred well before redundancy loomed. After two years, the workers' health status in general was 'normalising'. The Brenner model implies a continuous deterioration of health.

Many health studies have focused on the effects of long-term unemployment which, often being permanent, is much easier to research. McKenna and Fryer (1984) explored the effects of intermittent lay-offs. Union and management have negotiated these 'reduced working' agreements in preference to compulsory redundancy. They compared Factory A, where the workforce was made redundant on closure, with Factory B, operating rotating lay-offs of seven-weeks, then working for fourteen. Both were South Yorkshire engineering firms. Interviews were held in the fifth week after completion of work. Factory A produced a sample of 20 workers; another 20 workers declined to participate and in the research, being too distressed. Factory B had a sample of 39, its workers averaged six years younger, and had six years' less service. Health was assessed with the Nottingham Health Profile and the General Health Questionnaire (GHQ). The latter was used to evaluate psychological problems.

As expected, the perceived health of ex-workers from Factory A was worse than those of Factory B, and the control group of full-timers. However, those from Factory B suffered no health deterioration, which in some ways was better than the control group. They had laid contingency plans for the lay-offs to catch up on major house and car repairs and to extend their sporting habits. These strategies for filling 'breaks' are not novel. Occupational groups, like car workers and dockers, engaged in forceful strike activity in the 1960s, similarly filled their time; others used their skills in moonlighting networks. The official holidays for British workers are less than many of their European counterparts. Pahl (1984) and others have commented on the increasing investment in the domestic division of labour, in some ways counterbalancing the process of deskilling and deindustrialisation. The redundant workers from Factory A felt isolation, immobility, and shock, and lolled around the house.

The researchers offered reservations to these findings. This was the first period of lay-off for Factory B. The novelty of 'planned freedom' may wear off, especially if uncertainty sets in, and Factory B's trading position worsens. On the other hand, this mode of short-time working, could be for some an ideal preparation for the transition to an organised retirement.

Responses to unemployment have been translated, psychologically, into bereavement careers, popularised by death experts like Kubler-Ross. People mourn for the loss of their job, as they would for the death of a 'dear one', life becoming purposeless and unfair. Hayes and Nutman (1981), among others, have revived this metaphor, which was first used in pre-1939 research. Hayes specifies four stages. Immobilisation, characterised by feelings of powerlessness and difficulties in reasoning is followed by minimisation, with attempts made to construct reality in a form which 'explains' redundancy as not having taken place. Cushioned by redundancy payments, workers may go on expensive holidays, and on return 'expect' letters from firms offering employment. Cognitive dissonance sets in when the 'harsh' reality floods in. 'Letting go' is the final stage, when it is accepted that future employment is impossible and that unemployment is the only way of life.

If the unemployment findings are scoured, these responses can be found; but not necessarily scheduled in this determinate way. The bereavement career is not ideologically neutral. The final stage is a justification for passively accepting 'one's fate' when, by other means, like political activism, there is the possibility of change. Bereavement models are 'new' tools being built into the practices of the caring professions. If the unemployed do not subscribe to the rites of passage of bereavement, they can now be regarded as deviant. Medical treatments are geared to making people adapt to their social and economic predicaments.

As Seglow (1970) demonstrated, not all will mourn for their jobs: it all depends, as with a deceased, on the nature of the prior attachment. He studied the responses of two groups of workers to the closure of a cable factory. The carpenters conformed to the ideals of the Human Relations School of Management. They performed team work, took a serious interest in the quality of the finished product (drums for cables) and mixed with their mates outside work. When redundant, they experienced immobilisation. However, the wire drawers, who found their work isolating, repetitive and boring and had less frequent out of work contacts, adopted an aggressive posture to their redundancy and were more aware of their rights. The conclusion to be drawn is that 'over-attachment' to a firm can be deleterious when workers are made unemployed. Frictional industrial relations are a better preparation for future unemployment, fostering a combative attitude with the unemployment agencies. Beveridge (1960) noted a similar outcome; long-serving, loyal workers with no experience of other firms, become helpless when redundant. Like Job (in the Old Testament), they cannot understand their fate.

The strategies for passing time that the unemployed adopt influence their general health. Kilpatrick and Trew (1985) sampled 121 unemployed men in Northern Ireland, aged 25 to 45; they answered the Goldberg General Health Questionnaire and recorded for one day all their activities in a time-budget diary. Four groups were distinguished. A passive group, who retreated into the home and did little but watch TV, had the poorest psychological health. Another home-focused group, who busied themselves with domestic chores, had an improved health rating. A third group orientated to socialising *outside* the home, i.e. visiting relatives, had the next best health rating.

The group with the best health score were engaged in longer, 'work-simulated' tasks outside the home.

The authors are careful to warn that other intervening variables carry weight. The active group with the best health also consisted of many short-term unemployed; they also had the greatest percentage of working wives to supplement the household income. The passive, house-bound men with the lowest health scores were mainly married with young children. Some were geographically separated from their extended kin —an additional factor to hinge them to their own homes.

If the 'work attachment' thesis has general validity, then it would be expected that white-collar managerial and professional workers, who gain greater esteem from work, would experience greater stress and psychological difficulties when unemployed than would unskilled and semi-skilled workers. The comparison is complicated by the fact that the middle classes would be substantially cushioned by larger redundancy payments. Payne and others (1984) set out to test this proposition by sampling these two groups from the registered unemployed at 54 Unemployment Benefit Offices. The sample was highly selective, containing all white, married, able-bodied, aged 25–39 who had been unemployed for 6–11 months. They were given the GHQ, as well as being asked for self-reported details and for estimations of their strain rating on the preceding day.

The findings showed that there were no significant class differences in reported health and stress since unemployment. The working class did have more money problems and difficulties in usefully using their extra time. Suggestions offered by the researchers were that 'medium-term' unemployment homogenises the experiences of diverse groups. It is possible, however, that the middle class did experience greater health and stress problems, if they originally had a higher health status prior to unemployment. Their health may reduce further when they exhaust their financial advantage. One weakness of the multifarious unemployment studies is that most are anchored to a given temporal point; there are few longitudinal studies. Payne's class samples also turned out to have approximately the same employment commitment scores. (This is not wholly equivalent with either self-ascribed or organisationally acknowledged prestige.) Even if they won the premier pool prize, almost 70 per cent of both white-collar and manual workers said they would keep on working (if employed).

Suicide has been increasingly blamed on unemployment. Since 1976 the suicide rate in the UK has increased by approximately three per cent. Some coroners' verdicts have explicitly made the connection. It is fashionable for politicians wishing to stigmatise the Conservative government, to emphasise the link. The Labour MP, Allaun, did so at Question Time. The interpretation of suicide trends has long taxed the ingenuity of different methodologists. Before the unemployment enigma, phenomenologists had made severe criticisms of the Durkheimian tradition, which treats the official figures as social, concrete facts. The coroner's verdict, phenomenologists argued, reflected a host of untestable, moral assumptions about the suicide's motives. Another important consideration was the impact of the coroner's verdict on the living. The 'suspicious death' of the old and alone was more easily labelled 'suicide'. Thus the suicide statistics are socially manufactured.

In 1985 the Irish Republic resolved the dilemma by abolishing the verdict of suicide! Was it a coincidence that abolition corresponded with Ireland's post war peak of unemployment? Those who play the statistical game can point to Northern Ireland. Its unemployment rate especially long term, is higher than that of the mainland, but its suicide gradient is less. Nor are there any appreciable increases in mental illness. Explanations for this include: the 'spiritual comfort' gained from high rates of church going and the protection of sectarian communities which nullify the stresses of unemployment. Again, groups with high rates of public violence turn their aggression outwards, suicide being a product of 'inner-directed' aggression – the same argument can be used to explain the lower, black suicide rates in the USA. International comparisons of suicide movements, for testing Brenner, are therefore very difficult, compounded by lack of data. For instance, although long established, the national Australian figures do not record employment details at the time of death.

After the most meticulous scrutiny of the available official statistics, Platt (1984) concluded that the association between unemployment and suicidal behaviour (including 'parasuicide', with non-fatal outcome) is overwhelming. But the actual causal link is still elusive. His own longitudinal study of Edinburgh, 1968–82, showed a positive correlation between parasuicide rates and male unemployment. The longer the period of unemployment, the greater was the risk: for those unemployed for over 12 months the relative risk was 18.9 (compared with the employed) and 6.2 for those unemployed less than six months.

Also relevant are the availability of the means for suicide and the effectiveness of the organisational response by the health authorities to parasuicides. In the UK during the 1960s the correlation between unemployment and suicidal behaviour was not apparent. Domestic gas poisoning, a favourite means, was unavailable with North Sea gas. The use of drugs for self-poisoning has replaced gas. Oxford is one city which has pioneered treatment receptions for 'overdosers' and 'self-injuries' and these may themselves impact the statistics. Bancroft and others (1975) showed that the Oxford area, during 1969–73, had a 45 per cent increase in these parasuicides, and still more among women, with those in the semi-professions, such as nurses, being prominent. Much depends also on the method of classification. The frequent explanation given by self-poisoners is that they want a 'good' night's sleep, or to 'remove' pain, but they have no intention of dying.

Returning to Platt's review, he accepts the common psychiatric link made with suicide. Many USA and UK suicides are attributed to depressive illness, schizophrenia, personality disorders, addiction, alcohol abuse, etc., all of which make many of the victims unemployable. Platt elaborates this relationship by arguing that long-term unemployment, as an added stressor, is likely to impel the psychiatrically ill towards suicide. Also, if unemployment 'encourages' an increase in psychiatric illness and distress, thereby widening the pool of psychiatric cases, even with a constant *proportion* of 'psychiatric/suicides', the suicide rate will inevitably rise.

Platt calls for new longitudinal research on suicide to resolve these questions. The contrasting, explanatory models of suicide produce different causal emphases. He reveals the major weakness of most individual–cross sectional studies which look at the relationship with parasuicide. Many omit females, while others categorise all married women as 'housewives', irrespective of their employment position. Individual–cross sectional studies on suicide do show higher rates for the unemployed, but can often fail to reveal changes in unemployment levels or to use a control of employed suicides. Aggregate–cross sectional studies usually fail to reveal an ecological relationship between unemployment and suicide. Much depends on where the neighbourhood boundaries are drawn. Irrespective of employment levels, zones of transition, with a large number of mobile occupants of 'single status', produce above average numbers of suicides.

UNEMPLOYMENT AND WOMEN'S HEALTH

There are proportionately fewer studies made of unemployed women. (The same is true for the employed.) This can be largely attributed to male bias, the majority of researchers being men. There is the latent assumption that women's unemployment is less detrimental, economically and psychologically, because a greater proportion of women are part timers, doing 'less prestigious' work – the home always being a safe retreat. Studies of mass closure of steel works project the image of an all-male catastrophe, concealing considerations of women employees among the office staff and other service jobs. One major strand of research, continued from the 1930s, concentrates on maternal health and the effects of unemployment on children. The weight and height of children are accessible indicators. Najman (1984) and other members of the Mater Hospital, University of Queensland Study of Pregnancy research group studied 4,000 pregnant women in Brisbane. (Their conclusions are based on a final sample of 89.2 per cent.) Besides birth weight, the Delusions–Symptoms–States Inventory (a mental health measure, examining 'loss of control' over personal behaviour and checklist of symptoms), was used. Half had the father employed and the mother as housewife; 4.6 per cent had the father unemployed and the mother as housewife. Overall, 12 per cent of the women (including single parents) and 9 per cent of the men reported being unemployed.

Babies born to couples with both partners unemployed weighed 226 grams below the sample average. This difference is nullified, however, when adjustments are made for smoking habits, parity, and age, etc. This group also had fewer planned pregnancies and were more itinerant. Unemployed *women* had a greater tendency towards extremes of depression. Unemployed *couples* produced the highest levels of depression in women, even when other contributing factors were evaluated; but they had the same *average* level of anxiety as other categories of unemployed women. Couples with one partner unemployed had the intermediate range of depression, with employed couples having least. The authors conclude that women's mental health is more responsive to their *partner's* employment status than their own, with men 'passing on' their personal frustrations and miseries of unemployment and women soaking them up.

Macfarlane and Cole (1985) attempted to chart the effects of unemployment in England and Wales on mothers' and babies' health from the 1930s depression to 1983. Again, they faced the same problem of untying the Gordian Knot; what was the distinctive effect of unemployment as opposed to the general traits of poverty and inequality? The current maternal mortality total is so low that no statistical analysis is feasible for this differentiation. In the 1930s obstetric practices were of major significance. Macfarlane discovered that the maternal mortality in some London boroughs was the reverse of the unemployment thesis. Wives of professional men were at greater risk of dying in childbirth than those of unskilled workers. The obstetric techniques that middle-class women purchased carried high risks. They were also more likely to have their first child when older, introducing the age-risk factor.

Chamberlain and others (1975) 1970 survey of 15,000 births indicated that male unemployment raised the risk factor for women of each social class. They smoked more, were erratic attenders at antenatal sessions and were less likely to breast feed. Higher birth risk also hinged on whether the employed father was vulnerable to the possibility of unemployment around the time of birth.

Birthweight is a good indicator of deprivation – in 1984 Class I had the smallest proportion of low birthweight (under 2,500 grams), which then increased with social class, although it peaked in Class IV (semi-skilled), and not Class V. Mothers from India and Bangladesh had the highest proportion of low birthweight live births, 11 per cent, partly because of their physique. The highest proportion of high birthweight, live births (over 4,000 grams), 11.3 per cent, was to mothers of the Irish Republic. This was partly due to their high proportion of high parity births (*OPCS Monitor*, DH 385/5).

The height of primary school children has a class element, but in addition the children of unemployed fathers of each class are shorter. The children of poor Glaswegian families are smaller than their counterparts elsewhere. It is uncertain, however, when a given body height should be recognised as ill-health, although the nutritional relationship is obvious.

Although the father's occupation/unemployment is significantly related with infant and child mortality, Brennan (1978) introduces 'environmental factors' into this equation, and weights them heavily. Housing densities and their amenities also correlate significantly with child mortality under five years, allowing for social class and unemployment effects. But if the manual father is unemployed, the family has more chance of living in overcrowded conditions, with increased risks of infection.

The USA study of Hibbard and Pope (1985) sheds light on the complex interplay between women's employment and health. They compared the health status of similar housewives; these were not described as unemployed. They sampled 1,140 adult females, aged 18–64, using medical records over a seven year period. They also administered the Langner 22-item index of mental health and a self-reported health measure. Hibbard assessed women's work on three dimensions: the amount of support and integration with other workers; the challenge of the job and its decision making; and occupational status.

Women in high status occupations and those with high work

integration had better health. The major finding was, however, that age is a major discriminator. Employed women and housewives under 40 years have similar health indicators, but housewives over 40 years had the poorest health indicators. The significance of the cut-off point appears to be the stage of family development. Housewives under 40 years are occupying more multiple roles and have a selection of contrasting identities from which to accrue prestige. These possibilities diminish later. Older housewives, who maintain their range of alternative identities and sources of integration, have better health indicators than those without these status avenues. One extrapolation worth testing is whether 'isolated' unemployed women will have a poorer health status than those who are community orientated and 'activists'.

It must also be noted that there are other health trends not directly linked to unemployment. From the mid 1950s the mortality rate of stomach cancer in European women has declined, except for Poland. The highest rates are in Eastern Europe. However, breast cancer continues to rise; with Western Europe having higher rates than Southern Europe. Smaller families, oral contraceptives, hormone replacement therapy, increased alcohol and fat consumption have been indicted.

YOUTH UNEMPLOYMENT AND HEALTH

Employment has been the crucial status passage into adulthood. Unemployment is therefore a denial of this 'natural' right of 'maturity', the latter implying responsibility to self and society. Partly for this reason the government has focused the bulk of its manpower services on youth; at least to provide a 'taster' of work. Reasons for their unemployment are complex. Reduced recruitment by firms, intensified competition from women for light and service jobs, with the deindustrialisation of the 'heavy' base, are contributory factors. Also the employers' demands for better qualifications, although skill levels have not risen, has increased the pool of poorly-educated potential applicants, making it still more difficult for the young unqualified to enter employment.

As with adults, responses to unemployment vary. For those starting from the base of a 'delinquent culture' at school (with high absenteeism), unemployment, making out and fun morality are all part of the same continuum. For school leavers, who are imbued by the ideology of 'academic success equals proper job', unemployment is shameful and a kick in the guts. There is some evidence to suggest that the longer youths remain unemployed, the more their 'mental health' stabilises, even improving in some studies; this perhaps reflects Roberts' sociological picture of 'strategies of adaptation' being worked out. Again, much depends on the experience of unemployment.

Stafford and others (1980) psychologically tested, using the GHQ and other measures, 650 poorly qualified (with less than two 'O' levels) school leavers on leaving school and seven months afterwards. Those still unemployed offered a higher range of symptoms; many came from 'unemployed families', with fathers unemployed. At 15 months the sample was re-surveyed. The mental health of those permanently unemployed levelled off. Those becoming employed improved sharply in terms of mental health indicators. Those losing their job revealed a further deterioration in mental health symptoms. The latter group though, had high anxiety scores when first tested on leaving school.

CONCLUSION

Unemployment does not present a uniform set of experiences. The many variations make it impossible to be dogmatic about the health cause-effects. The Commission for Racial Equality report (1983) makes the additional connection between unemployment and homelessness, especially for black youth (omitting to record their health details). For instance 821 black unemployed were interviewed in the early 1970s: in Brent 35 per cent claimed they had been taken to the police station. Half of the black unemployed were not registered at either Career Offices or Employment exchanges, having no confidence in official sources for providing jobs. Authoritarian, West Indian fathers would sometimes eject from their home their unemployed sons at 16 years, expecting them to have been in work.

The deployment of such a diverse, research armoury produces competing versions of the effects of unemployment; ranging from the assertions of the vulgar Marxist macro-economic determinism, to the claustrophobic intensity of a few family-case studies which elaborate the permutations of their interpersonal, social algebra. Some were shocked and ill by their job loss, others not. Some delayed reproduction, others not, and so on. Researching unemployment merely highlighted the limitations of existing methodologies. Despite the thousands of previous studies made on the family, most have been at a 'distance'; only a negligible number have been undertaken from the psycho-social interior – where their 'real' decisions are made.

Help should not be withheld until we discover the 'precise', health consequences of unemployment. Increased drug, alcohol and tobacco abuse are clearly involved. Unemployment has exacerbated the various prior, structural inequalities, with clearly adverse effects on those involved. These should be tackled. To be 'fit for work' has been a crucial, medical indicator of recovery from sickness. Mass unemployment will condemn many to a 'permanent' sick role, unless steps are taken to devitalise the lingering, ideological potency of the work ethic. Removing the collective stigmata of being unemployed will assist in the construction of new and more acceptable criteria of normality, though this is inevitably a long-term process.

REFERENCES

Bakke E W 1933 *The Unemployed Man, A Social Study*. Nisbet & Co Ltd, London

Bancroft J H J, Skrimshire A M, Reynolds F, Simkin S, Smith J 1975 Self-poisoning and self-injury in the Oxford area. *British Journal of Preventive and Social Medicine* **29**: 170-7

Beveridge W H 1960 *Full Employment in a Free Society*. George Allen and Unwin, London

Brennan M, Lancashire R 1978 Association of childhood mortality with housing status and unemployment. *Journal of Epidemiology and Community Health* **32**: 28-33

Brenner M H 1971 Economic changes and heart disease mortality. *American Journal of Public Health* **61**: 606-11

Brenner M H 1973 *Mental Illness and the Economy*. Harvard University Press, Cambridge

Brenner M H 1979 Mortality and the national economy: a review of the experience of England and Wales 1936-76. *The Lancet* **2**: 568-73

Chamberlain R, Chamberlain B, Howlett B, Claireaux A 1975 *British Births: The First Week of Life*. Heinemann, London

Commission for Racial Equality 1983 *Unemployment and Homelessness: A Report*. London

Dumazedier J 1967 *Towards a Society of Leisure*. Free Press, New York

Eyer J 1977 Does unemployment cause the death rate to peak in each business cycle? *International Journal of Health Services* **7**: 27-35

Fagin L, Little M 1984 *The Forsaken Families, the Effects of Unemployment on Family Life*. Penguin, Harmondsworth

Firth R 1939 *We, the Tikopia*. Allen and Unwin, London

Forman C 1979 *Industrial Town, Self-Portrait of Saint Helens in the 1920s*. Paladin, London

Hayes J, Nutman P 1981 *Understanding the Unemployed*. Tavistock, London

Hibbard J H, Pope C R 1985 Employment status, employment characteristics and women's health. *Women and Health* **10**: 59–77

Jahoda M, Lazarsfeld P, Zeisel H 1972 *Marienthal: The Sociography of an Unemployed Community*. Tavistock, London

Kasl S V, Cobb S 1970 Blood pressure changes in men undergoing job loss. *Psychosomatic Medicine* **32**: 19–38

Kerr C 1984 Does unemployment cause ill-health? *New Doctor* **4**: 3–7

Kilpatrick R, Trew K, 1985 Life-styles and psychological well-being among unemployed men in Northern Ireland. *Journal of Occupational Psychology* **58**: 207–16

Komarovsky M 1940 *The Unemployed Man and His Family*. Dryden Press, New York

Macfarlane A, Cole T 1985 From depression to recession – evidence about the effects of unemployment on mothers' and babies' health 1930s–1980s. *Born Unequal*, Maternity Alliance, London

McKenna S P, Fryer D 1984 Perceived health during lay-off and early unemployment. *Occupational Health* **36**: 201–6

Najman J M, Keeping J D, Chang A, Morrison J, Western J S 1984 Employment, unemployment and the health of pregnant women. *New Doctor* **4**: 9–12

Pahl R E 1984 *Division of Labour*. Blackwell, Oxford

Payne R, Warr P, Hartley J 1984 Social class and psychological ill-health during unemployment. *Sociology of Health and Illness* **6**: 152–74

Platt S 1984 Unemployment and suicidal behaviour: a review of the literature. *Social Science and Medicine* **19**: 93–115

Roberts K, Noble M, Duggan J 1982 Youth unemployment: an old problem or a new life-style. *Leisure Studies* **1**: 171–82

Roy D F 1960 'Banana time': job satisfaction and informal interaction. *Human Organisation* **18**: 158–68

Seglow P 1970 Reactions to redundancy, influence of work situation. *Industrial Relations Journal* **1**: 7–22

Sinfield A, Bartley M 1984. In Draper P, Smart T (eds) *Health and the Economy, the NHS Crisis in Perspective*. Proceedings of a conference, 6th January, Guy's Hospital, London

Stafford E, Jackson P, Banks M 1980 Employment, work involvement and mental health in less qualified young people. *Memo 365 MRC Social and Applied Psychology Unit*. Sheffield University

Wedderburn D 1965 *Redundancy and the Railwaymen*. Cambridge University Press

Weiner H 1984 The concept of stress in the light of studies on disasters, unemployment, and loss: a critical analysis. In Zales M (ed) *Stress in Health and Disease*. Brunner/Mazel, New York

INDEX